ROUTLEDGE LIBRARY EDITIONS:
DEVELOPMENT

AID AND DEPENDENCE

AID AND DEPENDENCE
British Aid to Malawi

KATHRYN MORTON

Volume 11

LONDON AND NEW YORK

First published in 1975

This edition first published in 2011
by Routledge
2 Park Square, Milton Park, Abingdon, Oxon, OX14 4RN

Simultaneously published in the USA and Canada
by Routledge
270 Madison Avenue, New York, NY 10016

Routledge is an imprint of the Taylor & Francis Group, an informa business

© 1975 Overseas Development Institute

British Library Cataloguing in Publication Data
A catalogue record for this book is available from the British Library

ISBN 13: 978-0-415-58414-2 (Set)
eISBN 13: 978-0-203-84035-1 (Set)
ISBN 13: 978-0-415-59275-8 (Volume 11)
eISBN 13: 978-0-203-84014-6 (Volume 11)

Publisher's Note
The publisher has gone to great lengths to ensure the quality of this reprint but
points out that some imperfections in the original copies may be apparent.

Disclaimer
The publisher has made every effort to trace copyright holders and welcomes
correspondence from those they have been unable to contact.

Aid and Dependence

British Aid to Malawi

KATHRYN MORTON

CROOM HELM LONDON
in association with
THE OVERSEAS DEVELOPMENT INSTITUTE

First published 1975
© 1975 Overseas Development Institute

Croom Helm Limited
2-10 St John's Road
London SW 11

ISBN: 0–85664–024–7

CONTENTS

ACKNOWLEDGEMENTS

In the preparation of this study, I have benefited from the help and advice of a large number of individuals in official and unofficial capacities in both Malawi and Britain and I wish to thank all who gave such assistance. My research was guided throughout by Robert Wood, Director of ODI, and by members of a Steering Committee set up under the chairmanship of Professor Ian Little. To these I owe a special debt of gratitude. Finally, I wish to thank all my colleagues at ODI, who — variously — typed, read, corrected, commented on and discussed the study as it emerged. While this book could not have been produced without the assistance of those mentioned above, I am, of course, solely responsible for the opinions expressed and any errors of judgement or fact which it contains.

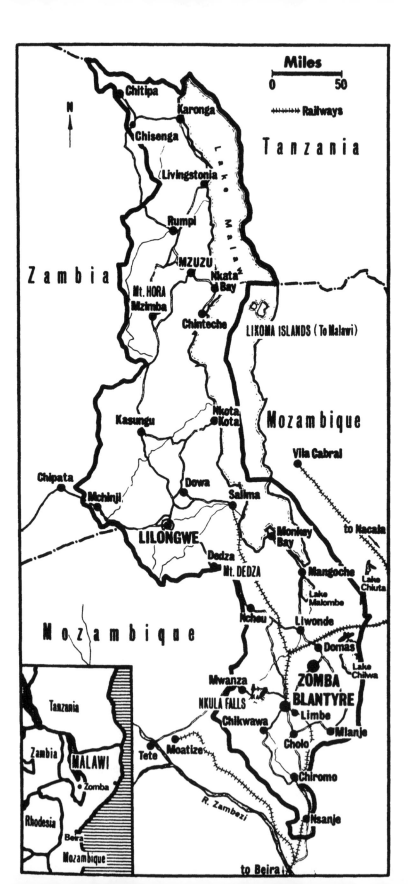

PREFACE

This study of British aid to Malawi is the first of a series which the Overseas Development Institute is undertaking with the help of finance from the Social Science Research Council. Others currently in progress include studies on Botswana, Lesotho, Swaziland and Kenya.

In embarking upon these studies we had two main aims. First, to examine the record of a particular donor country in providing bilateral aid to a number of recipients. The case against aid has two main planks: that the resources would be better used at home; that it does little to help and may even hinder the development of recipient countries. The ODI studies focus on the latter issue.

Does the receipt of aid sap enterprise and self-reliance, fostering instead a spirit of dependence? Does it favour the towns and the rich as against the countryside and the poor? Does it encourage an unreasonable expansion of the bureaucracy? Does it lead to ways of doing things which are inappropriate for the country and impossible to sustain? Are waste and corruption its usual concomitants?

Strong affirmative answers to these questions have come from commentators in both developed and developing countries over the years. In Britain, Professor Peter Bauer is the best-known exponent of the view that aid is either useless or harmful to recipients. And his assertions have been dramatic enough to receive considerable amplification by the media. They have, however, received surprisingly little scrutiny in the light of actual experience, and an important objective of the present studies is to provide this.

The second major aim of our series of studies is to indicate, through an analysis of past experience and recent trends, some lessons for British aid policy in the future. And we hope that such lessons will prove germane not only to Britain and to the particular countries under study here, but to other donors and other recipients too.

Most of the major questions at issue cannot be scientifically tested. Controlled experiments designed to show what would have happened with aid on the one hand or without it on the other, cannot be constructed. Careful assembly and analysis of data, and a proper understanding of the power and limits of both can, however, lead us far along the road to truth. Kathryn Morton has approached these tasks with a cool and sceptical intelligence, refusing allegiance to any particular camp, judging the evidence according to its weight.

'Progressives' will be disconcerted at the high marks she awards for its enlightened development policies to what many would regard as a reactionary government. Those who oppose aid because they believe it harms recipients will find little in the record of Britain's aid to Malawi to support their case, and substantial evidence — for instance with regard to the view that aid tends to diminish domestic savings — to controvert it. Those inclined to impute slackness, incompetence, and lack of guiding principles to the administration of British aid will find the weight of evidence against them. But aid administrators will receive a number of correctives to complacency in the judgements about the evolution of British policy and practice. Although this book's conclusions will not always be welcome, the care and scrupulousness with which they are presented have a persuasive force which even the most rigid of minds will find it hard to resist.

R.N. Wood
Director, Overseas Development Institute

INTRODUCTION

From a starting point of poverty, economic stagnation and insolvency, Malawi has experienced rapid economic progress since it gained its independence from Britain in 1964. At the same time, it has received substantial inflows of foreign aid, most notably from Britain. Indeed, aid receipts from Britain have exceeded Malawi's aid from all other sources, and in the initial years financed roughly half of all government spending. Malawi's achievements are by no means a rags-to-riches success story. The country is still poor and still needs a substantial inflow of foreign capital to sustain its economic growth. But its economic performance has been creditable by any standards, and particularly in comparison with many other similarly poor and agrarian developing countries. How far can Malawi's performance be attributed to its aid receipts? Did aid help or – as some critics argue – hinder the development process? It is these questions that this study examines. Specifically, it aims to assess the contribution of British aid to Malawi's economic development and so to derive lessons for future British aid policy.

For the purpose of this study, aid is defined as resources, primarily intended to assist economic development, transferred on concessional terms. As will be seen in Chapter 4, a small part of the resource flow under the British aid programme is thereby excluded.

The difficult question of defining economic development is tackled by adopting three criteria: growth in income per head, equity of income distribution and growth in income-earning opportunities. These are inevitably crude measures of what is here regarded as the objective of the development process: to raise the material living standards of the poor. The criterion, growth in income-earning opportunities, is chosen because of its value as a proxy measure of changes in income distribution. Given the political and administrative difficulties of redistributing income through fiscal policies in ldcs, the objective of equitable income distribution tends to be virtually inseparable from that of an increase in income-earning opportunities. Changes in income distribution itself are hard to assess because of poor data, though point estimates of the distribution of household incomes exist. Nevertheless changes in the composition of output and the probable outcomes of government policies and expenditure programmes provide a rough indication.

Obviously such criteria could be misleading if used *in vacuo*. The needs and problems of individual ldcs vary and will affect their development prospects — and should, hopefully, colour the donor's approach to aid-giving. In Malawi's case, it is important to note that, although the long-term goal of the government was to raise the material welfare of the 'mass of the ordinary people,' the achievement of greater economic, and hence political, self-reliance was considered of greater immediate importance. Although the pursuit of self-reliance may be both costly and illusory, in Malawi's case it was a reasonable medium-term objective. The country's ability to execute desired policies could have been seriously impeded by its extreme dependence and its ability to sustain any economic advance rendered vulnerable had it remained dependent on the scale of external support received in 1964.

The relationship between aid and development is complex — aid cannot be regarded as a neutral addition to a recipient's resources. Its availability, use and effectiveness are subject to donor-imposed conditions. The aid provided may be such as simply to permit the recipient to pursue its own development strategy. But it is likely that the process of aid giving and the type of aid provided will influence the course of development. Aid's impact on development can be evaluated by asking 'what would have happened to economic development in Malawi without the British aid contribution?' The answer to this question must clearly be a matter of judgement, and is approached here in two ways. The contribution of the British aid programme is assessed by looking at how the aid was and could be used and its observable, or likely, effects on the achievement of Malawi's development objective, Britain's objectives and the 'ideal' objectives implied by the criteria stated above. Secondly the situation had no British aid been received is considered on the basis of the various alternatives open to Malawi. Although quantitative factors are not ignored, the emphasis is — as it must be — on a qualitative evaluation of British aid.

1   BACKGROUND TO MALAWI

Colonisation and After

Malawi is a small state, roughly the size of Ireland, situated in Central Africa, with approximately 4.8m inhabitants. It constitutes a narrow mountainous strip of land some 520 miles long and between 50 and 130 miles wide. Lake Malawi forms its main border to the east. The southern end of the country is bounded on all sides by Mozambique while to the northwest lies Zambia and to the north Tanzania. By African standards, it is densely populated with an average of 130 people per square mile.

The formation of the modern state of Malawi followed the development of British interests in the region during the nineteenth century. The first Briton to enter Malawi was Dr David Livingstone, the Scottish missionary and explorer, who travelled there in 1858 as British Consul to the 'Eastern Coast of Africa and the independent districts in the interior.'[1] He found the area in a state of conflict brought about by tribal warfare and the Arab slave trade. It was his view, shared by other philanthropic Victorians, that the evils of the Arab slave trade and its results – the misery and degradation of African peoples – could, and should, be combated by the introduction of 'legitimate commerce' and 'civilising Christianity.' British interest in and concern for the peoples of Central Africa had already been roused by Livingstone's reports on the activities of the Arab slavers elsewhere in the region and the Universities' Mission to Central Africa (UMCA) was formed as a direct result of his appeals for action. In 1861, under the guidance of Livingstone, UMCA missionaries established Malawi's first mission at Magomero. This early missionary activity was unsuccessful, and it was not until the 1870s that either Christianity or 'legitimate commerce' gained a foothold in the region. Settlers and a few white hunters followed, and in 1883 the first British consul was appointed to 'the territories of the African Kings and Chiefs in the districts adjacent to Lake Nyassa.'[2]

Official British interest in the region, however, did not become marked until towards the end of the 1880s, when the pressures built up by the 'scramble for Africa' precipitated British action to secure the territory against the claims of other European powers. By 1891, after a series of political and commercial deals concluded with scant regard for local ethnic or geographical factors, the boundaries of present-day Malawi were defined and a British Protectorate over the area declared. Harry Johnston, who had been largely responsible for carrying out British policy during the preceding period, was appointed the Protectorate's Commissioner and Consul-General, entrusted with the task of bringing law and order to the country, and setting up an administration. He had to start almost from scratch with only a shoestring budget (the British government view then, as later, was that colonies should be self-financing), a handful of administrative officers and a small contingent from the Indian army. Yet, by the end of his administration in 1897, Johnston had virtually stopped the slave trade, had subjugated, by guile or force, most of the tribes, and had established a basis for modern government:

> ' . . . there were in 1897 nearly 400 miles of road suitable for wheeled traffic, there were some forty administrative-military stations, the postal services were running well, the official revenue of the country exceeded £40,000, a system of courts had been created and the foundation of the district administration, the Civil Service, and the central government departments had been established.'[3]

By 1904, the country was brought fully under British control. In 1907, it was renamed the Nyasaland Protectorate, a Governor was appointed, and Executive and Legislative Councils were set up. Later, during the interwar years, the system of indirect rule by traditional authorities was introduced.

After the energetic introduction to colonial rule provided by Johnston, Nyasaland's sluggish pace of economic development, its poverty, and its role as the supplier of African labour to the more prosperous territories of Central and Southern Africa earned it the reputation of being the 'Ireland of Central Africa — poor, scenic and with a ready supply of exportable labour.'[4] This reputation remained broadly unchanged by its inclusion in the Federation of Rhodesia and Nyasaland, despite the economic advantages that were supposed to accrue to the member states.

Such economic development as occurred in Nyasaland was largely confined to the agricultural sector and to the southern region[5] of the country. Cash crops were first introduced by the missionaries, and later by settlers. Initially coffee and rubber were the main crops but poor climatic conditions, pests and world competition combined to bring about their decline. By 1905, tobacco, cotton and then tea were the main cash crops and although there were shifts in their relative importance they remained the chief source of export earnings until the early 1950s. Then cotton, which had become the least important of the three, was supplanted by groundnuts. Tobacco and tea continued to account for some 75 per cent or more of total export earnings. By the 1920s, Africans had emerged as important producers of cotton and tobacco in the southern and central regions respectively, while Europeans concentrated on the production of tea and flue-cured tobacco in the same areas. The development of commercial and industrial activity, carried out mainly by Europeans and Asians, was limited and largely in the Blantyre area.

The provision of social services – education and health – was more widespread. Their existence was largely due to the missionaries, although in the 1940s the colonial government began to play a more active role in this area. Partly because there were few settlers in Nyasaland, the missionaries had arrived in relatively large numbers and were a major influence during the colonial period. They not only established mission schools, clinics and hospitals throughout the country but also sought to encourage African enterprise. They provided vocational training for crafts and trade and encouraged cash crop production amongst Africans. They also acted as spokesmen for African interests to the government and the settlers. Perhaps most important was that their various activities, stemming from a basic sympathy for the Africans, a belief in their ability to improve their lot, and a desire to help them improve it, stimulated political awareness amongst the African population. As Dr Banda later remarked, it was from 'the seed-bed of the Livingstonia Mission that the nationalist movement grew.'

Despite missionary efforts, there was a dearth of economic opportunity within the territory. This in turn was a factor in migration, which became a dominant feature of the colonial economy. From the late nineteenth century onwards, growing numbers of Nyasa workers, particularly from the northern and least developed region of the country, were recruited for the mines and plantations of nearby territories. By the mid 1930s, it was estimated that at any given time nearly one third of the able-bodied adult African males were working outside Nyasaland.[6] A combination of push and pull factors gave rise to this situation. Within Nyasaland, cash income was required by the Africans to pay the hut tax imposed by the colonial government. While in the southern, and later, to a lesser extent, in the central region the Africans had opportunities for wage employment and for cash crop production, in the northern region these were limited.[7] At the same time, the rate of economic expansion in neighbouring territories created a demand for labour which could not be satisfied by the local African peoples. The wages offered were usually higher than those prevailing in Nyasaland.[8] Active recruitment by extra-territorial employers, who often preferred Nyasa workers to local labour because of their better education[9] – and indeed their migrant status – also stimulated migration.

While the migration of labour may be thus briefly explained, the question that arises is why Nyasaland's economic growth failed to keep pace with that of the other territories of Central and Southern Africa. By 1954, for instance, average income per head in Nyasaland was only around £11 while in Northern and Southern Rhodesia, it was £51 and £54 respectively.[10]

The answer would seem to lie in the fact that Nyasaland, unlike the two Rhodesias, failed to attract significant numbers of European settlers, who, in those countries, were the chief agents of economic growth. Whereas the European population of Southern Rhodesia was 33,000 in 1923 and that of Northern Rhodesia over 5,500 in 1926, in Nyasaland the total European population – including a substantial number of missionaries[11] – was less than 2,000 until 1945. The basic reason for this failure was that Nyasaland was *relatively* unattractive. It offered little mineral wealth for exploitation, and while there was scope for cash crop production by settlers, there were constraints in both colonial policy and geography. The land and labour policies of the early administrations were designed to encourage European settlers, without whom, Johnston had said, 'Central Africa would be of no value.'[12] But they were also intended to protect African interests, and the resultant curbs on land alienation to Europeans and on methods of labour recruitment compared unfavourably – from the settlers' view point – with the policies adopted in neighbouring territories. At the same time because the main outlet to the sea lay in the south and access to the northern part of the country was difficult (and became more so shortly after the settlers' arrival[13]) potential settlement was limited to the southern and central regions. Meanwhile, the early crop failures of coffee, rubber and plantation cotton may well have been a further disincentive to settlement.

As time went by Nyasaland became even less attractive to intending settlers than other British territories in Central Africa. The larger settler population of the Rhodesias, particularly Southern Rhodesia, offered more economic opportunities to industry and commerce, while for intending settlers and investors, Southern Rhodesia had the political attraction of being more securely a 'white man's country' than Nyasaland.[14]

A process of cumulative causation thus reinforced Southern Rhodesia's position at the centre of economic activity for the region and Nyasaland's position on the periphery as a market for goods produced at the centre and as a supplier of labour to it.

A growth of African participation in the modern economy in Nyasaland might have compensated for the lack of settlers and countered the pull of the centre. But African participation was hampered by, amongst other things, lack of technical knowledge of cultivation methods or adequate transportation and marketing systems. Although the missionaries proposed, in 1903, that the colonial government should assist the development of African cash crop production, the government then lacked both the resources and the will to give such assistance. The British government's view was that colonies should be financially self-sufficient and that development should be undertaken by private enterprise operating within the framework of law and order provided by the colonial government. The revenues of the Nyasaland government barely financed the framework. These factors, together with opposition from the settlers, who feared that they would lose their labour supply if Africans had their own source of cash income, combined to produce virtual government inaction.[15]

After the First World War, the British government became more development minded, and the 1929 Colonial Development and Welfare Act provided a source, admittedly meagre,[16] of additional finance to the Nyasaland government. This and other factors, such as the research support provided to African cotton growers by the Empire Cotton Growing Association, assisted the development of African cash crop production. But the scale of support was small in relation to the needs of the country. Although, in 1954, African production accounted for 39 per cent of total agricultural production for sale in Nyasaland, as compared with 37 per cent and 14 per cent in Northern and Southern Rhodesia respectively,[17] the northern part of the Protectorate was still virtually untouched by any positive economic changes, and most African farmers elsewhere were still mainly subsistence producers. Such economic development was not enough to relieve the country of its basic poverty, or to prevent the flow of external resources and domestic labour to other parts of the region.

In 1953, Nyasaland became part of the Federation of Rhodesia and Nyasaland. The formation of the Federation was largely the result of pressures exerted on the British government over a long period by the settler populations of Northern and Southern Rhodesia. During the interwar years, the British had rejected the amalgamation of Northern and Southern Rhodesia, partly because of the differences in their policies towards the Africans. In Northern Rhodesia, as in Nyasaland, the twin principles of British colonial rule applied – the paramountcy of African interests in any conflict of interests between expatriates and Africans, and the trusteeship principle which looked to the eventual devolution of power to the Africans; in settler-ruled Southern Rhodesia, they did not. In place of amalgamation of the Rhodesias, two British government Commissions proposed closer links between Northern Rhodesia and Nyasaland.[18] After the Second World War, the idea of a weaker form of political union – federation – between the two Rhodesias was put forward. At the same time, the possibility of Nyasaland becoming a partner in the Federation was raised. Opinion amongst the European population in Nyasaland on the prospect of federation was divided: broadly, the missionaries were against, the settlers for, and the officials in doubt. Amongst the African population in Nyasaland, and in Northern Rhodesia, there was clear opposition to the idea, mainly on the realistic political grounds that federation with Southern Rhodesia would lead to the abandonment of the trusteeship principle and result in white settler domination.[19]

Why Nyasaland, where opposition to the federal idea was greatest, was finally included in the Federation is not wholly clear. It has been suggested that its inclusion was simply a 'condition of sale,' designed to relieve Britain of ever mounting development expenditure on an economically unviable territory, but the ill-founded belief that federation would provide substantial economic advantages to *all* partners[20] was probably also an important factor. Economically, the period of federal rule did not fundamentally change Nyasaland's position. Politically, it provided a focus for and stimulus to the African nationalist movement, which resulted in the achievement of independence.

Federation involved a division of functions between the territorial governments and the federal government. The latter's chief responsibilities were for external borrowing, defence, inter-territorial roads, power on a federal scale, the regulation of commerce and industry, health and European agriculture.[21] The territorial governments were responsible for most other functions. The territories shared a common fiscal system. While federation's economic effects on Nyasaland are difficult to assess without knowing what would have happened had the Federation not been formed, few now agree with the pronouncement made by the Jack Report in 1960 that 'the country's economic development has been accelerated in direct consequence of its federal association with the two Rhodesias and that the economic benefits which have been enjoyed have been substantial.'[22]

It is true that Nyasaland experienced economic growth after the Federation – though at a slower rate than the immediate preceding post war years – and gained financially from the large fiscal redistribution on current account that resulted from its federal association with Northern Rhodesia. It is also possible that the federal association with Southern Rhodesia resulted in safeguards for Nyasaland migrant workers, whose employment might otherwise have been subject to legal restrictions. On the other hand, the federal customs tariff did not favour Nyasaland: its impact was regressive and it reduced the customs revenue that would otherwise have accrued to the government to the extent that the tariff changes induced a switch of imports to federal products.[23] And although the federal fiscal arrangements and federal expenditure on public capital formation represented a redistribution of federal resources in favour of Nyasaland, it was a redistribution which favoured the white population rather than the Africans. Moreover it was too small to counter the increasing concentration of federal economic activity in Southern Rhodesia.

Opposition to the Federation had been based on African fears of settler domination and the abandonment of their political future, rather than on doubts as to its economic benefits. The fact that Nyasaland retained its Protectorate status and its government continued to be entrusted with the promotion of African political advancement did nothing to avert these fears. African opposition within Nyasaland continued, after the imposition of federation, under the leadership of the Nyasaland African Congress, which had promoted a campaign of non-violent resistance, including boycotts, nonpayment of taxes, and strikes. This campaign folded up in 1954 and between then and 1956 the voice of opposition was weak. In 1956, a four-year interim constitutional reform was enacted in Nyasaland to allow greater representation of Africans. The five Africans thereby elected to the Legislative Council were all members of the Congress, and opposition to federation was revived both inside and outside Council chamber. However, the younger members of the Congress wanted more positive leadership than they then had. 'What was needed was a kind of saviour, a prestigious father figure who would provide the dynamic leadership necessary for success.'[24] So Chipembere, one of the joint leaders of the African representation in Council, got in touch with Dr Hastings Kamuzu Banda.

Dr Banda had lived outside Nyasaland for most of his life. He was born around 1900[25] in the Kasungu district of the Central Province and was educated in mission schools. At about thirteen, he left the Livingstonia Mission school where he was training to be a teacher and travelled south, first working in Southern Rhodesia as a hospital orderly, and then as a mine clerk in South Africa, where he also attended night school. Sponsored by American missionaries, he went on to study philosophy and medicine in the USA. In order to obtain the British medical qualifications necessary to practise in Nyasaland, he took a further medical degree in Edinburgh, financed by the Church of Scotland and the Nyasaland government. The war prevented his immediate return to Nyasaland and he began to practise medicine in England, while keeping in touch with political developments at home. When he emerged as a significant figure in African politics, as a leading opponent of federation, Dr Banda, an elder of the Church of Scotland, was practising in a north London suburb. When federation was imposed, he moved to Ghana in order, he said, 'to give it [federation] a chance.'[26]

As an African who had made it in a white man's world, Dr Banda had prestige. He was also old enough to engender automatic respect. His grasp of the political issues surrounding federation was clear. Whether he could provide the dynamic *leadership* that the Congress lacked remained to be seen. In the event, his leadership was more dynamic than Chipembere and other younger members of the Congress probably bargained for: there is some suggestion that they had wanted a 'front man' rather than a true leader. He returned to Nyasaland in July 1958, after the moderate leader T.D.T. Banda (no relation) had been ousted, was elected President-General of the Congress, and toured the country, whipping up popular support for the abolition of federation. Membership of the Congress increased rapidly after Dr Banda's return.[27] At the same time tensions within the country increased and were heightened, in January 1959, by the Governor's failure to resolve the constitutional deadlock resulting from Banda's demands for a reform to allow an African majority on the Legislative Council — which inevitably would have resulted in a vote for secession from the Federation. In February, riots and disturbances broke out, particularly in the northern province, and a number of Africans were killed. Fiery speeches were made by the Congress leaders, and the government, fearing more violence if the constitutional reforms were not allowed, but unwilling to allow them when they might be construed as concessions to violence, 'was forced either to act or to abdicate.'[28] It acted: a state of emergency was declared, and the Congress leaders, including Banda, and many supporters were imprisoned. In the process, fifty-one Africans were killed, and disturbances continued for over a month.

After the enquiry into these events by a Royal Commission led by judge Sir Patrick Devlin, political opposition to the Federation could no longer be ignored by the British government. The report stated:

> 'It was generally acknowledged that opposition to Federation was there, that it was deeply rooted and almost universally held. We found it to be so.'[29]

In 1960, the Nyasaland constitution was reformed, allowing for a larger African membership of the Legislative Council, and elections were planned. In the same year, the Monckton Commission was set up to investigate conditions within the Federation, with a view to advising on the revision of the federal constitution that was to be considered later in the year. Again, 'widespread and sincere opposition' to federation in Nyasaland — and Northern Rhodesia — was observed. More importantly, the Commission's report[30] did not preclude secession as a solution to the political problems within the Federation. In 1961, elections were held in Nyasaland, and the Malawi Congress Party (the re-formed and renamed Nyasaland African Congress, which had been proscribed in the 1959 emergency) had an outstanding victory after campaigning on a

programme for secession. There was little possibility then that Nyasaland could remain in the Federation. In 1962, a constitutional conference was held in London, and it was agreed that Nyasaland should
become internally self-governing during 1963. Meanwhile, plans were
put into effect for the dissolution of the Federation. On 31 December
1963, the Federation was formally dissolved, or as Dr Banda more
colourfully put it, the Federation was 'now dead, cremated and thrown
into the Indian Ocean.' A few months before, the date for Nyasaland's
independence was set for 6 July 1964, exactly six years after Banda's
return to the country.

Malawi at Independence, 1964

'What those people who were saying we should not demand self-
government and independence because we were poor did not
realise is that we were poor because we were not independent. . . .
It is only when a country becomes independent that real *development* begins.'[31]

There can be no doubt that when Malawi achieved its independence the
will to develop was strong. Dr Banda had led the party and the country
to political independence, and now intended to lead the country in the
'fight against poverty, ignorance and disease'[32] through economic and
social change. The task was a difficult one, and Malawi's subsequent
achievements — and the role played by British aid — have to be set
against the background of the problems which faced the country at
independence.

There were factors in Malawi's situation which suggested that internal political divisions, at least, would not pose an obstacle to development, as they had in some other post-independence African countries.
Banda and the Malawi Congress Party (MCP) had a widespread popular
following. The original aims of the MCP had been essentially negative —
secession and the end of colonial rule. But once the party had achieved
power in 1961, and secession virtually obtained, the leadership, while
pressing for independence from Britain, had focused popular attention
on the task of development after independence. The slave trade,
defeats suffered from invading tribes and the colonial power in the
nineteenth century, and later, the modernising influences of education
and migration, had weakened tribal authority in Malawi. Tribalism was,
therefore, unlikely to become a divisive element after independence.
Meanwhile, the MCP had firm roots in most districts of the country and
was well organised to maintain interest in, and support for, the national
government's development endeavours.

Some outsiders, however, had misgivings about both the extent of popular support and the stability of the leadership of the MCP. The former stemmed from some unpleasant events in early 1964, when party members had resorted to strong arm tactics to win over a small minority, but the absence of support that caused them was relatively insignificant.[33] The latter misgivings arose from the belief that, although Banda appeared to be firmly entrenched as leader of the party and the people, his autocratic leadership would bring him into conflict with the younger men who had been in virtual control of the party up until his return. Now, they were very much the junior partners, referred to by Banda as 'my boys'. Their views on how the country should be run did not wholly accord with those of Banda,[34] and they still commanded popular support. Now that the need for unity in fighting for secession and independence had passed, they might attempt to draw on that support in order to reassert their position, with disruptive effects.

Poverty

The chief source of the misgivings felt by outsiders, and indeed by European residents of Malawi, was not the country's political stability after independence, but its economic survival. The country lacked the resources with which to maintain its present level of poverty, let alone to embark on development. Over most of the period after 1945, the country had experienced relatively rapid economic growth but, in 1964, Malawi still ranked amongst the poorest in the world. Its average gross domestic product (GDP) per head was only K39.5 (roughly £20).[35] Over 90 per cent of the African population lived in rural areas, and their main source of livelihood was subsistence agriculture, with the production of cash crops their chief source of money income: in 1964, smallholder cash crop production was valued at K13.4m, and non-monetary agricultural output at K63.0m. Only about 130,000 Africans were in wage employment, although some 200,000 or more were throught to be employed outside the country, and their remittances, amounting to K3.6m, provided an additional source of money income to rural dwellers – and of foreign exchange to the economy. The monetary economy was largely based on the agricultural sector: its output accounted for nearly 30 per cent of total monetary output, more than 95 per cent of domestic exports, by value and it provided a third of all wage employment. The manufacturing sector accounted for only 10 per cent of monetary output (see Table 2.1) and 7 per cent of employment.[36]

Since 1962, the economy had virtually stagnated, as a result of the uncertainties that had preceded and surrounded the dissolution of the Federation. In 1964, gross fixed capital formation amounted to less than 9 per cent of GDP, and stocks were being run down. Domestic savings (investment – including stock changes – minus imports, plus exports) amounted to K1m or 0.7 per cent of GDP. If one looked only at the monetary sector (in the subsistence sector, consumption and investment expenditure must equal production and income, by definition), the situation was worse: monetary domestic savings were negative, amounting to −K1.1m, while monetary national savings (after allowing for net factor payments abroad) were −K7.3m. The country was thus spending more on consumption than it earned by production. The reason lay with the level of the government's consumption spending. The central government accounted for nearly 30 per cent of total consumption expenditure and, with the rest of the public sector, roughly two-thirds of total gross fixed capital formation. Yet its domestic tax revenue amounted to only 40 per cent of its consumption expenditure. In 1964, the recurrent budget deficit of some K14m, together with most capital expenditure, had to be financed by grants and loans from Britain. Taxation amounted to 6.5 per cent of GNP, and 12.9 per cent of monetary GNP. Although there was some potential for increasing taxation levels, it was limited by poverty and the largely subsistence nature of the economy.

Federal Effects

Malawi's adverse budgetary position was an inheritance from federation. During the federal period, government services had increased far beyond Malawi's capacity to finance them from its own revenue, a situation made possible by the large fiscal subsidy received from the Federal government. With the dissolution of the Federation, Malawi had to finance not only the services provided by the territorial government, but also those previously provided by the Federal government. It also had to take over a portion of the Federal debts, and those pre-Federation debts for which the Federal government had taken responsibility.[37] Even with considerable economies, estimated expenditure on revenue account for 1964 amounted to K31.2m, two-thirds as large again as any previous estimate,[38] while estimated domestic revenue was only K16m.

The problems bequeathed by federation were not only financial. Like most countries emerging from colonial rule, Malawi possessed a government machine that was geared to ensuring law and order more than economic development. Meanwhile, the surrender of government functions that had occurred under federation gave Malawi an additional handicap. It not only had to finance new services, but also take over the running of federal services and provide the organisational structure and the administrative and technical skills for their operation. From the development angle, there were at least three important gaps in Malawi's government machinery. First, the country at independence had no central banking system, and its banking and financial sector was highly underdeveloped − an indirect consequence of control from Salisbury, as well as of Malawi's poverty. Thus the mobilisation of existing domestic resources was inhibited by lack of financial institutions. Secondly, although the territorial government had produced a development plan of sorts[39] for those sectors which lay in its control, Malawi lacked the expertise and the institutional capacity to prepare development plans. Finally, it lacked the statistical services necessary for planning purposes and for the management of the economy. The Federal government had halfheartedly collected statistics on Nyasaland's behalf, but these were seriously deficient for most purposes.[40] Thus economic policies would initially have to be formulated, to some extent, in the dark.

Lack of Skilled Manpower

The shortage of skilled manpower to formulate or execute *any* policies was, besides the budget deficit, the most important constraint on Malawi's development potential (assuming that external finance would be forthcoming). As Butler had earlier pointed out, there was 'a gap to bridge between the political aspirations of the Nyasaland people and the skills and expertise which they will need to bring them to fruition.'[41] The missionaries and later the colonial government had provided fairly widespread primary education, but until 1940 there were no secondary schools in the country. By 1959, there were only four. Expansion was more rapid thereafter but, in 1963, there were only about 3,000 pupils at secondary school and less than 400 candidates for the School Certificate. Opportunities for vocational training, except for teachers, were limited and teacher training capacity could not meet the needs of the existing educational system. A few technical and craft training opportunities existed in the missions, and a government trade school had been set up in 1960. Facilities for higher education and training, besides the teacher training institutes, were embryonic: the Staff Training College intended to provide in-service training for Malawian non-technical civil servants took its first students in 1963, the Polytechnic in 1964.

Thus, while there were many with primary education and manual skills developed while working abroad, at independence few Malawians had technical and professional skills. The country relied on the expatriate community for the functioning of its administration and much of its commercial and industrial life. In 1964, expatriates held all senior administrative posts in the civil service and predominated in most professional and technical spheres in the public and private sector. Although the MCP – if not Banda – had argued for the 'immediate Africanisation of the Civil Service' and opposed overseas recruitment for public or private sector activities in the heady pre-independence days,[42] there seemed little likelihood that Malawians could fill the gaps left by departing expatriates, let alone replace those that stayed. Meanwhile, the country had to acquire additional skilled manpower to meet the increased demands of a, hopefully, developing economy.

Physical Resources

Malawi's physical resources had potential but, like the country's other endowments, offered no easy road to riches. There were very few known mineral deposits of any commercial value. The chief of these — a large, if inaccessible, bauxite deposit on Mount Mulanje — was not likely to be exploited in the near future. On the other hand, the Lake, stretching alongside most of the country, offered a potentially cheap means of transport, compensating for the difficulties imposed by the country's mountainous terrain, as well as a valuable supply of fish protein. The water flowing from the Lake down the Shiré River could provide relatively cheap hydroelectric power. Capital expenditure was required, however, for such development. The beauty of the country was a potential tourist attraction, but a tourist industry would have to await the development of both internal and external communications. The most important of Malawi's natural resources at the time of independence was, however, its agricultural land.

Malawi covers a land area of some 36,000 square miles, most of it mountainous or otherwise uncultivable. The remainder is relatively fertile by African standards. Furthermore, the range of climatic, soil and vegetational conditions — a consequence of Malawi's varied topography — allow for a fairly wide variety of crops and forest products to be grown. So, unlike some less developed countries, Malawi's physical circumstances did not promote an excessive dependence on any one cash crop. But the country was also, by African standards, densely populated,[43] particularly in the Southern Region where there were 169 inhabitants to the square mile, as compared with 111 for the country as a whole. Estimates of the cultivable land area still free for cultivation varied but it was clear that pressure on the land was already dangerously high in some areas: continuous maize mono-cropping by peasant farmers was reducing soil fertility and causing soil erosion. If the estimated population growth of 3 per cent per annum continued and there was no change in production techniques, population pressure and reduced soil fertility would lead to an extension of the land area under subsistence cultivation. This in turn would limit the scope for increasing cash crop production — the main hope for economic development.

The Economic Infrastructure

The physical economic infrastructure — transport, communications and power — was in a state that reflected not only Malawi's basic poverty but also the southern bias of previous economic growth. If

Malawi was to develop its agricultural sector, the transportation system in particular would have to be improved and extended. Malawi's single track railway system was confined to the southern and central region, extending 289 miles from Salima to Nsanje, the southern exit leading to the port of Beira. Most of the track was in poor repair, particularly in the central region, yet it provided Malawi's only direct connection with an ocean port and its main transport link with other territories in Africa. The railway linked also with the Lake Service at the port of Chipoka, just south of Salima, thus providing a potential through service to the northern region. The existing Lake transport system, however, had never been adequately developed and was inefficiently organised: it ran consistently at a loss. And like the railway, the owner-ship and control of the Lake Service was not, at independence, fully in the hands of the Malawi government, and this posed problems for any plans to improve either service. A road network of some 6,000 miles extended throughout the country but less than 300 miles had a bitu-men surface, while between a third and a half[44] of the total mileage, including some main routes, was unusable in the rainy season. Although broadly sufficient for the country's immediate needs, many roads were badly aligned and poorly routed for the transportation needs of the agricultural sector.

Economic Dependence: Needs and Prospects

Malawi's domestic resources were limited in almost every respect. It seemed clear that without external support, both manpower and financial resources, the economy was more likely to collapse than to develop. The need to seek, and to rely on, external resources was not a subject for public debate in Malawi. With characteristic realism, it was accepted: the alternative course — a difficult period of retrenchment — was not an attractive proposition to a leadership that had promised economic advance. Thus in the 1965-9 Development Plan, published shortly before independence, it was stated 'it is essential for the fulfil-ment of the plans which are made and the attainment of the prospects that lie ahead for external capital to be made available to assist in the financing of economic development.' 'Fortunately,' it went on, 'Malawi is not without friends . . .'[45] That was so. Britain had given Malawi the assurance that 'it had in mind a substantial amount of aid for some years to come both for balancing the budget as well as for capital deve-lopment.'[46] West Germany had promised to make available a loan of just under K1m.[47] Malawi had received some technical assistance and very small quantities of financial aid from other sources and it had hopes, in particular, of obtaining more aid from the United States and of tapping World Bank resources (after it had become a member). Nevertheless, the prospects of attracting suitable external resources in sufficient quantities were not particularly favourable.

First, the aid generally on offer in 1964 was not of the kind that Malawi could easily use. Bilateral aid, including that of West Germany, Britain and the United States, was generally tied to the procurement of goods and services from the donor country. It was frequently tied to use for particular projects as well.[48] Much aid, moreover, was in the form of loans rather than grants. When the repayment terms of this aid were compared with commercial borrowing terms, it was clear that the actual gift element of the 'aid' was much below the nominal announced sum.[49] Yet since the kind of development projects envisaged by Malawi were likely to have a fairly low import content, and Malawi had few domestic resources with which to finance the local cost content of projects, procurement-tied aid would be of limited value.[50] Also, because the Malawi government had to eliminate its budget deficit, it had to be cautious about further debt servicing obligations whether to donors or to commercial creditors. The budgetary position, combined with the usual aid conditions, limited the range of projects that Malawi could offer to potential donors. Although Britain did not expect Malawi to balance its budget in the short term, both Malawi and Britain wished to reduce the size of the deficit. But expenditure on development account tended to lead to expenditure on recurrent account: schools once built have to be run, roads have to be maintained, and so on. Since donors generally provided only for the capital costs of development projects, their running costs would tend to burden the recurrent account unless projects were such as to generate their own running costs or to lead to a matching increase in revenue potential.

Second, Malawi was an unlikely candidate as an aid recipient, a commercial borrower, or a host to foreign private investment — which it hoped to attract as a complement to public sector activities. Donors, lenders and investors all hope for a return on their money. Leaving aside for the present the various motives and objectives that confuse the generally declared developmental object of aid giving, donors tend to expect to see results for their money in terms of economic development. Yet outsiders did not rate Malawi's developmental chances highly. The country verged on insolvency, the economy had been stagnating over the last few years, the government commanded few resources and was untried in important areas of economic management. At the same time, the hint of division within the leadership did not augur well for the country's future political or economic stability. Even if outsiders broadly shared Dr Banda's optimism, there was sufficient doubt as to the country's future to warrant prudence. Moreover, although with the dissolution of federation, commercial opportunities for outside investors were likely to increase, since the country would no longer have to depend on Rhodesian industry to supply its needs, the extent of the opportunities was not known. At the same time, the general poverty of the country, its small population and its poor communications with other markets were not encouraging to foreign investors.

Aid donors frequently have other reasons for providing assistance to less developed countries, which may lead them to support economic development despite uncertain prospects, or to extend funds with little regard to their use. Thus aid is given because the donor believes that economic development will combat the spread of communism or capitalism to the recipient, or so that the donor may retain strategic bases in the recipient. Malawi, however, was unlikely to benefit from this confusion of motives. Any donor, except perhaps Britain, looking for long- or short-term economic advantage through aid giving would scarcely light upon Malawi. The main political or strategic interest in Malawi lay in its potential role in any confrontation between white southern Africa and the newly independent black African states and in the support or otherwise of black liberation movements in the south. But Malawi's importance in this context was likely to be slight. Despite its geographical position, poised between white and black Africa, it would be difficult on logistic grounds to use Malawi as a base for any large-scale military or guerilla incursions into southern Africa.[51] Meanwhile the country's economic orientation towards white-ruled Africa rendered it vulnerable to the latter.[52] Since, moreover, Dr Banda had accepted this vulnerability, adopting a foreign policy which eschewed confrontation between black and white states,[53] he had effectively reduced the interest of both the white states themselves — which were more likely aid donors than the black states — and their supporters in giving aid to ensure, if not friendship, then at least the absence of open hostility. And Banda's foreign policy itself was a disincentive to those donors who opposed the racist southern African régimes, e.g. the Scandinavian countries. The country was, however, not completely without political or diplomatic interest to others: as an independent state it had a place in international affairs and China, at least, not reckoning with Dr Banda, thought that diplomatic recognition by Malawi would be worth some aid.[54]

The Development Strategy

Notwithstanding the uncertainties about the financing of development expenditure, Dr Banda was confident that once he had a plan, he would get money. But the 1965-9 Development Plan was scarcely a plan at all. There was no detailed presentation of its constituent projects, while little attempt had been made to show how the projects fitted together, and none to indicate precisely how or when they would be carried out.[55] The plan size — a total expenditure of K93.2m over five years — represented an annual development expenditure level more than double that in the years preceding independence. Even supposing the Malawi government were able to attract finance on that scale, it was doubtful that it would be able to use it productively. The government was aware of the document's shortcomings. It did, however, serve two purposes — providing donors with a statement of Malawi's developmental intentions and priorities, and an outline of the kind of projects for which aid was required, and giving evidence to the people of Malawi that their government was no cautious colonial government but meant to go into the development business in a big way.[56]

Although Malawi's ultimate development objective was to raise the living standards of the mass of the people, its immediate strategy had to be tempered by the resources available. If mass living standards were to be raised, it would have to be largely through their own efforts and through their responsiveness to economic opportunities. The government could afford few handouts.[57] The country's ability to attract foreign aid was realistically seen to be dependent on its economic performance, on its providing evidence of determination and self-sacrifice. Furthermore, the elimination of the budget deficit required an expansion of the tax base and a limit on the growth of consumption expenditure by the government. At the same time, Dr Banda was concerned that Malawi's poverty and external dependence should not lead to a timid approach to development.[58] Bold strokes were needed if development potential was to be realised throughout the country. Hence his proposals for the removal of the administrative capital from Zomba in the south to Lilongwe in the central region, for the establishment of a university in the northern region, for the building of a road from north to south along the Lake shore and of a railway link to a second port, nearer to the central region. Not all were incorporated in the Development Plan at the time of independence, but there was little doubt that, if Banda remained in power, these projects would have a high priority.

Although the individual projects contained in the Development Plan could not be taken as a guide to what, or when, projects would actually be implemented, the statement of priorities made there reflected fairly accurately the government's actual priorities. They were:

'(1)   the expansion of agricultural production (which accounts directly for over half the gross domestic product) so as to provide both for increased domestic production by the growing population and also for greatly increased exports;
(2)   the provision of greatly improved internal communications with a view to reducing transport costs and thus increasing the competitiveness of the country's agricultural exports in the world market;
(3)   a great expansion of the facilities for secondary and post-

secondary education so as to provide the skilled manpower which is essential for development, both in the Civil Service and in the private sector of the economy; and

(4)   the stimulation of the private sector of the economy and, in particular, the encouragement of industrial development.'[59]

These priorities broadly made sense in the context of particular development constraints that Malawi faced. It remained to be seen whether they could be translated into reality.

NOTES

1.   C.A. Baker, 'The Development of the Administration to 1897' in *The Early History of Malawi*, ed. B. Pachai, London, Longman Group Ltd., 1972, p. 324.
2.   *Ibid*, p. 324.
3.   *Ibid*, p. 338.
4.   W. Barber, 'Economic Aspects of Federation,' ed. Leys and Pratt, *A New Deal for Central Africa*, Heinemann, 1960, p. 96.
5.   Nyasaland (Malawi) is divided into three regions: South, Central and Northern, the latter being the least economically advanced.
6.   Central Office of Information, *Malawi*, HMSO 1964, p. 5. W.H. Hancock reports a figure of 120,000 in 1935, which was nearer a quarter of the adult male population. Roughly 20,000 were estimated to be working in Tanganyika, another 20,000 in South Africa, and some 75,000 in Southern Rhodesia. See Hancock, *Survey of British Commonwealth Affairs*, Part II, OUP, 1942, p. 92.
7.   Hancock noted that 'In the five northern districts of the Protectorate, the total sum collected in taxation amounted in one year to £18,379. The wages earned in those districts amounted to £13,000. The sale of crops brought in an additional £1,000. How could the natives secure the extra £4,379 which the government took from them in taxation?' *Ibid*, p. 115. It should be added, however, that, at the turn of the century, the settlers within Nyasaland pressed the administration to take measures to restrict labour migration because their own labour supply was insufficient. The administration accordingly sought to regulate and to limit the emigration but was overruled by the British government, acting in the interests of the labour recruiters of South Africa and Southern Rhodesia. See B.S. Krishnamurthy, 'Economic Policy, Land and Labour in Nyasaland, 1890-1914,' *The Early History of Malawi, op. cit.*, pp. 384-97.
8.   *Ibid.*, pp. 93-4.
9.   'The Nyasaland Native,' reported a Colonial Office investigator in 1938, 'has a reputation through South, Central and East Africa for intelligence and education.' *Ibid.*, pp. 119-20.
10.   A. Hazlewood, 'The Economics of Federation and Dissolution in Central Africa,' ed. A. Hazlewood, *African Integration and Disintegration*, London, OUP, 1967, p. 195. The figure for Nyasaland is based on a rough estimate of the population.
11.   In 1950, the missionaries were said to form 'well over a third of the European Community,' see J.G. Pike, *Malawi, a Political and Economic History*, London, Pall Mall Press, 1968, p. 109.

12. B.S. Krishnamurthy, *op. cit.*, p. 384.
13. Initially Lake Nyasa and the River Shiré provided a natural means of trans-portation, although porterage was necessary for part of the river's length,. from the northern region to the Zambesi, the Protectorate's outlet to the sea. But the water level of the Lake fell soon after the settlers arrived in Nyasaland and the Shiré be-came impassable in its upper and lower reaches.
14. Particularly after 1923 when Southern Rhodesia became self-governing.
15. B.S. Krishnamurthy, *op. cit.*, p. 385 ff.
16. Total expenditure under the Act between 1929 and 1940 came to only £6.5m. Cmnd. 4677, *CD&W Acts 1929-70: A Brief Review*, HMSO, 1971, p. 6.
17. Calculated from data in C.S.O. *National Accounts and Balance of Payments of Northern Rhodesia, Nyasaland and Southern Rhodesia 1954-1963*, Southern Rhodesia, C.S.O., 1964, Tables 56, 100 and 145.
18. The first Commission to investigate the possibility of closer association between the territories of Eastern and Central Africa was the Hilton Young Commission, which reported in 1929. The second, headed by Lord Bledisloe, produced its report in 1939.
19. Federation 'would mean domination by Southern Rhodesia instead of guardianship by the United Kingdom, since, by virtue of her much larger European population, the Native policy of the Federation would chiefly be determined by the attitude of the European settlers of that colony, which cannot be said to be favourable to full African political, cultural and social development . . . it would, in fact, be only the thin end of the wedge of amalgamation.' H.K. Banda and H. Nkumbula, *Federation in Central Africa*, p. 3, quoted in Pike, *op. cit.*, p. 114. They were not far wrong in guessing that the real aim of the settler leaders, Huggins and Welensky, was still amalgamation, see p. 117.
20. The belief was ill-founded because (a) 'in all the published reports, dis-cussions and debates which preceded the establishment of the Federation, there is no comprehensive – or even remotely adequate – treatment of the economic issues,' and (b) the arguments put forward to support the supposedly over-whelmingly economic case for federation were greatly overstated and, even so, not all of them led to the conclusion that political federation was necessary. See A.D. Hazlewood and P.D. Henderson, *Nyasaland: The Economics of Federation*, Oxford, Blackwell, 1960, pp. 18-30.
21. All agriculture in Nyasaland was under the territorial government.
22. Federation of Rhodesia and Nyasaland Government, *Report on Economic Survey of Nyasaland 1958-59* (Jack Report), Government Printer, Zomba, 1960, p. 1.
23. Hazlewood and Henderson, *op. cit.*, pp. 70-5.
24. Statement by Chipembere reported in Cmnd. 814, *Report of the Nyasa-land Commission of Enquiry* (Devlin Report), London, HMSO, 1959, p. 13.
25. There is some confusion as to Banda's date of birth: 1898 is the earliest date given, 1906 the latest.
26. Banda considered that if he stayed in London, he would continue in active opposition to federation. Devlin Report, *op. cit.*, p. 12.
27. It was estimated by the special branch of police in Nyasaland that, in the Northern Province alone, the number of Congress branches increased from thirty-seven to sixty-three during the six months up to January 1959. *Ibid.*, p. 23.
28. *Ibid.*, p. 37.
29. *Ibid.*, para. 43.
30. Cmnd. 1148, *Report of the Advistory Commission of the Review of the Con-stitution of Rhodesia and Nyasaland* (Monckton Report), London, HMSO, 1960.
31. Nyasaland Protectorate, *Proceedings of the Legislative Assembly*, Zomba, Government Printer, January 1968, pp. 1, 108-9.

32.　MCP slogan for the development struggle, as against the independence struggle.

33.　The small minority were the Jehovah's Witnesses, whose religion involved the rejection of any allegiance to political organisations. Consequently, they refused to become members of the MCP. The League of Malawi Youth, the militant wing of the MCP, attempted violent persuasion, and the sect suffered a number of deaths and hut burnings in the Mulanje district, Southern Region. Although Banda later supported the view that 'not to be with us, is to be against us,' in 1964 he intervened to stop the violence. Elsewhere, there were small pockets of political resistance to MCP domination but none really posed a serious threat.

34.　The future pace of Africanisation in Malawi, for instance, was a politically sensitive issue on which Banda and 'his boys' disagreed and were seen to disagree.

35.　After independence, Malawi's currency remained at par with £ Sterling. In 1971, decimal currency was introduced with one Kwacha equal to 100 tambala. Parity with sterling was retained with K2 = £1, until November 1973, since when the Kwacha-Sterling rate has averaged K1.96 (average of end of month parities to May 1974). K2 = £1 is the parity used here for conversion.

36.　Estimate of the C.S.O., Salisbury, for 1963.

37.　Malawi's additional budget liability for federal debt amounted, in 1964, to £236,000 for servicing costs and c.£1m for debt redemption. Federal services, leaving aside public debt payments, had been estimated to have cost £4.9m in Nyasaland during the financial year 1962/3. *Proceedings of the Legislative Assembly, op. cit.*, pp. 1090-4.

38.　*Ibid.*, p. 1095.

39.　Nyasaland Protectorate, *Development Plan 1962-1965*, 1962, Zomba, Government Printer. A document not without pretensions, but finally a 'project shopping list' plan.

40.　Perhaps the most basic deficiency was the fact that no one had troubled to carry out a population census in Malawi for nearly twenty years.

41.　Cmnd. 1887, *Report of the Nyasaland Constitutional Conference*, London, HMSO, 1962, para. 11.

42.　*MCP Manifesto*, 1961.

43.　According to UN figures for 1971, the average population density in Africa was twelve persons per square kilometre, in Malawi it was thirty-eight, in neighbouring Tanzania, Zambia and Southern Rhodesia it was fourteen, six and fourteen respectively.

44.　The classification depended on drivers' standards and tastes.

45.　Malawi Government, *Development Plan, 1965-69*, Zomba, Government Printer, June 1964, p. 7.

46.　Statement made on 17 December 1963 in the House of Commons, UK, quoted by the Minister of Finance (Mr Phillips) in his 1964 Budget Speech, *Proceedings of the Legislative Assembly, op. cit.*, p. 1104.

47.　*Ibid.*, p. 1104.

48.　Q.v. I.M.D. Little and J.M. Clifford, *International Aid*, London, George Allen & Unwin, 1965, p. 61.

49.　*Ibid.*, pp. 63-5.

50.　And total project costs tend to be raised if the recipient tries to minimise the local cost content: 'For instance, a farm institute was built in Nyasaland for £48,000 with untied "Freedom from Hunger" money. The proposal for the institute had been fully explored with AID [the US aid agency]. Financed by them the cost would have been £73,000, with an AID [tied] contribution of £40,000.' I.M.D. Little, *Aid to Africa*, Pergamon Press, 1964.

51.   Malawi is landlocked and had only one, vulnerable, link with a port, yet most supplies would have to be imported.

52.   Malawi's supply line passed through Mozambique; Rhodesia and South Africa accounted for nearly half its imports and 20 per cent of its domestic exports, while the majority of Malawians working abroad did so in white southern Africa. While in all these areas a *quid pro quo* existed between Malawi and southern Africa, the economic sanctions that could be applied by the latter countries were potentially more damaging to Malawi than vice versa.

53.   At the OAU Conference in July 1964, Dr Banda had pointed out that Malawi simply could not afford to follow any resolution demanding the severance of economic, diplomatic or cultural relations with southern Africa. His 'dialogue' policy, which rendered the expedient desirable, was pronounced shortly afterwards.

54.   China's offer of aid conditional on diplomatic recognition was referred to as a 'naked bribe' by Banda.

55.   Detailed phasing of projects was 'likely to be misleading,' 1965-1969 Development Plan, *op. cit.*, p. 5.

56.   Banda related that when 'his boys' first brought him the plan, its size was K26m. Banda 'was furious' and sent them away to produce a plan of at least K80m. 'I am not a colonial government,' he had said. See Malawi Goverment, *Hansard*, 29 October 1964. This also illustrates the arbitrary formulation suggested by the relatively large plan expenditure.

57.   Universal primary education, for instance, part of the MCP election platform, represented an important unsatisfied popular demand: yet its provision would require largely consumption expenditure, and it was therefore dropped from the immediate development strategy.

58.   Equally aid should not be accepted if it compromised Malawi's political and economic independence.

59.   Development Plan, *op. cit.*, pp. 5-6.

2 MALAWI'S ECONOMIC PERFORMANCE AFTER INDEPENDENCE

In 1964 Malawi faced economic problems as severe as any confronting any newly independent country. This chapter summarises the main aspects of Malawi's economic performance since that time, as a background to the examination of British aid. It begins, however, with a short account of political developments in the country.

Crisis and Consolidation

Less than two months after the independence celebrations, Dr Banda's dominance was challenged. The crisis was precipitated by a clash between Dr Banda and the majority of his Cabinet, who specifically opposed a number of his policies, and generally opposed his autocratic style of leadership, which tended to preclude due Cabinet consultation. Whether or not a showdown was intended is not clear: at first, some compromise seemed possible.[1] But what initially appeared to be a domestic squabble swiftly turned into a confrontation. The ministers, who had the support of a large section of educated Africans and also some popular backing, either resigned or were dismissed from Dr Banda's government, and several months of political unrest followed. At one point, the administrative capital – Zomba – was virtually in the hands of the dissidents and in February 1965 an armed insurrection led by the leader of the 'rebel' ministers, Chipembere, came near to toppling Dr Banda. However, Chipembere was defeated and went into exile along with the other 'rebel' ministers and Dr Banda emerged as victor.

The situation posed a serious threat to Malawi's development prospects – not to mention the personal power of Dr Banda. Malawi was dependent on external support, both financial and in the form of expatriate skills. Neither would be forthcoming if outsiders had little confidence in the political stability of the country. And the domestic development effort could have been dissipated by political uncertainties and lack of leadership. While such uncertainties might have been ended quickly if Dr Banda had been toppled, it is more probable that unrest would only have been protracted. Chipembere was by no means the only contender for leadership of the rebels and even if Dr Banda had gone quietly into exile (as he maintained he would, had popular support favoured the rebels), it is unlikely that all of his followers would have transferred their allegiance. Further, whether or not Chipembere and the other ex-ministers would have toned down their anti-European and anti-southern African sentiments when in power and whether or not political stability was achieved, the local expatriate community would certainly have been less willing to remain had they attained power.

Since this threat to Dr Banda's position, his power has steadily increased. Although Malawi retains British-style institutions of government and law, constitutional amendments have whittled away their powers. In 1966, Dr Banda became President of Malawi and the MCP was made the only legal political party; thus organised opposition was banned. Dr Banda has acquired sole control over the membership of Parliament,[2] of the Cabinet, of the Party and its Executive: a power which he has used, together with the detention laws to curb possible opposition and ensure that the four cornerstones of his regime — loyalty, obedience, discipline and unity — did not crumble again. In 1971, when nearing the age of seventy, Dr Banda was made Life President. No vice-president exists nor has any politician been permitted to emerge as his probable successor.

Certain observers in Western liberal circles have likened Dr Banda's régime to such régimes as that of François Duvalier in Haiti. Such comparisons have much to do with Dr Banda's foreign policy — often misconstrued — of dialogue and *détente* with the white-dominated régimes of Southern Africa and the lack of *détente*, until recently, between Malawi and the black African states on its borders. Inside Malawi there is some justification in that strong arm methods are used, and while party loyalists do not receive direct economic rewards, there has recently been a notable accretion of economic power amongst party officials and politicians. But, on the whole, the comparisons lack justification. While Dr Banda's régime has certain repressive and unpleasant features,[3] his retention of power is based on the widespread popular support he enjoys. Partly this support derives from personal loyalty, but it is also a consequence (as well as a cause) of the development momentum that has been built up in Malawi under his leadership. And his political strength has had one major advantage. It has resulted in a degree of political stability that is unequalled by many developing countries, and is all the more impressive because the development strategy entailed a considerable restriction of current consumption growth, which could easily have caused popular dissent and political instability.

General Economic Performance

Under Dr Banda's leadership, Malawi has pursued its development strategy with some success. Economic growth, measured in terms of GDP at current market prices, averaged 12 per cent a year between 1964 and 1973. With the population growing at 2.5 per cent a year, average income per head has been increasing by 9 per cent a year, representing a growth of over 4 per cent a year at constant prices. Exports of goods and services by value have increased by nearly 15 per cent a year. Investment rates have been high and Malawi has received substantial inflows of private and official foreign capital. Meanwhile the recurrent budget deficit, financed by grants from Britain, has been eliminated. However, incomes per head are still very low: in 1973, GDP per head was estimated to be only K89.5 at current market prices — roughly £45.

The growth rate since independence has been far from even. The economy had been virtually stagnant since 1962 and in 1964 was at an extremely low ebb: there may even have been a decline in GDP in that year. In 1965 economic activity began to return to normal, and good agricultural conditions, higher public spending and a large increase in private sector investment produced a rapid rate of growth in 1966. Between 1964 and 1966 GDP expanded by 26 per cent at constant prices. Growth slowed in 1967, and in 1968, when bad climatic conditions were added to financial and physical constraints, GDP at constant prices actually declined. There was a revival in 1969, and over the two succeeding years and despite poor weather conditions in 1970, GDP at constant prices increased by 17 per cent. Since then the annual rate of expansion has slowed to 4 per cent a year in real terms. As output was abnormally low in 1964, the average growth rate through to 1973 overstates the real expansion in Malawi's productive capacity. Nevertheless, and despite the fluctuations in growth, Malawi's economy has clearly acquired a substantial growth momentum.

Output

Non-monetary output in Malawi accounted for nearly half of GDP at factor cost in 1964 and 35 per cent in 1973 (see Table 2.1). The existence of a large subsistence sector in Malawi poses problems in considering economic performance, for while calculating the value of subsistence output may indicate the order of magnitude, it cannot accurately show changes occurring in the subsistence sector.[4] Yet, it is reasonable to suppose that, with the rapid expansion of monetary output, the pattern of subsistence activity has changed, since those living in rural areas are characteristically participants in both the subsistence and the cash economy. For instance, with a greater division of labour being encouraged by monetisation, certain activities may have declined while increased opportunities for cash earnings and purchases may have stimulated non-monetised investment activities. Such changes must be a matter of speculation. Nevertheless, despite the recorded decline of

Table 2.1 Non-monetary Gross Domestic Product by industrial origin. Total GDP and Gross National Product 1964-73.

Sector	Km (current prices)									
	1964	1965	1966	1967	1968	1969	1970	1971	1972*	1973**
Agriculture	63.0	71.1	78.8	78.4	79.1	81.4	87.9	110.2	116.9	119.8
Manufacturing	4.4	5.3	5.5	6.2	6.3	6.1	6.5	7.0	7.5	7.7
Building and construction	2.3	2.7	2.8	3.3	3.4	3.5	3.6	3.5	3.8	4.0
Storage	0.4	0.5	0.5	0.7	0.7	0.7	0.7	0.7	0.7	0.8
Ownership of dwellings	2.2	2.4	2.5	2.8	2.9	2.9	3.0	n.a	n.a	n.a
Total non-monetary GDP (factor cost)	72.3	82.1	90.1	91.4	92.3	94.5	101.7	121.4	128.9	131.5
% Total GDP	49.3	47.8	46.7	45.0	43.4	40.7	39.2	38.0	36.8	34.6
Total monetary GDP (factor cost)	74.2	89.8	102.8	111.5	120.4	137.5	157.8	193.3	221.4	248.4
% Total GDP	50.7	52.2	53.3	55.0	56.6	59.3	60.8	62.0	63.2	65.4
Total GDP (factor cost)	146.6	171.9	192.9	202.9	212.7	232.0	259.5	314.7	350.3	379.9 (403.9)†
Plus net indirect taxes	4.9	6.9	9.9	10.9	11.1	13.5	17.2	21.2	23.3	25.0†
Total GDP (Market prices)	151.4	178.8	202.9	213.9	223.8	245.6	276.7	335.9	373.6	428.9†
Plus net income paid abroad	− 6.2	− 4.3	− 5.6	− 7.8	− 7.0	− 5.7	− 6.0	− 1.2	+ 2.7	− 3.1†
Total GNP (Market prices)	145.3	174.4	197.3	206.1	216.9	239.9	270.7	332.7	376.3	425.8†

* Estimates
** At 1972 prices
† Estimate at 1973 prices
n.a. not applicable

Sources: N.S.O. *National Accounts Report 1964-1969*, Zomba, 1971; and *Economic Reports 1972, 1973 and 1974*, Zomba, 1973 and 1974.

subsistence output relative to total output, its continuing importance in Malawi's economy must be stressed. Most of the rural dwellers in Malawi – the majority of the population – still rely on their own production to meet their subsistence needs and as their main source of real income: cash crop production is essentially a marginal activity for many small farmers, with sales depending on the size of their surplus production.

Having increased by over 15 per cent a year,[5] monetary output now constitutes 65 per cent of total GDP (factor cost) in Malawi. The agricultural sector continues to be the mainstay of the economy although production has grown slightly more slowly than total monetary output (Table 2.2). The most striking sectoral growth has been in manufacturing industry, which doubled its share of monetary GDP, while the most striking decline, in relative terms, has been in public administration and defence, whose share of GDP dropped from 18.6 per cent in 1964 to 8.4 per cent in 1973 – a symptom of Malawi's budgetary restraint.[6]

Agricultural output has fluctuated considerably from year to year, mainly because of the variations in smallholder cash crop production. The most important smallholder cash crops are maize, groundnuts, sun/ air and fire-cured tobacco and cotton. (Rice, millet, wheat, sunflower seed, cassava and coffee make up most of the remaining crops that are marketed.) Both in quantities produced for sale and their value, output of these crops has been erratic, owing to climatic variations and price fluctuations. But since 1968 total smallholder cash crop production has begun to rise in value. The production of estate crops, chiefly tea, flue-cured and Birley tobacco, has steadily increased, from K5.9m in 1964 to K22.3m in 1973. The production of sugar as an estate crop after independence contributed to this increase.

The main growth in manufacturing output has occurred in import substituting consumer goods industries, a growth which is reflected in the fall in consumer goods imports (see Table 2.7). In 1964, roughly half of the manufactured output of firms employing twenty or more persons[7] was from the processing of agricultural exports, chiefly tea and tobacco, while consumption goods accounted for 40 per cent. By 1969, production of manufactured consumption goods, including beer, soft drinks, matches and clothing, accounted for nearly 60 per cent of a considerably expanded total. Intermediate goods production, mainly textiles and building materials, increased its share from 10 per cent to 19 per cent.

Most other sectors of the economy have expanded fairly steadily, although none, with the exception of banking and finance (which made a negative contribution to total output in 1964), at the rate of the manufacturing sector. The growth of the banking system is indicated by the rise in commercial bank advances and deposits since 1965 (which

Table 2.2 Monetary Gross Domestic Product by industrial origin, 1964-73

Sector	1964	% total	1965	% total	1966	% total	1967	% total	1968	% total	1969	% total	1970	% total	1971*	% total	1972*	% total	1973*†	% total
Agriculture																				
smallholders	15.9	21.4	21.7	24.2	21.8	21.2	24.2	21.7	21.9	18.4	26.0	18.9	25.1	15.9	32.3	16.7	36.1	16.3	32.5	13.1
estate/government	5.9	8.0	6.4	7.1	7.0	6.8	7.3	6.6	9.0	7.5	11.1	8.1	11.4	7.2	15.2	7.9	19.0	8.5	22.3	9.0
Total	21.8	29.4	28.1	31.3	28.8	28.0	31.6	28.3	30.9	25.7	37.1	27.0	36.5	23.1	47.5	24.6	55.1	24.8	54.8	22.1
Manufacturing	7.8	10.5	10.1	11.2	13.5	13.2	15.6	14.0	17.6	14.7	21.6	15.8	34.5	21.9	33.0	17.1	39.5	17.8	48.6	19.6
Building and construction	3.3	4.4	3.8	4.3	6.1	6.0	5.3	4.7	6.8	5.6	8.6	6.3	10.2	6.5	13.2	6.8	15.8	7.1	20.6	8.3
Electricity and water	1.1	1.5	1.3	1.5	1.7	1.7	2.0	1.8	2.3	1.9	2.5	1.8	2.9	1.8	3.6	1.9	4.2	1.9	4.7	1.9
Total	12.2	16.4	15.2	17.0	21.4	20.8	22.9	20.6	26.8	22.3	32.9	23.8	47.6	30.2	49.8	25.8	59.5	26.8	73.9	29.8
Distribution	11.9	16.1	14.8	16.5	15.7	15.2	15.5	13.9	19.3	16.0	22.6	16.4	25.9	16.4	37.9	19.6	42.4	19.1	45.6	18.4
Banking and finance	−0.2	−0.3	0.4	0.5	0.3	0.3	0.4	0.4	0.5	0.5	0.5	0.4	}		3.2	1.7	4.3	1.9	5.7	2.3
Transport and communications	5.2	7.0	6.5	7.3	8.4	8.1	9.9	8.8	9.7	8.1	9.7	7.1	9.9	6.3	15.1	7.8	17.8	8.0	23.9	9.6
Rents	1.5	2.1	1.8	2.1	2.0	1.9	2.4	2.1	2.7	2.2	3.0	2.1	3.1	2.0	6.8	3.5	7.8	3.5	8.3	3.3
Domestic and other services	4.0	5.4	4.4	4.9	5.0	4.9	5.8	5.2	6.0	5.0	6.6	4.8	7.5	4.8	n.a.	n.a.	n.a.	n.a.	n.a.	n.a.
Total	22.4	30.6	27.9	31.1	31.4	30.5	34.0	30.5	38.2	31.7	42.4	30.8	46.4	29.4	63.0	32.6	72.3	32.6	83.5	33.6
Public administration and defence	13.8	18.6	13.9	15.5	15.7	15.3	17.2	15.3	17.7	14.7	18.2	13.3	19.1	12.1	18.6	9.6	20.0	9.0	21.0	8.4
Education	2.8	3.8	3.1	3.5	4.0	3.9	4.2	3.8	5.0	4.2	5.3	3.9	5.5	3.5	6.3	3.3	6.7	3.0	7.0	2.8
Health	1.1	1.5	1.4	1.6	1.5	1.5	1.6	1.4	1.7	1.4	1.8	1.3	2.7	1.7	3.0	1.6	3.2	1.4	3.4	1.4
Total	17.7	23.9	18.4	20.4	21.2	20.6	23.0	20.6	24.4	20.3	25.3	18.4	27.3	17.3	27.9	14.4	29.9	13.5	31.4	12.6
Total monetary GDP at factor cost	74.2	100.0	89.8	100.0	102.8	100.0	111.5	100.0	120.4	100.0	137.5	100.0	157.8	100.0	193.3	100.0	221.4	100.0	248.4	100.0
															(97.4)		(97.4)		(98.1)	

(For 1970 the value 25.9 / 16.4 under Distribution is combined with Banking and finance.)

* Individual items do not add to the total; and data for domestic and other services not available. Percentages based on total not on the sum of individual items.

† At 1972 prices.

Source: As for Table 2.1

was the year in which the Reserve Bank of Malawi was established). Demand deposits increased 130 per cent over the six year period from December 1971, savings and time deposits 186 per cent and advances 250 per cent. The two main financial institutions outside the banking system, the Post Office and the New Building Society, also expanded their operations: savings deposits at the Post Office increased by 130 per cent, Building Society deposits 116 per cent.

Building and construction output has fluctuated widely, reflecting changes in the level of domestic fixed investment. Distribution has expanded slightly faster than total output, but has been fairly sensitive to shifts in agricultural production. Surprisingly, an absolute decline in output occurred in 1967, which was a good agricultural year: the Farmers' Marketing Board (now the Agricultural Development and Marketing Corporation – ADMARC), which normally contributed a quarter of value-added in the distribution sector, made a heavy loss owing to its miscalculation of the maize price. Mining and quarrying, which is included in manufacturing, still accounts for only a small fraction – 0.1 per cent – of monetary output. No decision has yet been reached regarding the exploitation of the bauxite in Mount Mulanje, which, despite vigorous exploration – mainly by the government – remains the only known mineral deposit of any major significance.

It is difficult to give an accurate picture of how production is organised. Available data show that government output declined from 29.1 per cent of monetary GDP in 1964 to 23 per cent in 1969. However, this figure understates the extent of public sector involvement in production, both directly through public sector enterprises and indirectly through the participation of public corporations, most notably ADMARC and the Malawi Development Corporation, in private sector enterprise. Further, the rapidly increasing interests of the MCP-owned private enterprise venture Press Holdings,[8] into which some ADMARC profits have been channeled, represents an extension of government control in the economy. Thus, although the private large-enterprise sector has apparently grown fastest, its increased share of output overstates the growth of wholly private production. The share of small-scale enterprises and production on own account – mainly smallholders – has declined, from 39.8 per cent in 1964 to 35.8 per cent in 1969.

Employment

Statistics on employment are available only for large-scale industries in the monetary sector, and show that it has not kept pace with the rate of growth in GDP. But as these industries are more capital-intensive, employment trends in them cannot be taken as a guide to what happened elsewhere. Average annual employment in such enterprises — employing twenty or more persons — and in government increased from 134,500 in 1968 to 215,000 in 1973, up 60 per cent as compared with a growth of monetary GDP at constant prices of nearly 70 per cent over the same period. Employment in government service increased relatively slowly — by 45 per cent — mainly because of budgetary restraint. This depressed the total growth rate since it accounts for about a third of wage employment: numbers employed in the private sector rose by 68 per cent. In the manufacturing sector, however, employment increased by only 47 per cent, so that, while the sector's output was 23 per cent of total monetary output (excluding smallholder agriculture) by 1973, it accounted for less than 12 per cent of total wage employment (in larger enterprises).

Government development policy aims to create jobs: economic growth, and particularly agricultural development, has been the chief means for increasing work opportunities. Within the organised sector, a system of investment allowances — although not overly generous — actually favours capital-intensive activities. The National Wages and Salaries Policy, introduced formally in 1969, but partially effective since 1966, provides some counterweight by attempting to curb wage increases in the large-scale industrial sector. The fact that average earnings in the organised sector have risen slowly, barely exceeding inflation since 1968, suggests that the policy has had some effect; but for various reasons earnings data are a poor guide to movements in wage rates.[9] It is difficult to say whether this policy, which is designed chiefly to narrow the gap between rural and urban incomes and to prevent wage inflation, has actually had any impact on industrial employment: certainly there has been no discernible downward movement in the capital/labour ratios of new enterprises receiving industrial licences.[10]

The growth of employment in enterprises employing less than twenty persons and the growth of self-employment is hard to gauge: little data exist and none are comparable. The relatively slower growth of output from smaller enterprises and enterprises 'on own account' (including smallholder agriculture), and the fact that Malawi continues to export labour in large, and probably increasing, numbers to neighbouring countries[11] suggest that employment opportunities have not risen rapidly.[12] And indeed the availability of relatively lucrative job opportunities outside the country is an important factor in Malawi's avoiding the problem of urban unemployment.[13]

Localisation in Malawi has proceeded slowly compared with some other African countries, partly because of the rapid expansion of economic activity and partly because of the acute shortage of local skilled manpower. The number of expatriates employed in the public sector, where most effort to localise has been made, has remained more or less constant (while declining in relative terms), but in the private sector has probably increased since independence. In 1971, it was estimated that 16.8 per cent of total skilled manpower, and 31 per cent of private sector skilled personnel, were non-citizens.[14] It is at the top management and professional level that expatriates are most important.

Investment, Consumption and Savings

The rate of investment expenditure in Malawi since independence has been high for such a poor country: only in 1964 was fixed investment expenditure less than 10 per cent of GDP (at market prices) and since 1968 it has not been below 16 per cent. Fixed investment in the subsistence sector is estimated to have increased from K1.3m in 1964 to K2.5m in 1973. Taking the monetary sector alone, investment has generally been between 25 per cent and 30 per cent of GDP, increasing from K11.9m in 1964 to K87.5m in 1973 (see Table 2.3).

Public sector investment (i.e. by the central government and statutory corporations) has predominated throughout the period. Private sector investment has, however, grown faster: in 1964 and 1965 it stagnated at around K4m but has since increased, with some fluctuation, to a record level of K26.8m in 1971, nearly half of total monetary investment in that year. Recorded fixed investment in the monetary sector probably understates the total investment that has taken place; a substantial proportion of government 'consumption' expenditure, for instance in the education and extension services, has raised the country's productive capacity.

Much of the investment in both the private and public sector has been financed by capital inflows and transfers from external sources. The importance of external finance in the public sector is indicated by the fact that roughly three-quarters of development account spending (not all capital expenditure) by the central government since independence has been financed by foreign grants and loans. The precise contribution of external resources to private sector investment is not known but almost all larger enterprises in Malawi are wholly or partially foreign owned.

Britain has been the main source of Malawi's public and, probably, private external finance. After 1966 other countries began to make significant aid contributions. Malawi now receives inter-governmental aid from six main sources besides Britain: the International Development Association, South Africa, the United States, West Germany, Denmark and the African Development Bank. Besides British investment, private external finance appears to come mainly from Denmark, Rhodesia, South Africa and Portugal.

However, an increasing proportion of investment has been financed

Table 2.3 Domestic Resources and Uses 1964-73

Km (current prices)

	1964	1965	1966	1967	1968	1969	1970	1971	1972*	1973*
GDP at market prices	151.4	178.8	202.9	213.9	223.8	245.6	276.7	335.9	373.6	428.9
Import surplus	11.1	21.3	29.2	20.8	31.6	34.3	37.2	34.5	46.1	44.2
Total domestic resources	162.5	200.1	232.1	234.7	255.4	279.9	313.9	370.4	419.7	473.1
Consumption total	151.2	175.1	197.4	205.7	218.6	230.1	255.4	309.7	347.6	387.6
of which:										
non-monetary	70.2	80.2	86.9	88.2	89.5	91.9	99.8	117.8	128.8	138.3
monetary:										
government	23.8	26.8	31.6	34.5	36.7	38.6	37.7	44.0	50.7	53.2
private	56.5	68.0	78.2	82.5	92.4	101.5	117.8	147.9	168.1	196.1
Fixed investment total	13.2	19.3	29.4	25.5	37.4	49.0	50.2	53.2	66.1	87.5
of which:										
non-monetary	1.3	1.6	1.6	1.9	2.0	2.0	2.1	2.1	2.5	2.5
monetary:										
public	7.9	13.4	16.1	13.5	18.1	24.1	28.6	24.7	29.6	43.5
private	4.0	4.3	11.6	10.0	17.3	22.9	19.5	26.4	34.0	41.5
Stock changes	− 1.2	5.8	6.0	4.0	− 0.7	− 1.0	8.3	7.5	6.0	− 2.0
of which:										
non-monetary	0.8	0.4	1.6	1.2	0.8	0.6	0.4	4.5	1.0	0.0
monetary	− 2.0	5.4	4.4	2.7	− 1.5	− 1.6	7.9	3.0	5.0	− 2.0
Total uses	162.5	200.1	232.1	234.7	255.4	279.9	313.9	370.4	419.7	473.1

*   Provisional estimates.

Sources: Malawi Government *National Accounts Report 1964-69; Economic Report*, 1974.

from domestic savings. Whereas in 1964 monetary domestic savings were negative, as a result of the large budget deficit, in 1973 Malawi's domestic savings covered 47 per cent of domestic investment expenditure (including stock changes). And national savings (i.e. domestic savings plus net factor payments abroad), which were negative until 1969, covered about a third of total investment requirements in 1973 (viz. domestic investment, amortisation payments on external debt and changes in reserves). Consumption spending meanwhile has been relatively restrained, particularly government consumption, which increased at an average annual rate of just over 9 per cent between 1964 and 1973, only slightly more than the rate of inflation – roughly 8 per cent.

A breakdown of domestic investment by industrial sector is not available. In the government sector the major part of investment-type spending has been in transport and agriculture. Elsewhere in the public sector, capital spending has been mainly on the expansion of services for the urban industrial sector. Data are also not available on the regional location of investment, which would allow an evaluation of the government's success in redressing regional imbalance. However, the main focus in both private and public sector investment has clearly been in the southern and central regions. Urban industrial development by both sectors has mostly taken place in the southern region, as in the colonial era. However, the transportation system, the building of the new capital at Lilongwe and agricultural projects will shift the balance more to the central region. And the new large-scale agricultural project in the northern region, together with the development of road and lake links with the north, are likely to increase growth prospects there.

Public Finance and Administration

The Malawi government has moved from its post-independence position of insolvency when its recurrent budget deficits were financed by British budgetary aid, achieving a balanced budget in 1973-4. This is the result of a combination of expenditure restraint, tax effort and economic growth. 'Non-developmental' government recurrent expenditure, for instance on general administration and health, has been held back, civil service salaries have been subject to a freeze[16] since 1966 and various expenditure control devices have been introduced to encourage the efficient use of available resources. Between 1964 and 1972-3, recurrent account expenditure increased by about 75 per cent while tax revenue was more than trebled. This latter increase is due to the imposition of new, mainly indirect, taxation as well as the expansion of the tax base with economic growth and inflation. Total tax revenue accounted for 16.4 per cent of monetary GNP in 1972-3 as compared with 12.9 per cent in 1964.

Table 2.4   Malawi Government Expenditure on Revenue and
Development Accounts 1964-5 and 1970/1-1971/2
(annual averages)

	Annual average 1964-5		Annual average 1970/1-1971/2		Percentage change between 1964-5 and 1970/1-1971/2
	Km	% total	Km	% total	
General services	9.0	22.8	12.3	15.1	36.7
Natural resources	3.1	7.8	11.1	13.6	258.0
Manpower	8.2	20.8	15.5	19.0	89.0
of which:					
Education	(5.2)	(13.2)	(10.6)	(12.9)	103.8
Health	(2.0)	(5.1)	(3.4)	(4.2)	70.0
Community development	(1.0)	(2.5)	(1.5)	(1.8)	50.0
Communications	4.8	12.2	15.1	18.5	214.6
Other services	4.3	10.9	14.5	17.8	237.2
Public debt charges	5.5	13.9	7.4	9.1	34.5
Unallocable	4.6	11.6	5.7	7.0	23.9
Total	39.5	100.0	81.9	100.0	107.3
Total excluding public debt charges and unallocable	29.4	74.4	68.8	83.9	134.0

Sources: N.S.O. *Malawi Statistical Yearbook 1972*, Zomba, 1972; E.P.D.
Economic Report 1973, Zomba, 1973.

Central government development expenditure (which includes a significant element of recurrent 'developmental' expenditure) meanwhile
increased rapidly, from K5.4m in 1964 to K26.7m in 1972-3,[17] a
growth permitted by Malawi's success in attracting external aid finance.
Total government expenditure has more than doubled (see Table 2.4):
consistent with development priorities, spending on natural resources,
education and communication has grown most rapidly, along with
expenditure on 'other services' (which include the new capital).
    The need both to curb recurrent expenditure growth and to obtain
external support has reinforced the incentive for efficiency in the

government service. The Malawi government has concentrated on the problem of getting things done and has administered the country and implemented its development programme with considerable efficiency, and with a marked absence of corruption. Compared with other ldcs, the standards of honesty and efficiency in Malawi's public service are considered to be high by donor government officials and other expatriates. And certainly, there is little evidence of bribery or the misappropriation of funds within the service. Planning has received less attention, partly because Malawi's needs were initially fairly obvious and partly because of the shortage of data and expertise and the reliance on donor finance.

That reliance, together with a decline in external grants, has resulted in the growth of external public debt outstanding from K47m in 1964 to K170m in 1973, of which the central government's debt was K40m and K143m respectively. The terms of the government debt have improved, reflecting relatively soft loans after independence: in 1964, the average interest rate was 4.9 per cent and the average redemption period 15.9 years: in 1973, they were 2.1 per cent and 24.9 years respectively.[18] Malawi has also gained from changes in exchange rate parities — which in 1971, for example, reduced the debt by K3.9m.

Nevertheless servicing of the total external public debt has risen steadily since 1965 (in 1964 it was abnormally high because of the federal debt settlement): from K4.1m to K8.6m in 1973, and is expected to reach K11.5m by 1975.[19]

Balance of Payments and External Trade

The rapid growth of mainly cash crop exports since independence has been a key factor in Malawi's economic growth. Exports of goods and services increased by 15 per cent a year between 1964 and 1971, and represented approximately 37 per cent of monetary GDP in both years. Imports, however, increased at a slightly faster rate — and Malawi's deficit has grown over the period from K21m in 1965 to K41m in 1973. As can be seen from Table 2.5, apart from the factor income payments, the current account has been in surplus owing to government and private transfers from abroad. These transfers have fallen, however, mainly reflecting the reduction of budgetary grants-in-aid, and the total current account deficit has increased in most years since independence. This deficit has, however, usually been covered by foreign capital inflows and only in 1966 did foreign exchange reserves fall substantially. Malawi's reserves have given import cover of slightly over three months on average, except in 1973 when it was over six months.

Malawi's merchandise exports are still predominantly agricultural. In 1973 cash crops accounted for roughly 95 per cent of domestic exports,

Table 2.5 Balance of Payments of Malawi 1964-73 (in Km)

Current account	1964	1965	1966	1967	1968	1969	1970	1971	1972	1973*
1 Merchandise:										
Exports	24.4	28.5	34.6	40.4	40.0	43.2	47.9	58.3	62.6	75.8
Imports (f.o.b.)	28.6	40.9	54.1	50.2	57.0	61.0	68.4	75.3	89.4	98.9
Balance	-4.3	-12.4	-19.5	-9.7	-17.0	-17.8	-20.5	-17.0	-26.8	-23.1
2 Non factor services:										
Exports	3.2	4.1	6.3	7.4	8.0	7.7	10.8	13.0	14.2	19.6
Imports	10.0	13.1	16.0	18.5	22.5	24.2	26.2	30.5	33.5	37.6
Balance	-6.8	-9.0	-9.7	-11.1	-14.5	-16.5	-15.4	-17.5	-19.4	-18.0
3 Factor income:										
Receipts	3.9	5.5	5.3	5.1	5.6	8.0	10.0	13.3	14.8	15.8
Payments	10.1	9.8	10.9	12.9	12.6	13.7	16.1	15.9	16.7	18.9
Balance	-6.2	-4.3	-5.6	-7.8	-7.0	-5.7	-6.0	-2.6	-1.9	-3.1
4 Net balance										
(1) + (2) + (3)	-17.2	-25.7	-34.8	-28.6	-38.5	-40.0	-41.9	-37.1	-48.0	-44.2
5 Private transfers:										
Receipts	1.3	2.1	1.2	1.6	1.8	2.0	2.1	2.0	2.5	2.7
Payments	1.2	1.2	0.5	0.2	0.3	0.3	0.2	0.1	0.1	0.1
Balance	0.1	0.9	0.7	1.3	1.6	1.7	1.9	1.9	2.4	2.6
6 Government transfers										
Receipts	18.1	26.4	16.3	16.6	15.1	14.0	11.2	8.8	8.7	9.0
Payments	-	0.1	0.1	0.1	0.2	0.2	0.2	0.2	0.2	0.2
Balance	18.1	26.3	16.2	16.4	14.9	13.8	11.0	8.6	8.4	8.8
7 Net transfers	18.1	27.2	16.9	17.7	16.5	15.6	12.9	10.5	10.8	11.4
8 Current account										
balance (4) + (7)	0.9	1.5	-17.9	-10.9	-22.0	-24.5	-29.0	-26.7	-37.2	-32.8
Capital account										
Long-term private										
Inflow	1.4	2.8	3.7	4.7	8.0	10.0	6.3	12.4	8.7	20.4
Outflow	0.3	0.7	0.5	1.1	0.3	1.4	9.2	1.5	2.0	3.6
Balance	1.1	2.1	3.2	3.5	7.6	8.5	-2.9	11.0	6.7	16.8
Long-term official:										
Inflow	5.3	3.1	7.3	11.8	13.0	17.4	32.6	20.2	26.0	27.0
Outflow	4.3	3.2	2.1	2.7	1.3	2.3	3.1	3.5	5.5	2.8
Balance	1.0	-	5.2	9.1	11.7	15.2	29.5	16.6	20.4	24.2
Net short-term capital	-0.4	1.3	1.9	-0.8	3.2	1.4	5.5	1.0	9.8)	
Net monetary										)19.1
movements	-0.6	1.2	1.0	0.5	0.1	1.0	2.1	1.3	1.4)	
Capital account										
balance	1.2	4.6	11.3	12.3	22.7	26.2	34.1	29.9	38.3	60.1
Errors and omissions	1.3	1.5	2.1	-2.0	1.0	-2.0	1.7	-2.4	3.0	n.a.
Change in reserves	-3.4	-7.6	+4.5	+0.5	-1.6	+0.3	-6.8	-0.8	-4.1	-27.3

* Provisional figures. Errors and omissions are included in the combined total of net short-term capital and net monetary movements.

Sources: N.S.O. *Balance of Payments 1970 and 1972*, Zomba, 1972 and 1974; E.P.D. *Economic Report 1974*.

Table 2.6 Composition of Merchandise Exports 1964-73

	1964	1965	1966	1967	1968	1969	1970	1971	1972	1973†
Smallholder crops										
tobacco*	5.8	7.9	6.4	5.1	6.0	6.4	8.4	11.7	11.7	12.1
%	(25.2)	(29.1)	(23.1)	(15.4)	(17.8)	(17.6)	(20.7)	(23.5)	(21.2)	(17.7)
groundnuts	2.2	3.3	2.6	6.9	4.6	5.6	4.2	5.9	7.1	6.7
%	(9.6)	(12.2)	(9.4)	(20.8)	(13.8)	(15.3)	(10.5)	(11.7)	(12.9)	(9.8)
cotton	2.0	2.2	2.2	1.4	1.3	1.7	2.8	2.5	2.6	1.7
%	(8.7)	(8.1)	(7.9)	(4.2)	(3.8)	(4.7)	(6.8)	(5.1)	(4.7)	(2.4)
other**	2.2	2.1	3.6	5.6	5.5	4.3	2.5	3.6	4.9	8.3
%	(9.6)	(7.7)	(13.0)	(16.9)	(16.4)	(11.9)	(6.2)	(7.3)	(8.8)	(12.1)
Total smallholder crops	12.2	15.5	14.8	19.8	17.4	18.1	17.9	23.7	26.3	28.8
%	(53.0)	(57.2)	(53.4)	(57.4)	(51.8)	(49.4)	(44.2)	(47.8)	(47.7)	(42.1)
Estate crops										
tobacco***	2.6	2.4	2.6	3.3	4.6	6.2	8.2	10.4	13.3	18.1
%	(11.3)	(8.8)	(9.4)	(10.0)	(13.7)	(17.0)	(20.2)	(21.0)	(24.0)	(26.5)
tea	6.6	7.5	8.8	9.0	9.7	9.5	10.9	11.9	12.0	13.7
%	(28.7)	(27.7)	(31.8)	(27.2)	(28.9)	(26.0)	(26.9)	(24.0)	(21.8)	(20.1)
Total estate crops†††	9.9	10.6	12.0	13.0	14.5	16.2	19.7	22.9	25.8	34.7
%	(43.0)	(39.1)	(43.3)	(39.3)	(43.3)	(44.3)	(48.5)	(46.1)	(46.7)	(50.8)
Other exports††	1.0	1.0	0.8	1.1	1.6	2.3	3.0	3.0	3.1	4.9
%	(4.0)	(3.7)	(2.9)	(3.3)	(4.8)	(6.3)	(7.3)	(6.1)	(5.6)	(7.2)
Total domestic exports	23.0	27.1	27.7	33.1	33.6	36.6	40.6	49.6	55.1	68.3
Re-exports	2.0	1.6	7.2	7.8	6.5	7.4	9.1	9.7	9.4	11.1
Total exports	25.0	28.7	34.8	40.9	40.1	44.0	49.7	59.3	64.5	79.4

*   Dark fined, fine-cured, sun/air-cured and oriental tobacco.
**   Includes pulses, maize, cassava, rice, sunflower seeds and coffee.
***   Flue-cured and Burley tobacco.
†††   Includes tung oil, sisal and sugar.
††   Includes cattle cake, cement, wooden boxes, clothing and footwear.
†   Provisional.

Source: E.P.D. *Economic Report 1974*, p. 18.

as compared with 96 per cent in 1964, with the two key commodities, tobacco and tea, still representing nearly two-thirds of domestic export earnings (see Table 2.6). In all, Malawi's domestic export earnings have increased at an annual rate of nearly 13 per cent between 1964 and 1973.

This increase in earnings is remarkable, given the difficulties usually faced by ldc exporters of agricultural goods. Malawi has, however, had two advantages. First, as a relatively small producer it does not generally face the problem of having to restrict output to prevent a decline in world prices. A major exception to this rule is in sun/air and fire-cured tobacco (23 per cent of domestic exports) since, in a fairly slow growing market, Malawi is an important supplier. Second, while world prices for some of its exports, for instance, tung oil and rice, have declined, Malawi has on balance gained from favourable price movements for its major export crops in recent years.[20] Smallholder crops have particularly benefited: for — leaving aside quality improvements — they have increased in value by 6.4 per cent p.a. between 1964 and 1970, whereas volume rose by only 2 per cent; estate crops exports increased by 12.2 per cent and 8.5 per cent p.a. respectively. Rhodesia's unilateral declaration of independence (UDI) and subsequent sanctions have been an important factor in the improvement in prices for Malawi's estate crop — tobacco. And the 1973 commodity boom brought further price gains to many of Malawi's crop exports, with the major exception of tea. But Malawi's gain from world price movements has not been passive: the responsiveness of producers and of the government has been important, as witness the efforts to expand the estate production of tobacco and sugar, the development of marketing facilities for cassava and the quantity of particular smallholder crops offered for sale in different years.

The share of re-exports in total visible exports has increased from 8 per cent in 1964 to 14 per cent in 1973. Much of that increase is attributable to the poor relations between Zambia and Rhodesia after UDI, which led to a growth in transit trade, mainly in petroleum and tobacco, with Zambia. The balance of payments gain from the value-added in Malawi is estimated at approximately one-fifth of total re-export earnings.

While the pattern of exports has not changed significantly since independence, this has not been the case with merchandise imports. As would be expected, the share of consumer goods has dropped, from 49 per cent in 1964 to 28 per cent in 1973, while that of investment goods — capital equipment and materials for building construction — rose from 21 per cent to 30 per cent and intermediate goods from 29 per cent to 41 per cent (see Table 2.7). These changes were not smooth, being affected by variations in investment expenditure and domestic

Table 2.7 Imports by End Use, 1964-73*

	Km									
	1964	1965	1966	1967	1968	1969	1970	1971	1972	1973†
Goods mainly for final consumption										
Motor cars and bicycles	1.5	2.0	2.1	2.2	2.0	2.1	2.4	2.8	2.3	3.4
Piece goods	3.9	6.5	5.3	4.4	4.0	3.8	3.5	3.9	4.1	5.2
Motor spirit	0.6	0.5	0.6	0.7	0.9	0.9	1.9	2.3	2.6	2.9
Other	8.0	11.5	12.5	12.8	12.6	12.0	14.5	15.5	18.1	20.1
Total	13.9	20.5	20.5	20.1	19.6	18.8	22.4	24.5	27.1	31.6
% of total imports	(49)	(50)	(38)	(40)	(34)	(31)	(27)	(27)	(26)	(28)
Capital equipment										
Transport equipment	2.2	2.6	5.0	5.0	7.0	7.4	9.6	9.7	14.5	12.3
Other	2.0	3.5	6.9	5.0	8.8	8.0	9.8	10.4	12.3	12.5
Total	4.2	6.2	11.9	10.0	15.8	15.4	19.4	20.0	26.8	24.8
% of total imports	(15)	(15)	(22)	(20)	(27)	(25)	(23)	(22)	(26)	(22)
Materials for building construction	1.8	2.7	3.4	3.4	4.3	6.0	6.1	7.1	10.3	9.7
% of total imports	(6)	(7)	(6)	(7)	(7)	(10)	(7)	(8)	(10)	(8)
Intermediate goods										
Petroleum products n.i.e.	1.0	1.1	1.4	1.5	2.2	2.3	4.5	5.3	5.8	6.9
Parts, tools and miscellaneous appliances	0.6	0.8	1.1	1.3	1.6	1.8	3.4	4.0	3.1	3.5
Other	6.7	8.9	14.9	13.4	13.4	15.8	25.3	27.0	28.6	35.6
Total	8.3	10.8	17.4	16.2	17.2	20.0	33.2	36.4	37.4	46.0
% of total imports	(29)	(26)	(32)	(32)	(30)	(32)	(40)	(41)	(36)	(41)
Other	0.5	0.6	1.0	1.2	1.2	1.4	1.5	1.4	1.4	1.1
% of total imports	(1)	(2)	(2)	(2)	(2)	(2)	(2)	(2)	(2)	(1)
Total imports	28.6	40.8	54.3	50.9	58.2	61.5	82.5	89.8	103.0	113.3

* 1964-9 imports valued at f.o.b.; 1970-3 valued at c.i.f.
† Provisional.

Source: E.P.D. *Economic Report 1974*, Zomba, 1974.

output: for instance, K5.2m of the recorded increase in intermediate goods in 1970 was attributable to the poor maize harvest which necessitated imports from Rhodesia. Nevertheless, despite yearly fluctuations, an underlying trend over the period is reasonably clear, reflecting the growth of import substituting industries and the high level of investment.

While Malawi has gained from higher prices for its exports, its terms of trade have worsened in recent years because of a rapid increase in the unit value of imports. Having improved since 1967, Malawi's terms of trade deteriorated from 1970: the index was estimated at 85 in 1973 as compared with 100 in 1970. The rise in oil prices will undoubtedly reinforce this trend.

Britain, Rhodesia and South Africa continue to be Malawi's main trading partners, but their shares have changed since 1964, most markedly on the import side (see Table 2.8). There has been some geographical diversification of Malawi's export trade since 1968 but Britain continues to dominate, buying between 41 and 55 per cent of Malawi's domestic exports in any one year. The rise in the share of exports to the USA reflects the increase in sugar exports under the US Sugar Agreement.

Table 2.8 Direction of Malawi's Visible Trade 1964-73 (% of total)

	1964	1965	1966	1967	1968	1969	1970	1971	1972	1973†
Domestic exports to:										
UK	48	47	48	55	51	46	48	44	43	41
Rhodesia	14	10	6	4	5	7	8	7	6	6
South Africa	5	4	3	3	5	3	4	5	6	4
USA	3	3	3	3	5	6	3	5	5	10
West Germany	1	1	3	2	3	3	3	2	2	2
Zambia	1	1	2	2	2	8	4	5	3	4
Other countries	28	34	35	31	29	27	30	32	35	33
Imports* from:										
UK	23	25	31	28	31	30	27	28	30	25
Rhodesia	39	36	23	21	18	17	22	15	16	14
South Africa	6	5	7	8	11	14	13	11	13	16
USA	2	3	3	3	6	4	5	4	2	2
West Germany	2	3	2	3	4	4	4	4	3	3
Zambia	4	2	10	7	4	4	4	4	4	4
Other countries	24	26	24	30	26	27	25	34	32	36

*   Include on consignments. The data are f.o.b. until 1970 and c.i.f. thereafter.

†   Estimated on the basis of the first nine months.

Source: N.S.O. *Monthly Bulletin of Statistics*, June 1972, and *Economic Report*, 1974.

With the dissolution of Federation, Malawi's abrogation of its trading agreement with Rhodesia in 1965, and the growth of import-substituting industries, the share of imports from Rhodesia has fallen from 39 per cent in 1964 to 14 per cent in 1973, with the exception of an increase in 1970 due to the unusual purchase of maize imports. The British share rose shortly after independence, since when it has fluctuated. Imports from South Africa have increased in relative terms, reflecting the development of diplomatic and trade relations between the two countries and the purchases associated with South African aid. Two other major donors to Malawi — USA and West Germany — have tended to increase their share of Malawi's imports. There have, however, been considerable yearly fluctuations in Malawi's imports from different sources and these, as well as the overall diversification (the combined share of imports from Rhodesia, South Africa and Britain dropped from 68 per cent to 53 per cent in 1971), reflect in part the growth and changes in Malawi's receipts of foreign capital. They are also said to reflect attempts by Malawian buyers to seek out cheaper supply sources, but the extent of these efforts is not clear, and, whatever the case, the procurement restrictions imposed by some aid donors limit such possibilities in the public sector.

Invisible exports are not a major source of earnings, accounting for only 12 to 13 per cent of total exports of goods and services during the 1960s and rising to 18 per cent in 1970, partly as a result of statistical revisions. No single item dominates: tourism, for instance, long mooted as an important foreign exchange earner, contributed only 13 per cent of invisible earnings in 1970. Invisible imports on the other hand have constituted between a quarter and a third of total imports, the most important item being freight and insurance.

Malawi's net factor income position has improved since the mid-sixties, despite the rise of foreign private investment earnings (although a huge proportion of these are reinvested and reappear as a credit item in the capital account) and public debt servicing. Two main factors have been responsible: the decline in pension and gratuity payments to expatriates by the Malawi government, and the increase in remittances from migrant workers, from K4m in 1968 to over K12m in 1972. This export of migrant labour has also boosted invisible earnings since migrants to South Africa are carried by Air Malawi charter flights.

Malawi's net inflow of private and official capital has risen sharply since independence, from K2m to K41m, offsetting the decline in transfer receipts (see Table 2.5); net inflows fluctuated, between 1968 and 1970, mainly as a result of the arrangements for the financing of the rail link with the Mozambique port of Nacala: this was financed by private contractors, hence the large inflow of private capital in 1968 and 1969, which was repatriated in 1970 on completion of the link. An aid loan from South Africa received in 1970 – hence the large inflow of official aid in that year – was used to make the final payment of nearly K10m to the contractors. Since 1969, the rate of private capital repatriation has increased, possibly as a consequence of Malawi's increased emphasis on local participation in, and localisation of, the private sector. Official capital outflow has also risen in recent years, from K1.3m in 1968 to K5.5m in 1972, and will continue to do so, as more repayments on aid loans become due.[21]

Development of the Infrastructure

The post-independence years have witnessed a considerable expansion of Malawi's economic infrastructure. The most significant infrastructural development so far as the rural areas were concerned has been the improvement of the transportation network – to which roughly a quarter of central government development has been devoted. The major part has been spent on the improvement and extension of arterial roads, to facilitate the transport of agricultural inputs and outputs over the long distances between the producing regions and the points of exit from and entry to Malawi in the south. Between 1964 and 1971, some 407 miles of main roads – gravel or tar – were reconstructed or newly constructed. The two most important road developments have been the reconstruction of the main road between Zomba and Lilongwe, and the construction of the Lake shore road,[22] still not wholly complete, between the northern and southern regions. The first road links the rich agricultural area of the central region with the south, while the second is intended to stimulate development by opening up previously neglected areas. In all over 1,000 miles of road have been newly constructed between 1964-71, including 869 miles of crop extraction earth roads, and some 400 miles have been subject to major reconstruction. Further major road developments are currently being planned.

The main railway project – the construction of the link with the Mozambique port of Nacala – was, like the major road developments, intended to redress the regional imbalance of the transport network, which was previously geared to the populous southern region. It has also helped to reduce Malawi's vulnerability as a land locked country with – formerly – only one outlet to the sea via the overcrowded port of Beira. But it has had an adverse effect on Malawi Railway's financial position,[23] and the implementation of the project has led to considerable criticism, chiefly on the grounds that it was 'premature.'

Although Malawi has devoted some of its resources to the improvement of airport facilities and the expansion of its airfleet, it has until recently avoided the temptation of building a prestige international airport or operating costly long distance services via its national airline.

This restraint, coupled with the income accruing from the charter arrangement with the South African importers of Malawian labour, resulted in an operating profit for the airline until 1972, when the introduction of new aircraft resulted in a loss of K0.1m. A new international airport was, however, implicit in the plan to move the capital to Lilongwe and plans are now going ahead for its construction. The site of the existing airport at Chileka (Blantyre) makes it unsuitable for some long haul jets but it is dubious whether the costs of the new airport will be justified by returns — unless national pride is weighted heavily among the benefits. The inflow of Malawi's tourist traffic, for instance, is largely from within the central and southern African region. Similar doubts must be voiced in respect of the decision, put into effect in 1974, for Air Malawi to operate a long haul jet service between London and Blantyre.

With the expansion of economic activity in the organised sector, there has been a fairly large public sector investment programme to provide the requisite services. ESCOM's installed electricity capacity has risen from 14.3 megawatts in 1964 to 39.4 megawatts in 1971, mainly through the development of hydroelectric capacity: a 16 megawatt power station is currently being installed on the Shiré River. Water supplies and sanitation systems, mainly in Blantyre and Lilongwe, have been improved and expanded. The capacity of the post and telecommunications network has been increased. Some K3.5m[24] has been invested in public housing between 1965 and 1971, mainly in the southern region, but increasingly in the central region with the construction of the new capital.

Development of Social Services

The budgetary restraint imposed by the need to phase out British budgetary assistance has restricted spending on the two main social services — education and health. Most central government investment expenditure on education has been on the development of higher educational and training facilities designed to reduce the acute shortage of local skilled manpower at the middle levels. The primary education and health systems have been relatively neglected since the services thereby provided have been regarded as consumption goods, as compared with the investment role of post-primary education.

Consequently primary school enrolment has barely increased: in 1964 there were 359,891 pupils enrolled in primary schools, in 1971, 350,000 and in 1973, 347,174.[25] The proportion of children of school age actually attending primary schools is only about a third — the lowest in Commonwealth Africa — and the majority of pupils do not complete the full eight year course of primary education. However, efforts have been made to improve the quality of primary education by curricula changes and teacher training: in 1964 only 60 per cent of the 8,464 primary school teachers had had any training while in 1970 83 per cent of the 9,057 primary school teachers were trained, although the majority had not completed the four year secondary school course. Plans now exist to expand and improve primary education facilities.

Secondary school enrolment has meanwhile more than doubled, from 5,823 in 1964 to 13,276 in 1971. Roughly one in ten primary school leavers actually gets to secondary school and still fewer make it to the higher education institutions developed since independence — the university and the various technical and vocational training schools: these have an annual intake of a few hundred. Some training opportunities for primary school leavers and for farmers have been developed: for instance, the Malawi Young Pioneer (MYP) training bases now provide mainly agricultural training to roughly 2,000 MYPs a year, and the rural training centres, short (usually one day) training courses to nearly 70,000 farmers a year. Further, the Correspondence College was set up in 1965 to provide education to those unable to attend secondary school: its total enrolment of nearly 25,000 by 1972 is an indication of the demand. The major part of Malawi's educational investment expenditure has been directed towards the provision of formal academic and vocational education facilities at the post-primary school level, which benefit relatively few young Malawians. This balance is somewhat redressed in total government expenditure on education, but in 1972-3, primary education accounted for only 35.5 per cent as compared with 18 per cent on secondary education,[26] and 40 per cent on higher education and vocational training.[27]

The running of the largely curative health service in Malawi is shared about equally by the government and the religious missions. There has been little expansion of government health facilities since independence: most investment expenditure has been devoted to the repair and reconstruction of dilapidated hospitals and clinics. It is unlikely that mission health facilities have expanded significantly. In 1970, there were approximately 1.7 hospital beds per 1,000[28] of the population, somewhat less for the rural inhabitants. In the absence of adequate data on morbidity, the hospital bed occupancy rate indicates the kind of demand for curative health services that exists: government hospitals, which are generally free, had a bed occupancy rate of 102 per cent, mission hospitals, which charge fees, had one of 80 per cent. Recently expenditure has been increased on preventive medicine and health education generally, but the largest item on the health budget is the construction of a new hospital in Lilongwe.

Land and Population

Malawi's population was estimated to be 4.8m in 1973. According to the 1966 population census, the non-African population accounted for 0.5 per cent of the total, with 7,395 Europeans and 11,300 Asians. Roughly half the population lived in the southern region – as compared with 40 per cent in 1911 – 37 per cent in the central and 12 per cent in the northern region, whence immigration has been greatest. As in most developing countries, over 40 per cent of the population was aged fourteen and under and only 18 per cent over the age of forty. Life expectancy in 1971 was 42.4 years; rural dwellers and males have slightly shorter life expectation at birth.[29]

The population is estimated to have grown by 2.5 per cent a year from independence to 1971, and 2.6 per cent since, with urban and rural rates of 4.7 per cent and 2.4 per cent respectively. There has been no official policy to limit population growth, partly because Dr Banda – despite external criticism – has felt that such demands could not be made while health services were poor and infant mortality high: in 1972 infant mortality (per 1000 live births) was estimated at 142.1 nationally and 150.9 in the rural areas.

Population density has increased from 105 per square mile in 1964 to 130 in 1973. In 1964, it was clear that population pressure seriously affected agricultural productivity in certain areas of the country. Even though rural population growth has been slower than the national average, it is some tribute to smallholders and to government development efforts in agriculture that cash crop output has been maintained and that maize production has in most years sufficed to meet the country's subsistence needs (see Table 2.9). Much of the expansion of subsistence production and the maintenance, and in some cases increase, in cash crop output is attributable to the extension of the acreage under cultivation, although development efforts, including the increased sale of farm inputs, in particular fertiliser, are thought to have been a key factor. Thus in the more densely populated areas of the central and southern regions land only marginally suitable for cultivation is being brought into production.

Although land use surveys suggest that much unused cultivable land remains, a large part is marginal and/or poses special cultivation problems, because of the soil and/or the topography.[30] As the rural population increases – and some estimates suggest it will exceed 7 million by the year 2,000 – more of this marginal land will be drawn into cultivation, unless the productivity of land currently in production is considerably increased. Although with improved farming techniques crop yields can be greatly improved, and controlled acreage expansion (via settlement schemes, for instance) can minimise the problems of soil

46

degradation, both processes tend to be slow and often costly. In a country whose inhabitants, and growth prospects, will continue to be largely dependent on agriculture, the problems posed by an increasing population and limited land resources are formidable.

Table 2.9   FMB/ADMARC Purchases of Main Crops from Customary Land Farmers, and Fertiliser Sales by Quantity, selected years

	1964	1965	1967	1968	1970	1972	1973
			'000 short tons				
Maize	30.8	24.2	100.0	92.2	9.1	73.5	66.5
Pulses	16.7	30.0	23.3	3.8	8.9	17.9	7.5
Paddy	4.0	5.6	5.1	2.3	9.9	21.9	19.0
Groundnuts	19.5	25.2	47.6	25.1	29.8	43.2	33.0
Seed cotton	14.9	22.7	13.1	12.8	23.5	24.1	17.9
Tobacco	9.2	20.3	17.5	9.7	13.1	19.5	16.6
Fertiliser sales	2.2	6.2	9.5*	10.8*	17.1*	n.a.	n.a.

*   Crop year.

Sources: Ministry of Agriculture data for *Annual Report*, 1972; N.S.O. *Compendium of Agricultural Statistics 1971*, Zomba 1971: E.P.D. *Economic Report 1974*, Zomba, 1974.

Conclusion

As stated in Chapter 1, the dominant objectives of the Malawi government over the period considered have been the elimination of the budget deficit and the expansion of economic activity. Both have been achieved with remarkable success, given the country's economic position at independence. It is true that Malawi has relied heavily on external finance to achieve these objectives. But it has also made a substantial domestic effort, through the restraint of government consumption expenditure, the rapid increase in tax revenue and the growth of domestic savings. There can be no doubt that Dr Banda's leadership has been an important factor in this achievement, both in encouraging and directing the national development effort, and in ensuring political stability, without which external finance – both private and official — would have been slow to arrive.

To some extent, however, Malawi's economic growth is due to external factors, such as favourable movements in world prices and the Rhodesian UDI. Furthermore, it is somewhat exaggerated by the fact that at the start of the period the economy was slack. There are, too, certain features which are not particularly encouraging for the future: for instance, the low rate of expansion in employment opportunities in the organised sector; the large part played by the extension of cultivated acreage in agricultural growth.

With a fast growing population, pressures on land will grow and cash crop output will suffer unless productivity in the agricultural sector increases at a faster rate, and the urban sector can absorb more of the new entrants to the labour force. And this difficulty would be exacerbated should political circumstances lead to a repatriation of migrant labour.

Malawi's long-term development objective of raising the living standards of the mass of the ordinary people has been somewhat overshadowed by the government's concern to achieve financial solvency. And although a large part of public expenditure has been directed towards the rural sector where the poorest people live, the main gains from rapid economic growth have accrued to the organised sector and specifically to those owning and working for the larger enterprises, and the opportunity for such gains has been considerably enhanced by public sector policy and expenditure. Nevertheless, while attempting to encourage savings and investment by its direct taxation policies, the government has contained the growth of the rural-urban income imbalance by its wages policy.

While real incomes in the rural sector have increased, the gains have been unevenly distributed. Most opportunities for increasing farm incomes have occurred in regions of relatively intensive development efforts, where only a minority, albeit substantial, of the rural population live. But the maintenance of agricultural services to the non-project areas and the uniform crop pricing policy have been offsetting factors. Given the constraints under which the government was operating, the apparent imbalance that has occurred with economic growth should not be too severely criticised. The test of the government's good intentions will have to be made in later years.

NOTES

1.   The first two of the four main issues – Africanisation, foreign policy, civil servants' pay, and a charge for treatment in government hospitals – reflected ideological disagreements between Dr Banda and 'his boys.' One suspects that if the ministers had been faced with the realities of policy making, they would eventually have adopted similar, if more stiff-necked, localisation and foreign policies than those of Dr Banda. And he himself amended his policies on pay and hospital charges after the crisis.

2.   Dr Banda selects the candidate for election from the list of possible candidates submitted by the individual constituencies: some constituencies are without representation, having failed to submit suitable candidates.

3.   The severe persecution of Jehovah's Witnesses in 1972 is a case in point.

4.   Malawi's methods of imputing a value to agricultural subsistence output are, however, more sophisticated than those of many developing countries where estimated changes in output tend to be based on estimated changes in population in the subsistence sector.

5.   Measured at factor cost in current prices between 1964 and 1973.

6.   Because of statistical revisions, output data from 1971 onwards are not wholly comparable with earlier years.

7.   It is estimated that these firms currently account for roughly 80 per cent of total manufacturing output.

8.   In which Dr Banda is the majority shareholder.

9.   See Malawi Government *Economic Report*, 1973, p. 57.

10.   The average capital/labour ratio of enterprises granted licences since 1967 has fluctuated between K1,400 and K4,800 (per employee). New enterprises require a licence if they employ more than ten persons or machinery of more than 25 horse power.

11.   In 1966, there were some 265,000 Malawian (mainly adult males) working outside the country against an average of 175,000 in employment throughout the year in Malawi. In 1969, it was estimated that a total of 329,000 were in South Africa and Rhodesia. The number of Malawians working in South African mines under contract rose from 32,620 in 1964 to 99,849 in 1971. In 1974, however, Dr Banda banned further recruitment of Malawians to South African mines. The reasons behind this action, precipitated by an air crash in which seventy-seven returning Malawian migrant miners were killed, are not yet known, although various political motives have been postulated. See the *Guardian*, 12 August 1974.

12.   On the other hand, labour shortages are reported on some agricultural projects.

13.   Even so, the squatter population of Blantyre does pose problems; the urban population there is thought to be growing somewhat faster than the 8 per cent official estimate.

14.   *EPD Manpower Survey 1971*, Zomba, 1972. Unfortunately this survey is not really comparable with previous attempts to estimate Malawi's stock of skilled manpower.

15.   Implied by the price index used to deflate national income.

16.   A pay rise of 6 per cent was allowed in 1973.

17.   This was in fact a drop compared with the immediately preceding years. Estimated expenditure for 1973-4 is K34.3m.

18.   *Malawi Government Public Sector Financial Statistics 1969*, Table E.1 and *Economic Report 1974*, p. 67.

19.   *Malawi Government Statement of Development Policies 1971-80*, Zomba, 1971, p. 114.

20.   The index of the unit value of exports rose from 80.74 in 1967 to an estimated 107.3 in 1973 (1970 = 100).

21.   The figure of K2.8m, from Malawi Government *Economic Report* 1974, given in Table 2.5 is almost undoubtedly an error. Scheduled public sector amortisation payments were K5.0m according to the same source (p. 68).

22.   A key part of Dr Banda's personal plan — named the Gwelo plan after the Rhodesian jail where he conceived it in detention — for Malawi's structural transformation.

23.   The construction standards and hence the cost of the link were high, and the aid loan borrowed from South Africa to finance its construction has put a substantial debt servicing burden on Malawi Railways. The link has also reduced the freight mileage within Malawi and hence the revenue earned by Malawi Railways.

24.   *M.H.C. Annual Report 1971*, June 1972.

25.   The 1973 figure excludes pupils in unassisted primary schools, which accounted for c. 12 per cent of enrolment in 1970.

26.   Including 1.2 per cent on the Correspondence College.

27.   Including 32.7 per cent on the University of Malawi. Data from Malawi Government *Education Plan of Malawi 1973-1980*, Zomba, 1973, Table 8.3.

27.   *Malawi Statistical Yearbook*, p. 16. A lower estimate of 1.3 beds per 1000 is given by the *Malawi Yearbook 1971*, p. 80.

29.   See *Malawi Government Economic Report 1974*, p. 7.

30.   A recent survey based on aerial photograph data indicated that 20.6 per cent of land was under cultivation, and that 11.42 per cent was uncultivable. Of the remainder, 15.3 per cent was recent fallow; 15.5 per cent was long fallow (4-20 years); 18.2 per cent was potentially cultivable, over twenty years fallow; 5.3 per cent was swamp or marshes and *dambo* (seasonally waterlogged, lowlying grassland) and 13.6 per cent posed special cultivation problems because of soil and topography.

3 BRITAIN AS DONOR

Britain has a long tradition of providing financial and technical assistance to countries now designated less developed and the size of its annual aid programme puts it among the leading Western donors.[1] This chapter aims to provide a general picture of Britain's aid policy towards Malawi, as a background to the more detailed examination of different aspects of that policy in later chapters. For comparative purposes it begins, however, with a brief consideration of Britain's bilateral aid policy over the period since Malawi's independence.

General British Aid Policy

Until the late fifties, the main focus of Britain's development aid was on its colonies, with relatively small contributions being made to non-Commonwealth countries and to multilateral aid agencies. Then, in keeping with growing international recognition of the development needs and difficulties of independent developing countries and with the growing pace of decolonisation, Britain began to expand its aid to independent ldcs. Before 1964, however, it was impossible to talk of a British aid programme or policy: responsibility for aid giving was split among a variety of government departments and ministries according to the type of aid provided and the political status of the recipient, and there was no overall aid management or strategy. Then, in 1964, the Overseas Development Ministry (ODM)[2] was formed by the newly elected Labour government and was given responsibility for virtually all British aid. Efforts have since been made to evolve a coherent aid policy towards the Third World. Nevertheless, the provision of aid is still by no means governed by an all-embracing and consistent aid policy.

The objectives of the aid programme have always been diverse and, to some extent, conflicting. The first policy statement of the new Ministry, however, attempted to bring the development purpose of aid firmly to the fore, announcing that 'the objective of the British aid programme is to help developing countries in their efforts to raise living standards,'[3] and that aid was not 'a means of winning friendship' or 'an insurance against political tension'. Even so, the policy makers did refer to some other non-developmental purposes which could be achieved through aid although, they stressed, these were to 'be secondary to the primary (development) purpose of aid'.[4] Subsequent policy statements have been less altruistic. In 1969, for instance, the Minister of Overseas

Development stated:

'The (aid) programme is based on moral considerations and on the interests of the UK which, particularly in the longer term, centre on security, stability and prosperity . . . It is also a consideration that we have important investment and trading interests in the third world from which many materials of importance to us are supplied. Balance of payments considerations add to the importance of maintaining and developing these very substantial and other economic interests and of maintaining the stable political and economic conditions on which they depend.'[5]

and he added:

'While aid must of course be used for projects and services which are to the benefit of the recipients, it is also right to seek to promote British exports.'[6]

It has been argued that the small size of the aid programme — in relation to the Third World's needs and Britain's wealth — and its relatively slow growth can be traced in part to the variety of inconsistent objectives it has sought and failed effectively to fulfil.[7] And certainly, the existence of non-developmental objectives has helped to limit the potential impact of British aid on Third World development through their effect on both the distribution of aid between ldcs and the terms and conditions of aid.

With the expansion of the aid programme in the late fifties, increased attention was paid to the need to adopt developmental criteria to decide the distribution of aid between ldcs. In the process, a conflict emerged — on paper at least — between the desire to ensure that aid was used productively for development and the desire to focus aid efforts on the poorest countries, whose need for development was greatest, since it was observed that the poorest countries were often the least able to use aid effectively. This conflict was left unresolved by the ODM. It stated that preference was to be given to 'those countries and regions where (aid) will have the greatest effect in the long run,' taking account of the resources being supplied by other donors, the aid available from the UK, the recipient's own resources and efforts *and* its poverty relative to other countries.[8]

The actual allocation of Britain's bilateral aid — which accounts for some 90 per cent of total aid — has not, however, been significantly influenced either by a concern for the needy[9] or a preference for the speedy. Partly, this has been because the conflict between the two criteria has never been resolved, but mainly it has been because various other non-developmental considerations have a major influence on aid allocation. Britain's special responsibility for its colonies, its commercial and political interests in its ex-colonies, reinforced no doubt by ties of sentiment and some continuing sense of responsibility, has resulted in allocation of nearly 90 per cent of Britain's gross bilateral aid disbursements to Commonwealth countries each year (see Table 3.1). It is true that the Commonwealth contains many of the world's poorest countries *and* peoples, but the allocation of aid between these countries does not correspond closely with either relative needs or relative performance. And the allocation of aid to non-Commonwealth countries reflects more Britain's particular political and commercial interests than any attempt to compensate the non-Commonwealth poor and needy for the overwhelming bias of its aid towards Commonwealth countries. It should be added, however, that since ODM drew up its allocation criteria Britain's total aid flows have virtually stagnated and this, of course, has limited the extent to which a reallocation of aid according to such criteria was possible.

If ODM brought little change in the distribution of British aid, it did bring a distinct change in the terms and conditions on which aid was provided. Broadly, Britain provides aid of three types: grants and loans for development projects, grants and loans for non-project purposes (e.g. budgetary aid, import finance, pensions and disaster relief), and technical assistance, which is mostly grant aid. In 1963, the type of aid offered and its terms and conditions were governed largely by the political status of the recipient. Britain's colonies tended to receive aid on relatively generous terms as grants or as soft loans for development projects, and for the purpose of financing budgetary deficits or emergency expenditures and the aid was subject to few formal procurement restrictions. On the other hand, independent countries, particularly Commonwealth countries, tended to receive tied aid on near commercial terms, although rarely for specific projects. Some concessions both on terms and tying were made to take account of particular difficulties of individual recipient countries, but on the whole the extent of tying and the hardness of lending terms of aid to independent countries made it clear that it paid to be a colonial aid recipient.[10]

The differences between colonial and non-colonial aid reflected in part the *ad hoc* way in which Britain had accommodated the aid requirements of independent countries. They also indicated Britain's reluctance to interfere, or to appear to interfere, with the policies of independent countries, and its particular sensitivity on the issue of sovereignty with regard to newly independent countries. The use of hard financial terms was to some extent a substitute for the more paternalistic means — employed in respect of colonies — of ensuring that aid, taxpayer's money, was productively used. But because hard, procurement tied loans were not generally appropriate to the needs of the independent ldcs and because their machinery for planning and implementing development programmes was frequently weak, there was insufficient assurance that the development objective of such aid would be achieved or that the British taxpayer would be satisfied.

With the establishment of ODM, concern over the sovereignty of aid recipients was modified and interest in the effective use of aid increased. It was announced that:

> 'if Britain contributes substantially to the flow of aid, she has a right to ask that the resources transferred shall be used to the best effect . . . the keynote of our efforts will be partnership . . . together with (ldcs) we shall be more active in identifying particular opportunities for providing aid which may assist or, indeed, generate development . . .'[11]

This shift in policy put Britain on a par with most other donors dealing with ldcs. Although there are individuals who argue for a purely automatic approach to aid giving, viz. providing the resources but leaving it to the ldc to do what it sees best with the funds, while accepting that not all aid funds will be used well or in accordance with the donor's ideas as to how they should be used, no donor formally accepts this approach. In any case, the type of aid and the criteria on which it is provided will inevitably affect the outcome, whether or not the donor takes an interest in the use of aid. Britain's increased interest in the use of aid has had several consequences for the way in which aid was given.

First, there has been an attempt to ensure that the financial terms of aid are more suited to the economic conditions prevailing in individual countries, i.e. that the aid *can* be used effectively.[12] As a result the financial terms of aid have been significantly softened. Interest free loans were introduced in 1965, and the use of these loans, which had long maturity periods, and of grace periods for interest and amortisation payments increased over the sixties. In 1972, 86 per cent of loan commitments, by value, were interest free and 98 per cent of these had maturity periods of twenty-five years and grace periods of seven years.[13] The idea that loans — even very concessional loans — promote more effective use of aid than grants has persisted and, partly also because of budgetary and balance of payments constraints, Britain has increasingly favoured loans (see Table 3.1). Even so, the gift or grant element in British aid has increased: in 1964, it was estimated at 74 per cent of total aid commitments, in 1972 at 87 per cent.

Secondly, the ODM has tended to increase the amount of aid tied to specific projects or purposes [15] as compared with that given as general support to the recipients' development programmes (see Table 3.1). At the same time, ODM has attempted to improve the assessment of individual recipients' need for aid, with the aim of bringing about a situation where the provision of aid does not represent a passive response to a request, but rather the result of an active — and joint — consideration of the recipients' needs. So far as individual types of aid have been concerned, the main change in assessment procedures has been in respect of project finance. And it was not until 1969 that any systematic attempt was made by ODM to appraise the overall requirements of individual recipients. Then country policy papers were introduced as a means of bringing together the various considerations (such as the country's economic situation, its ability to use aid, its own development efforts and British interests — development and otherwise — in the country) thought appropriate to the formulation of a coherent aid policy towards individual ldcs. Aid administration has meanwhile continued to be focused in London. Given the assumption of a more active donor role, this situation is open to criticism. Many decisions on aid made in London have to be based to a large extent on information from overseas. The required transfer of information is not only a cumbersome process but may also reduce the effectiveness of aid because of administrative delays, and because of the remoteness of the decision makers.

Nevertheless, the fact that many recipients are ex-colonies does enhance the likelihood of an awareness of their problems in Britain. And recently, overseas administrative representation has been increased with three new Development Divisions[16] (including one covering Malawi) being added to the two existing Divisions covering the Caribbean and the Middle East. Apart from these Divisions, ODM overseas representation in recipient countries is the function of individual officials, working on a full- or part-time basis on aid matters, in diplomatic missions.

The practice of procurement tying — that is the provision of aid which has to be used for the purchase of goods and services from Britain — has, however, persisted and, in recent years, increased.[17] This practice reflects Britain's concern to protect its balance of payments and to promote British exports: it does nothing to further development. Tying not only reduces the real value of aid[18] but may also have adverse effects on development, particularly when linked with the practice of tying aid to projects. Procurement tied aid is inappropriate to many areas which have or should have priority in ldcs' development, for instance, agriculture and education. What characterises expenditure in these areas is its low import content: aid provided mainly for offshore costs creates a bias away from such areas. Although the precise effects of tying will vary according to the particular conditions of the recipient country, those countries which have few local resources and few sources of external finance and receive mainly project finance are likely to suffer most from the increased costs and distorting effects of tying. Britain is aware of this problem but, with the balance of payments concern dominant, its concession has been restricted to the provision of

Table 3.1 British Aid Programme 1964-72 (£m)

	1964	1965	1966	1967	1968	1969	1970	1971	1972
Total Aid Flows									
Gross disbursements	191.2	194.8	207.2	200.9	203.0	210.8	213.8	268.9	305.2
Disbursements – net of amortisation	173.4	168.5	173.6	173.3	173.0	179.7	186.2	230.9	243.3
Disbursements, net of amortisation & interest	151.8	144.8	148.1	146.5	146.3	155.4	162.3	203.9	215.4
Gross Disbursements									
Multilateral	15.7	18.5	19.8	19.0	18.7	33.1	20.0	30.4	51.1
(% total)	(8.2)	(9.5)	(9.6)	(9.5)	(9.2)	(15.7)	(9.3)	(11.3)	(16.7)
Bilateral of which:	175.5	176.2	187.4	182.0	184.3	177.8	193.6	238.6	254.3
Financial grants	57.9	61.2	56.6	56.9	46.7	42.9	39.7	48.4	69.9
Loans	85.9	74.7	93.2	83.8	86.8	77.3	99.6	121.6	109.5
Technical assistance	25.3	31.7	30.4	33.5	41.4	43.7	45.4	53.4	60.8
CDC exchequer advances	6.4	8.6	7.2	7.8	9.4	13.9	8.8	15.2	14.1
Project aid commitments as percentage of bilateral commitments of financial grants and loans	53.2	35.8	30.6	50.2	58.1	47.6	47.7	55.7	58.1
Commonwealth countries share of total gross bilateral aid disbursements %	89	88	88	89	89	88	89	88	83 *

* Pakistan included with non-Commonwealth aid recipients in 1972.

Source: ODM/ODA *British Aid Statistics 1963-1972*, HMSO

local costs 'in exceptional circumstances and to a limited extent.' 19 Similarly, little provision was or is made for the financing of recurrent costs of projects, except through the supply of tied import finance and budgetary aid. This, in turn, may create a bias towards capital-intensive projects, which are generally unsuited to ldcs' development needs.

In summary, the British aid programme over the period since 1964 has been subject to a number of changes designed to improve the effectiveness of aid for development. The objectives of British aid remain somewhat confused and the actual conduct of the programme has been influenced by a variety of non-developmental as well as developmental considerations. The question of how far the aid programme to Malawi conforms with this general view and how far the various shortcomings and improvements in policy have affected Malawi's potential benefits from aid receipts must now be addressed.

Britain's Aid Programme to Malawi

Consistency of Objectives

Malawi has been a major recipient of British aid, in terms both of its share in total bilateral aid and of its aid receipts per head.20 In most years since independence, only India, Pakistan and Kenya have received larger quantities of British aid than Malawi. And in terms of British aid receipts per head Malawi has generally had a place among the top ten recipients.21 Given Britain's stated criteria for the allocation of aid, Malawi has been and is a deserving case. It is a poor country, initially with few local resources for development while aid from other donors was not forthcoming. Further, its government announced from the start its resolve to mobilise what local resources it possessed for development and has done so with some success. However a variety of considerations to do with Britain's national interests, as well as its humanitarian concern for poverty and development, govern both the allocation and the type of aid proffered to individual recipients. It is therefore necessary to ask whether Malawi's relatively large receipts of British aid reflect something more than a desire to assist Malawi's economic development, since the objectives of British aid giving may in turn have affected the usefulness of aid. In considering this question, attention will be focused on the consistency of Britain's objectives: areas of potential conflict will be signposted but discussion of how such conflict affected policy will be reserved for later chapters.

From Britain's stated objective in giving aid to Malawi, it is clear that economic development was of prime concern. But development was perceived as means to an end for Britain as well as an end in itself. Thus, the brief of ODM's economic mission to Malawi in 1965 was to examine policy (in Malawi) and aid requirements 'for the expansion and development of Malawi's economy with a view to the elimination of the budgetary deficit *and Malawi's dependence on external aid for recurrent expenditure.*'[22] Britain also wished to bring about a situation where the provision of aid to Malawi was an international rather than a specifically British responsibility.[23] It is possible to conceive of situations where such objectives could be inconsistent with the object of development. However Britain did in fact see economic development as the chief means to their achievement: incomes would have to rise to permit higher revenues while successful development efforts would increase Malawi's chances, which were otherwise limited, of attracting outside aid.

The existence of these two objectives helps to explain the large flow of British aid to Malawi. Britain accepted special responsibility towards Malawi, arising from its obligations as the ex-colonial power and the particular economic circumstances obtaining in Malawi at independence. Until the late fifties, Britain tended to take literally the legal and constitutional truth that its special responsibility for the economic welfare of a colony ceased at independence. From 1960 onwards, it became the practice for Britain to make fairly generous provisions of aid to newly independent Commonwealth countries under independence settlements. Nevertheless, while clearly accepting a greater measure of responsibility for ex-colonies than for foreign ldcs, Britain still attempted a sharp distinction between its aid policy towards independent Commonwealth countries and that towards colonial territories: having received their independence settlements, the former had no special claim on Britain's aid resources, though in practice they could generally expect more favourable treatment than countries without past colonial connections with Britain.

Malawi's economic position prior to independence was such that the normal independence settlement — development grants and/or loans plus provisions regarding the retirement and the continued employment of expatriate civil servants — would have been insufficient. With the break up of the Federation, Britain had resumed full colonial responsibility for a territory which was unable to meet its recurrent government expenditure out of local revenue. The prospect of economic viability — a condition equated with a balanced budget — was generally thought to be distant, despite one optimistic estimate that it would only take five years. On the other hand, the political circumstances were such that independence could not easily be delayed. With no other donor ready to finance Malawi's expenditures, it was clear that if Britain gave Malawi the standard treatment the economic welfare of the country would be severely jeopardised. Britain's response was to accept the quasi-colonial responsibility of providing budgetary assistance 'for some years to come' as well as providing 'development' aid. It was a considerable, though not unique, extension of the *de facto* aid policy towards newly independent colonies. Like the latter policy it had its basis in a sense of moral obligation which, in Malawi's case, was doubtless heightened by the fact that the discrepancy between its economic requirements and its political demands could be attributed to a large extent to Britain's mistaken policy on federation.

This acceptance of a post-colonial responsibility committed Britain to providing economic support to Malawi in accordance with Malawi's absolute needs rather than with its needs relative to those of ldcs elsewhere or in accordance with other factors which generally affect the allocation of British aid between ldcs.

That Britain was unhappy with its quasi-colonial role is revealed by the objectives stated earlier. Britain's main concern in this respect was to end budgetary aid, which had two major disadvantages. First, Britain considered that, in providing such aid, it was put in a situation where it was too closely involved in the affairs of a sovereign state. Second, the commitment to provide budgetary aid was open ended: the very type of commitment that governments try to avoid with their own citizens let alone other governments. Despite Britain's desire to encourage development and the fact that higher incomes were perceived as the chief way of ending Malawi's budgetary dependence, it is possible that the short-term aim of ending budgetary aid may have conflicted with the longer-term objective of raising the living standards of the people of Malawi, by encouraging, directly or indirectly, a pattern of development inconsistent with the latter. This possible conflict will be considered in the next chapter. Broadly, however, the aims of British aid policy towards Malawi stated so far, focus on development. How far were Britain's political and commercial interests in Malawi consistent with these aims?

As might be expected, Britain's commercial interests in Malawi were, and are, relatively small compared with its interests elsewhere in the Third World. Its merchandise trade with Malawi constituted only 3.8 per cent of total exports to and 5.1 per cent of imports from the Third World in 1965-6. Its private capital in Malawi accounted for only 0.8 per cent of total British overseas assets in developing countries in 1965.[24] While obviously Britain had an interest in protecting and if possible expanding its trade and investment in Malawi, the view taken by aid policy makers was that a growth in Malawi's material prosperity was the best means of so doing. And this view is reflected in the terms and conditions of the aid provided to Malawi.[25]

Britain's chief political interest in Malawi relates to the country's position as a buffer state between black and white Africa. The interest is strategic in a political rather than a military sense and derives from

Dr Banda's pursuit of the dialogue policy with South Africa. Britain has a stake in the peaceful coexistence of white and black dominated African states not only because it has a general desire for global peace and security, but also because it wishes to avoid a situation where it must choose between its fairly evenly balanced interests in these two political groupings. The importance of the dialogue policy in reducing tensions between the two groups is debatable. Black African states are sceptical of the sincerity of Dr Banda's policy which, given Malawi's economic ties with, and its aid receipts from, southern Africa has every appearance of being simply expedient. It has not been conspicuously successful as an example to other black African states. And there is little doubt that Malawi's idiosyncratic approach to the problem of southern Africa would not be an obstacle to concerted black African action to end white minority rule — should such a move be decided. Despite these shortcomings, however, Britain supports the dialogue policy.

Britain's interest in the success and continuance of the dialogue policy could affect the conduct of the aid programme in two ways. First, it could bring about a situation where the amount of aid provided was influenced by Malawi's aid receipts from, and other links with, southern Africa: the object being to counter the latter's influence in Malawi. Secondly, it could result in aid being given in order to sustain Dr Banda, the chief exponent of the policy. Dr Banda's generally sympathetic attitude towards Britain, his encouragement of both foreign and domestic private enterprise and his promotion of harmonious race relations add to Britain's interest in his political survival.[26] But the possibility of conflict between this latter interest and Britain's interest in Malawi's development is small. Dr Banda's power depends primarily on his popular support, which in turn depends largely on the success of Malawi's development policies. If his political survival were ensured purely or mainly by repressive means, his effectiveness in most areas of interest to Britain would be reduced. Coming from a domestically unenlightened despot, the dialogue would carry even less weight with the black African states, while his sympathy towards British subjects with economic interests in Malawi would not make up for the political uncertainties that would attend a repressive régime or for the lack of commercial opportunities. A similar line of reasoning suggests that Britain would not boost its aid flows to Malawi simply to provide a counterweight to South African influence without having regard to the developmental impact of such aid.

There is a greater possibility of conflict between the developmental objective of aid giving and two other short-term objectives. The first relates to Britain's balance of payments policy, which has clearly influenced both the quantity and quality of the aid programme over the sixties. It is the quality of aid that is of concern here. Three factors in Malawi — its dependence on British aid, its lack of local resources and its development priorities — rendered the country extremely vulnerable to the adverse effects of procurement tied aid. As will be seen below, however, British aid to Malawi has not been formally subject to restrictive procurement requirements. The official ODM view is that the use of procurement tying to minimise the balance of payments cost of aid is inappropriate to Malawi's case and that if there is to be balance of payments gain from aid, it must be derived from increased trade with a country made more prosperous as a result of British aid. It is, of course, possible that Britain may have sought by less formal means — such as project selection — to minimise the balance of payments cost of aid to Malawi.[27] But in formal terms, Britain's procurement policy towards Malawi has been dictated by Malawi's rather than Britain's need.

The second short-term consideration is more specifically related to Malawi: namely, Britain's objective of ensuring cordial relations with Malawi so as to assist the smooth running of the aid programme and to protect British subjects and interests in Malawi.

Since Britain has had reason to be strongly interested in Malawi's development and its provision of budgetary aid has entailed a close involvement with Malawi's domestic affairs, the potential for friction between the two countries is obvious. On the one hand, Britain could be expected to attempt to ensure that Malawi's policies agreed with its own views on what policies were necessary. On the other hand, because of the extent of Malawi's financial dependence on Britain, its government could be expected to be more than usually sensitive to any attempts by Britain to exert leverage to ensure that its policies were 'correct.' This conflict between the development objective and the diplomatic objective could occur if Britain's views as to what policies and projects were required for Malawi's development differed from those of the Malawi government. It is clear, however, that some compromise on the developmental side would be required, given that Britain felt morally obliged to assist Malawi: if diplomatic considerations were always to be over-ridden by developmental considerations then Britain might find itself in a position of having its aid totally rejected — Dr Banda is not averse to telling donors to keep their aid, if he considers that they are guilty of attempting undue interference in Malawi's affairs.[28]

British Aid to Malawi: the Facts

Volume

Britain's total disbursements to Malawi under the aid programme between 1964 and 1972 have amounted to £80.3m gross and £68.5m net of interest and amortisation payments to Britain. Malawi's net aid receipts from Britain have averaged roughly £1.80 per head of Malawi's population per year. In consequence, Malawi has ranked as a major recipient of British aid while Britain has ranked as Malawi's most significant donor. The relative importance of Britain as a donor and Malawi as a British aid recipient has declined, however, over the period. In 1964, Malawi's net aid receipts accounted for some 8 per cent of Britain's total bilateral aid disbursements, net of interest and amortisation, while British aid accounted for over 98 per cent of Malawi's gross aid receipts and financed nearly half of total government expenditure. By 1972, Malawi's share of net British aid disbursements had dropped to roughly 4 per cent while British aid accounted for only 40 per cent of Malawi's gross aid receipts and 14.6 per cent of government expenditure.[29]

This broad quantitative picture has to be modified to the extent that not all Britain's aid flows can properly be regarded as aid — that is resource flows that are concessional and primarily intended for development — and that the recorded aid receipts of the Malawi government include some non-aid flows from other 'donors' and exclude technical assistance transfers made in kind. Malawi has received financial aid from relatively few sources besides Britain — Denmark, West Germany, the International Development Association (IDA), South Africa and the USA being the most prominent. It has, however, received transfers in kind from a much larger number of countries and agencies[30] and Britain has been relatively less important in this category. The quantitative significance of non-cash aid, valued according to donors' estimates of actual costs, has been small — but of increasing importance: available data indicate that in 1964 it was approximately 4 per cent of Malawi's total gross cash and non-cash aid receipts and 10 per cent in 1968.[31]

To eliminate the non-aid component from the British 'aid' total, it is necessary to examine the different kinds of resource flows which made up the aid programme. Broadly, these can be classified under five heads: budgetary grants-in-aid; 'development' grants and loans; technical assistance; finance for pensions, commutation and compensation; and Commonwealth Development Corporation (CDC) assistance. Budgetary grants-in-aid were obviously concessional but less obviously intended for development in that a major purpose in their provision was to prevent economic decline in Malawi. However, although traditionally the developmental role of recurrent expenditure had scarcely been taken into account in the provision of budgetary aid, this has not been the case so far as Malawi was concerned. That the supportive was combined with the developmental intent is evidenced by Britain's willingness to allow Malawi's recurrent expenditure to rise while it was receiving budgetary aid. 'Development' grants and loans were both concessional and primarily developmental – as the epithet implies – although the distinction between this type of aid and budgetary grants-in-aid is in fact somewhat blurred: a point which will be considered later. British technical assistance to Malawi, provided in grant form, may be regarded as an adjunct to both budgetary and 'development' assistance. The remaining two categories – finance for pensions, etc., and CDC finance – do not readily conform with the definition of aid used here and require further consideration.

Between 1964 and 1971, Britain provided a number of grants and loans to compensate former colonial service officers employed by the Nyasaland government for their loss of career after independence, and to pay pensions to such officers. Part of the pensions could be commuted to capital sums and Britain has also provided finance for this purpose. The precise amount made available to Malawi is difficult to determine from British aid statistics. Using Malawi government revenue account data,[32] the total compensation and commutation loans received from Britain from 1 January 1964 to the end of March 1971 amounted to £3.6m (K7.2m), while grant payments amounted to £2.9m (K5.8m). Commutation loans have been made at interest rates ranging from 6 to 8 per cent generally repayable over twenty-five years with a seven year grace period, while compensation loans have been interest free with similar capital repayment terms. The 1972 DAC recommendation[33] on aid terms requires that any given transaction must have a grant element of at least 25 per cent before it may be considered as genuine development assistance. Taking this yardstick, all but the commutation loans with 8 per cent interest charges qualify as aid.[34]

But to be termed aid, resource flows have to satisfy the second criterion, namely that they are primarily intended for development. This the various grants and loans fail to do. The object of providing such finance was to permit the independent Malawi government to discharge the responsibilities of the former colonial government to its employees. In effect such finance (which includes a contribution to the interest charges) represents a payment to the British government and to British subjects – not for their present services to Malawi but largely to meet contractual obligations arising from their past services to Nyasaland. It is hard to see why the Malawi government should have to make payments for services rendered to a régime that members and supporters of the present government fought to overthrow. And certainly, the

Table 3.2 British Aid to Malawi

	1964	1965	1966	1967	1968	1969	1970	1971	1972
Gross disbursements									
Grants of which:									
Financial	6,747	8,382	4,499	4,165	3,131	2,729	2,624	5,068	441
Technical assistance	1,195	1,113	1,283	1,370	1,683	1,734	1,685	1,742	2,822
Loans	2,957	1,464	3,162	3,061	3,015	2,689	3,400	3,241	4,934
of which: CDC	623	914	908	310	202	234	120	575	529
Total	10,899	10,959	8,943	8,596	7,829	7,152	7,709	10,051	8,197
Amortisation payments	114	81	126	230	282	458	528	4,485	619
of which: CDC	(10)	(9)	(-)	(71)	(117)	(291)	(302)	(239)	(217)
Gross disbursements net of amortisation	10,785	10,878	8,817	8,366	7,547	6,694	7,181	5,566	7,578
Interest payments	304	416	498	530	584	595	580	825	535
of which: CDC	(147)	(192)	(248)	(276)	(322)	(331)	(326)	(317)	(359)
Gross disbursements net of amortisation and interest	10,481	10,462	8,319	7,836	6,963	6,099	6,601	4,741	7,043
% Total British bilateral disbursements net of interest and amortisation*	-	-	6.4	6.3	5.5	5.2	4.8	2.8	4.4

*   Including net CDC disbursements

Source: *ODM/ODA British Aid Statistics 1964-1972*, HMSO

receipts from Britain to facilitate such payments cannot be regarded as aid but rather — to the extent that they are not all grants — as a burden. Britain has now recognised this point of view.[35] In 1971, an agreement was concluded with Malawi by which Britain took an increased share of pensions and related payments to expatriate officers while all outstanding compensation and commutation loans were cancelled. This cancellation is the reason for the increase in gross British aid to Malawi in 1971 (see Table 3.2) and the large return flow of amortisation payments in that year: the debt cancelled amounted to nearly £4m (K7.9m).[36] Between 1971 and March 1974, Britain has disbursed some £1.4m under the pensions 'pick-up' agreement.

Resources provided by the CDC tend to be regarded as part of the aid programme. They are, however, separately administered by the CDC, whose activities are only minimally under the supervision of the government minister concerned with aid. By statute the CDC financial provisions are supposed to assist development but it is also under an obligation to operate on commercial lines, taking one year with another. Thus, although primarily developmental, CDC finance has rarely been particularly concessional. This is certainly true in Malawi's case where the majority of CDC resources provided has been in the form of fairly hard loans to public sector enterprises: for example, a loan to a subsidiary of the Malawi Development Corporation had a grant element of only 12 per cent. The net flow of CDC resources to Malawi, as recorded by ODM, has consequently been small in relation to the gross inflow: £641,000 between 1964 and 1972 as compared with £4,415,000. Although not qualifying as aid, CDC resource flows to Malawi have a flavour of aid. For this reason and because they are formally part of the British aid programme, a brief account of CDC activities will be given in the appendix to this chapter.

A figure for the *aid* component of British disbursements to Malawi is hard to determine precisely. Roughly, however, gross aid disbursements by Britain probably amounted to about £64m between 1964 and 1972 while net *aid* was probably just over £60m.

Terms and Conditions of Aid
Financial aid
In Malawi — as elsewhere — a distinction is drawn between recurrent and development expenditure, the latter being largely but not wholly investment expenditure. The distinction holds broadly for accounting purposes but would be hard to justify as a means of classifying developmental and non-developmental expenditure. This is not only because some capital expenditure is at most only indirectly developmental but also — and mainly — because much recurrent expenditure actually increases the productive capacity of the country or provides the infrastructural services necessary for development to take place. British aid

has, however, been formally directed to either the recurrent or the development account and the terms and conditions have varied accordingly.

The most significant category of British aid, in quantitative terms, has been budgetary assistance — that is, aid provided to finance Malawi's deficit on recurrent account. As will be seen from Table 3.3, there has, apart from 1965, been a continuous decline in budgetary grants-in-aid from 56 per cent of Malawi's gross cash receipts from Britain in 1964 to 6 per cent in the financial year 1971-2, which was the last year in which Malawi received budgetary aid. Total budgetary aid[37] to Malawi between 1964 and 1971-2 has amounted to £27.9m, 45 per cent of its gross cash receipts from Britain. This budgetary assistance has been wholly in grant form but, since 1966, 50 per cent of any savings in the budgetary aid agreed for a given year could be converted into an interest free loan for development projects in Malawi, subject to Britain's approval. This arrangement was designed to provide an incentive to the Malawi government to pursue its and Britain's objective of phasing out budgetary aid. Grants-in-aid have not been subject to any procurement restrictions but under a 'gentleman's agreement,' Malawi was committed to using recurrent revenue for the purchase of British goods wherever possible.

Budgetary grant-in-aid is not the only assistance to Malawi's recurrent account. Besides the financial arrangement associated with ex-colonial officers, Britain has made small grants towards the financing of agricultural and fisheries research stations, and certain of its technical assistance payments are made via the recurrent account. These payments are included under UK grants 'other recurrent' in Table 3.3; the technical assistance component is by far the most significant.

British aid finance for development — or more accurately finance towards expenditures carried out under Malawi's development account is best seen from the breakdown provided in Table 3.3. British aid statistics do not distinguish between non-aid loans and development loans or general budgetary grant aid and grant aid specifically for development account expenditure. In the first two years of Malawi's independence, Britain provided development grants only. From 1966 onwards Britain has provided increasing quantities of development loan finance and, until 1970-1, no further development grant aid. The grants drawn between 1964 and 1966 were of three kinds: CD&W grants largely for the continuation of projects already embarked upon, an independence gift of £3.0m towards the financing of the Development Programme, and a £1.5m grant to be spent on projects approved by the ODM. The development loans have all been interest free with a twenty-five year repayment period, for financing projects to be agreed later between the Malawi government and the ODM. As from 1972-3, the capital repayment terms have been improved by an adjustment of the grace period provisions, thereby increasing the concessionality of UK development loans[38] from having a grant element of 73 per cent to a grant element of 77 per cent. Both the development grants (excluding the independence gift) and loans have been tied to procurement in Malawi or in Britain, thus allowing the financing of local costs as well as offshore costs (in Britain). Britain's first loan to Malawi, of £7m to be drawn over 1966 to 1968, was available for the total costs of any agreed project. The second and subsequent loans cover only 90 per cent of the total costs of an agreed project, while the remaining 10 per cent has to be financed by Malawi out of local resources.[39] Recently, Britain has provided further development grant aid to Malawi (see Table 3.3). This does not represent a return to the earlier practice of providing development grants, but, in fact, arises from an agreement, made in 1965, to provide a £1m grant towards the capital cost of establishing the University of Malawi, which project, for reasons considered later, was delayed.

The final category of aid provided by Britain has been technical assistance. The total disbursements of British technical assistance have increased slowly, as can be seen from Table 3.2. It has been provided as grants and, by its nature, tied to British goods and services. Basically, British technical assistance to Malawi has had three components: the financing of British personnel working in Malawi, of Malawians training in Britain, and of equipment, usually provided in support of British personnel in Malawi. Of these, the first has been the most important, and by far the greatest number of British personnel working in Malawi have done so in established civil service posts, under the supplementation schemes, chiefly the Overseas Service Aid Scheme, the British Aided Conditions of Services scheme and the British Expatriates Supplementation Scheme whereby the Malaw government pays them the local salary, and makes other contributions, while Britain 'tops up' the salaries to roughly British levels and makes other payments associated with overseas service. Between 1964 and 1971, 800-900 British personnel worked under these arrangements, the numbers increasing between 1965 to 1967 and declining thereafter from 916 in post in 1967 to 736 in 1972. More than three-quarters of these personnel have been employed in education, public administration and works, and communications. Since 1967, there has been a significant decline in the numbers employed in public administration.

Wholly funded British personnel operating in an advisory capacity in Malawi represent, by contrast, only a minor though increasing part of Britain's technical assistance contribution. At the end of 1964, there were sixteen such personnel working in Malawi: at the end of 1972, forty. The number of volunteers financed under the British aid programme has been slightly greater: there were twenty-eight in 1964-5

Table 3.3 Gross British Financial Aid Compared with Total Gross Financial Aid Receipts of Malawi Government 1964-72/3 (in Km)

	1964	1965	1966	1967	1968	1969*	1970/1	1971/2†	1972/3†
1. *Gross Loans Total*	2.4	1.3	6.0	6.9	8.5	15.2	32.4	24.3	20.5
of which:								(21.6)	(18.8)
UK compensation and commutation	1.7	1.3	1.0	1.2	1.1	0.8	0.6	0.1	-
UK development	-	-	3.4	4.3	4.5	5.0	6.6	8.6	6.7
UK other	0.7	-	-	-	-	-	-	-	-
UK Total	2.4	1.3	4.4	5.5	5.6	5.8	7.1	8.7	6.7
Denmark	-	-	0.2	0.2	0.7	0.9	0.5	1.0	0.8
West Germany	-	-	1.4	0.9	0.2	0.5	1.2	1.4	0.6
IDA	-	-	0.1	0.2	1.8	4.9	7.8	7.2	5.2
USAID	-	-	-	-	0.1	0.1	3.1	1.8	1.8
South Africa	-	-	-	-	-	3.0	12.6	3.1	2.0
ADB	-	-	-	-	-	-	0.1	1.1	0.8
Canada	-	-	-	-	-	-	-	-	1.1
UNDP	-	-	-	-	-	-	-	-	0.1
Other	-	-	-	-	-	-	-	-	1.5
Non-UK Total	-	-	1.7	1.3	2.8	9.4	25.3	15.6	13.8
2. *Cash Grants Total*	15.6	21.1	10.3	11.1	9.3	7.9	7.3	4.3	n.a.
of which:								(3.6)	(3.7)
UK grant-in-aid	10.0	11.9	8.5	8.3	6.4	5.6	4.2	0.8	-
UK other recurrent	2.7	2.0	2.0	2.4	2.7	2.0	2.0	2.1	n.a.
UK development	2.7	6.8	0.6	-	-	-	0.2	0.9	n.a.
UK Total	15.4	20.7	10.0	10.7	9.1	7.6	6.4	3.9	n.a.
Non-UK Total	0.2	0.4	0.3	0.3	0.2	0.2	1.1	0.5	n.a.

Table 3.3 (Cont.)

(Km)

	1964	1965	1966	1967	1968	1969*	1970/1	1971/2†	1972/3†
3. *Total Cash Grants and Loans*	18.0	22.4	16.3	18.0	17.8	23.1	39.8	(25.2)	(22.5)
Of which:									
UK	17.8	22.0	14.4	16.2	14.7	13.4	13.5	12.6	n.a.
% Total	98.9	98.2	88.3	90.0	82.6	58.0	33.9	43.9	n.a.
4. *Total Gross Expenditure by Malawi Government***	37.4	41.7	48.6	49.0	54.3	60.5	82.1	(81.6)	(83.7)
% Financed by Cash Aid Receipts	48.1	53.7	33.5	36.7	32.8	38.2	48.5	(30.9)	(26.9)
% Financed by UK Aid Receipts	47.6	52.8	29.6	33.1	27.1	22.1	16.4	14.5	n.a.

* The financial year was changed in 1970 to run from April to March instead of January to December. 1969 data refers to estimates for the calendar year based on actual data for the fifteen month period January 1969 to March 1970.

† Revised estimates used for these years. Figures in brackets refer to final estimates of receipts and expenditure for which no detailed breakdown is available. All other data are final estimates.

** I.e. total gross expenditure on revenue and development account.

Sources: M.G. Ministry of Finance, *Public Sector Financial Statistics 1970; Economic Reports 1972 and 1974; Accountant General's Report on Public Accounts 1964-1968; Approved Estimates of Expenditure on Development Account 1973/74.*

and since 1967-8 between seventy and one hundred. In most years, more than half of them have been engaged in teaching.

In terms of total technical assistance disbursements, the amount spent on providing training and tuition to Malawians in the UK has been relatively small, though it has increased from less than 1 per cent of the total in 1965 to c. 10 per cent in 1970. The number of Malawian students and trainees in Britain has increased from 37 in 1965 to 118 in 1971. In 1972, the number of students dropped to fifty-six while that of trainees increased to forty-eight.[40] Engineering, medicine, education and the social sciences have been the main field of study.

The terms and conditions of British financial aid compare favourably with those of other major donors to Malawi. The grant element of British aid is relatively high. Partly this reflects the fact that Britain has provided a greater proportion of its aid in the form of grants. But the grant element of British loans has also been greater than all but IDA, USAID and, until 1972, Denmark, whose loans have had a grant element of 88 per cent, 79 per cent and 77 per cent respectively. The first South African loan to Malawi was virtually on commercial terms and, with a grant element of 8.4 per cent, cannot be regarded as aid. Its second loan, however, had a grant element of 62 per cent. The terms of loans from West Germany have varied, but the majority have had a grant element ranging between 62 and 73 per cent. Malawi's loan from the African Development Bank (ADB) had a grant element of only 35 per cent.

The conditions attached to British aid have generally been less restrictive than those of other major donors. So far as its 'development' aid has been concerned, Britain has been prepared to finance the whole cost of any approved project (later 90 per cent of the cost), it has not formally distinguished between local and offshore expenditure and it has been prepared to finance both small and diffuse projects often for fairly long time periods. Meanwhile, unlike other major donors' aid, a large proportion of Britain's aid has been untied and available for unprojectised recurrent expenditure. Apart from Denmark, all other donors have provided aid on the basis of individual project requests and they have shown a marked preference for large projects. Some donors have sought to limit their contribution to project costs, and particularly to *local* project costs, via procurement restrictions and limits to the proportion of costs that can be financed by aid. ADB aid, for instance, has been wholly tied to offshore procurement while American aid has largely been tied to procurement in the USA or approved ldcs: only 7 per cent of the largest US loan ($ 7m) to Malawi was allowed towards local costs. The full conditions of West German and South African aid are not clear but tying exists, and this is borne out by the import content of some projects and the level of Malawian local cost contributions to others. IDA, however, does not tie its aid and requires a local contribution of only about 15 per cent of total project costs. Denmark, meanwhile, is prepared to finance total project costs and, like Britain, makes a total loan commitment for projects to be agreed later. It does however require that 75 per cent of its aid be spent on Danish goods and services.

Although the terms and conditions of other bilateral donors' aid to Malawi and of ADB aid tend to be less favourable to Malawi than those of Britain, they do tend to be more favourable than those generally proffered to ldcs. This is also true in Britain's case and bears out the conclusion of the preceding section that Britain's interest in Malawi's development was of over-riding concern so far as its aid programme was concerned.

Scope for Leverage

The quantity, terms and conditions of British aid to Malawi indicate a responsiveness to and concern for Malawi's development needs. But the provision of such aid is – as critics of aid giving are swift to point out – no guarantee that it will be effectively used for development. Before moving on to a more detailed consideration of how the different kinds of aid affected Malawi's development progress, it is of general interest to consider how far Britain's aid policy was designed to ensure – in the words of the 1965 White Paper – 'that the resources transferred (were) used to the best effect.'[41]

Obviously, to the extent that Malawi and Britain shared the same objectives and had similar views as to how they might be achieved there was little need to attempt to exert influence. *Ex post* both governments appear to have agreed on major issues. They jointly placed a high priority on the ending of budgetary aid, and it was agreed that this required an expansion of the revenue base through economic growth – which in turn required an expanded recurrent budget – and a close watch on government consumption expenditure. Similarly, they agreed that the focus should be on the agricultural sector with transportation investment largely in support of agricultural development, on secondary and higher education and on providing suitable conditions for private sector industrial growth. The extent of the apparent agreement between donor and recipient is not, however, proof of the relative absence of leverage or of the need for its exertion. There were, in fact, areas of disagreement not only on detail but also on fairly major questions, for instance, Britain was opposed to both the new capital and the Nacala rail link project.

The conduct of its aid programme to Malawi has been such as to enable Britain to exert some control over the use of aid in a number of ways. Until 1972, budgetary aid was only agreed after the Malawi government's annual estimates had been subjected to ODM scrutiny and Britain had been satisfied as to Malawi's requirements. Agreed 'development' finance has only been disbursed for specific projects and purposes approved by ODM, and other forms of aid have similarly been tied to specific purposes. Efficient use of past aid has always been a factor, known to Malawi, in future aid allocations. And Malawi's use of aid funds has been subject to a certain degree of financial and administrative control from Britain. Meanwhile, visits by ODM advisors and aid missions to Malawi and the presence of a full-time representative in the British High Commission in Blantyre have enabled Britain to maintain some field level check on the implementation of aid financed projects and on general development progress in Malawi. And the Development Division now established in Blantyre will increase this capability. Through the various contacts in the aid giving process, Britain can make known its views on issues specifically related to British aid and on Malawi's general policy. But the use of aid conditions as a means of influencing general policy has been rare: the most important instance[42] being the change from 100 per cent to 90 per cent project financing, which, by effectively limiting Malawi's capability to carry out non-aided projects, increased Britain's influence over its total development expenditure. Britain has, however, undoubtedly exerted an influence on Malawi's policy choices at an indirect level by virtue of being Malawi's most important aid donor. With future aid at least partially dependent on both the effective use of past aid and, generally, on satisfactory development progress, Malawi could not afford to disregard Britain's views on such matters.

Britain's actual scope for influence has been subject to some limitations. For the first few years after Malawi's independence the administrative machinery for aid giving was relatively weak. Although aid was provided for a variety of purposes, the main British concern initially was with budgetary grants-in-aid. British involvement in project selection and implementation then increased but technical assistance provisions were until recently largely the result of a passive response to Malawi's requests. The increasing focus on project tied aid itself could be viewed as a limiting factor in that the donor tends to look at the effectiveness of spending on the specific project it finances, rather than the other expenditure which its aid may allow by releasing local or foreign resources.

But, in practice, this possibility has been restricted, particularly in the early years (when ironically Britain was paying less attention to actual project selection and implementation), by the shortage of local resources in Malawi and the type and purpose of aid provided by other donors. In any case, since Malawi's development programme has been essentially a list of projects, Britain would have found it difficult not to focus on projects.

Britain's ability to influence Malawi's development policies more generally has been subject to a number of constraints. In the earlier years when, as virtually the only donor to Malawi, Britain was apparently in a strong position to exert leverage, the lack of information on broader development issues within both Malawi and ODM limited the leverage potential. At the same time, the need to exert leverage beyond the rejection of certain projects was limited also by the fact that Malawi found it difficult to obtain finance to support policies or programmes of which Britain disapproved, and there was anyway broad agreement on the type of policies to be pursued. Later, the presence of other donors (in particular South Africa) with whom there was little coordination and, to a certain extent, a lack of common interest, acted as a constraint on Britain. Although Britain could and did refuse to finance 'undesirable' projects, the fact that Malawi had alternative sources of finance limited the efficacy of this policy. Further, Britain could not threaten to curtail aid, since the danger that it would be forced to use this sanction was considerable and the consequences self-defeating in terms of Britain's aid objectives. The London based, project oriented aid administration might also have limited the potential for leverage, had not the main constraint been Britain's reluctance on principle to attempt to influence Malawian affairs against the wishes of the government; a reluctance arising from its sensitivity on the issue of sovereignty, which was heightened by the fact that Malawi was in a position of neo-colonial dependence on Britain.

Conclusions

Britain's aid to individual ldcs is by no means governed by a consistent or uniform set of policies. Nevertheless, certain general features, or at least tendencies, of Britain's bilateral aid programme are identifiable. Compared with these, Britain's treatment of Malawi has been exceptional — although not unique — in several respects. The development objective of providing aid has, in Malawi's case, been remarkably untrammelled by non-developmental considerations. Both the quantity and the quality of aid have been determined largely by Malawi's development needs rather than by the pursuit of Britain's national interests. This reflects the special nature — traceable to Malawi's economic dependence on Britain — of the relationship between the two countries. Although Britain's aim in providing aid to Malawi was not solely that of development, it was chiefly *through* Malawi's development that Britain's desire to relieve itself of its quasi-colonial role could be achieved. Britain's aid policy towards Malawi has therefore been such as to allow development to take place, and, in keeping with shifts in its general approach to recipients, Britain has sought to ensure that aid was well used and that development *did* take place. These efforts have, however, been subject to certain limitations — the most important arising from Britain's special relationship with Malawi. Paradoxically, Malawi's neo-colonial dependence on Britain, which led to Britain's close involvement with and concern for Malawi's development, has also restricted the scope for the exercise of influence to ensure development. The extent to which such influence was needed will be considered in the chapters which follow, where the developmental effectiveness of the British aid programme to Malawi will be examined.

3   Appendix: CDC'S ROLE IN MALAWI

As stated earlier, the activities of the CDC are regarded as part of the aid programme, but the nature of its resource flows are such that they do not accord with the definition of aid used here. Both in general and specifically in relation to Malawi, CDC resource flows do, however, possess some aid characteristics. For this reason and for the sake of completeness, a brief description of the CDC and its activities in Malawi is given below.

The CDC was set up in 1948, as the Colonial Development Corporation, to bridge the gap between government development finance to the colonies and private investment. Colonial was changed to Commonwealth in 1963 so that the CDC could extend and continue its operations in newly independent Commonwealth countries (excluding India and Pakistan). Since 1969, it can, with ministerial approval, operate outside the Commonwealth and in India and Pakistan. Subject to the necessity of operating on commercial lines, taking one year with the other, the CDC can undertake a wide variety of projects, alone or with others; it can provide loans or equity finance; it can furnish managerial and advisory services; and the terms of its finance may be varied. The CDC receives its finances mainly from the Treasury, though it can borrow outside the government. Its borrowings from the Treasury, and in total, at any one time are subject to a ceiling (£130m and £160m respectively from 1963 onwards, increasing to £205m and £225m in 1969), and since 1965 its annual drawings from the Treasury have come within the aid ceiling. As the finance it receives has been on relatively hard terms, its provisions to ldcs have not been particularly concessional. Until 1965, its activities were subject to the general, but in practice minimal, direction of the Secretary of State for Commonwealth Relations and for the Colonies. After 1965, the Minister for Overseas Development – or his equivaient – took over this role. Though the CDC's Exchequer finance has come within the aid ceiling, this fact does not seem to have had much impact on CDC's relative autonomy.

The CDC describes its activities as 'overseas investment with some flavour of aid.'[43] In some respects CDC's operations have advantages over aid. The finance provided, though on relatively hard terms, is untied, it is often closely linked with the provision of technical assistance, and its administration is decentralised.[44] Balance of payments concerns and Britain's short-term political objectives do not appear to have influenced CDC's activities to the extent that they have the aid programme.

Unlike the rest of Britain's aid, the emphasis in CDC's assistance has always been that of an active 'partner' in development. The need to operate commercially can obviously conflict with its statutory object of assisting economic development, not only in the type of projects undertaken but also in the allocation of its finance between countries. The requirement is, on the other hand, a built in incentive to efficiency,[45] and it does not automatically follow that this type of assistance is any less likely to further development than aid provided for export promoting and political reasons.

Since its independence, Malawi has received a gross inflow of CDC finances of £4.4m, approximately 3 per cent of CDC's gross investment in ldcs over the period. Net of amortisation and interest payments, Malawi's CDC receipts amounted to £0.6m. The assistance has been of four distinct types: loans made directly to public sector enterprises or to commercial enterprises in which the public sector had major interests; the provision of equity finance; direct sponsorship of development projects; and the provision of operational and advisory personnel. The major part of CDC's support to Malawi has been in the form of loan finance with commitments up to 1972 amounting to £6.3m. The terms have varied but generally repayment periods have been less than twenty years and interest rates over 7 per cent, with some use of waiver and grace periods for debt servicing. Nearly two-fifths of total commitments have been made to the Electricity Supply Commission of Malawi (ESCOM) to finance the development of hydro-electric power facilities and a fifth have been made to the Malawi Housing Corporation towards the construction of urban housing (see Table 3.4). The remaining 42 per cent of loan commitments has been made in support of two agricultural projects run by statutory authorities (27 per cent); two commercial enterprises and a development finance company (13 per cent); and a water supply project run by a statutory body (2 per cent). In 1973 CDC approved a further £3m in loans towards the extension of the two agricultural projects (£0.5m) and of the hydro-electric power schemes (£2.5m). In all, eleven separate projects have received fresh CDC loan support.[46]

CDC's provision of equity finance has been relatively insignificant, amounting to £450,000 gross over the period and £250,000 net. In the process, CDC acquired equity in two firms in which the Malawi Development Corporation was the major shareholder, and in the Investment and Development Bank in which the Malawi government has a substantial equity interest. CDC has also made loans to all these bodies.

CDC has been in direct control of two agricultural projects, the Vipya Tung Estates and the Kasungu Tobacco Estates. The former,

Table 3.4   CDC Finance to Malawi, 1964-72
(£000)

	1964	1965	1966	1967	1968	1969	1970	1971	1972	Total
Loan commitments										
Power*	1850	-	65	-	-	-	500	-	-	2415
Housing**	-	-	-	-	450	-	-	800	-	1250
Agriculture†	-	-	-	220	-	-	600	866	-	1686
Industry††	-	150	-	150	-	175	-	-	375	850
Water***	138	-	-	-	-	-	-	-	-	138
Total	1988	150	65	370	450	175	1100	1666	375	6339
CDC disbursements										
Gross	623	914	908	310	202	234	120	575	529	4415
Net of interest & amortisation	466	713	660	-37	-237	-388	-508	19	-47	641
Equity finance†††	-	200	-	25	-	(-200)	-	100	125	450 (250)

*   Direct loans to the Electricity Supply Commission of Malawi.
**   Direct loans to Malawi Housing Corporation.
†   Direct loans to Smallholder Tea Authority and Kasungu Flue Cured Tobacco Authority.
††   Direct loans to David Whitehead and Sons Ltd., and Malawi Hotels Ltd., (MDC subsidiary), and the Investment and Development Bank.
***   Direct loan to Mudi River Water Board, supplement to previous commitment of £1.3m.
†††   Figure in brackets under 1969 refers to sale of CDC equity holding in David Whitehead & Sons Ltd., and under Total refers to net equity investment on the period. Other equity investment was in Malawi Hotels Ltd., and the Investment and Development Bank.

Sources: Loan commitments and equity finance from CDC *Annual Reports 1964-1971*; loan disbursements from ODM/ODA *British Aid Statistics*.

started in 1948, was liquidated in 1968 after a continuous operating loss during the post-independence period.[47] The latter was taken over by a statutory crop authority in 1965, after which CDC continued to provide the management for the scheme. Advisory technical assistance has been supplied for appraisals of smallholder tea growing schemes to be run by the Smallholder Tea Authority, which itself was established on CDC's recommendation.

CDC has been a useful source of finance and, to a lesser extent, technical assistance to Malawi and most ventures in which the CDC has been involved appear to be successful — in financial terms at least. The availability of CDC funds has, moreover, helped Malawi to attract funds from other sources, as for instance, for the consortium financed housing schemes of the Malawi Housing Corporation. The chief criticism of the CDC activities in Malawi is one which has been made of CDC activities generally, viz. that its role has been more akin to that of a finance house than of a donor or private investor. Most of its financial provisions have been in the form of low risk, near-commercial loans to public utilities serving the urban industrial sector, rather than in more risky ventures, particularly in the rural sector, where the developmental impact could be greater.

Partly this bias in CDC activities reflects the terms in which CDC itself is financed, although a change was made in 1967 so that CDC might better fulfil its statutory function.[48] As it is, however, the CDC has played a somewhat conservative role in its developmental investment activities in Malawi.

NOTES

1.   Only the United States, France and, recently, West Germany, provide a greater volume of aid to the Third World than Britain.
2.   When the Conservatives returned to power in 1970, the ODM ceased to operate as a separate Ministry, becoming a functional wing — known as the Overseas Development Administration (ODA) — of the Foreign and Commonwealth Office. With the return of a Labour government in 1974, a separate ministry — ODM — was re-established. To avoid confusion here the British aid administration will be referred to as ODM throughout.
3.   Cmnd. 2736, *Overseas Development: the Work of the New Ministry*, London, HMSO, 1965, p. 6.
4.   *Ibid.*, p. 7.
5.   Cmnd. 285, *Select Committee on Overseas Aid, Sessions 1968-69, 1969-70 Minutes of Evidence*, London, HMSO, 1971, p. 2.
6.   *Ibid.*, p. 2.
7.   See, for example, Dudley Seers and Paul Streeten 'Overseas Development Policies,' *The Labour Government's Economic Record 1964-70*, ed., W. Beckerman, London, Duckworth, 1972. Continuing balance of payments problems also played their part in restricting growth.
8.   Cmnd. 2736, *op. cit.*, p. 6.
9.   There was in fact a positive correlation between aid receipts per head and income per head in 1971. See *Report from the Select Committee on Overseas Development, Session 1972-73*, Vol. II, HMSO, 1973, p. 320.

10.   For a full description of the variety of British aid in the early sixties see ODI *British Aid – 2, op. cit.*

11.   Cmnd. 2736, *op. cit.*, pp. 39-40.

12.   This move also marked a change from the colonial aid policy of adapting aid terms to colonies according to the type of project rather than to the colony's general ability to service the aid receipts. It should be noted that some move towards softening aid terms had been made prior to 1965.

13.   ODA *British Aid Statistics 1968-1972*, London, HMSO, 1972, p. 20. This excludes Commonwealth Development Corporation loans.

14.   Estimates from OECD, *Development Assistance Reviews 1967 and 1973*, p. 77 and p. 48 respectively. The grant element is calculated as the face value of a loan less the discounted cost to the recipient of the flow of future service payments; the discount rate used is 10 per cent.

15.   The provision of import finance to India is a notable exception to this approach.

16.   These were established between 1972 and 1973 to cover British aid recipients in East Africa, Central and Southern Africa and South East Asia.

17.   In 1969, 54 per cent of Britain's bilateral aid (excluding technical assistance and certain categories of financial aid to which the procurement issue is not applicable) was formally completely or partially tied to the purchase of British goods and services. In 1970 and 1971, the proportion was 64 per cent, and in 1972, it was 67 per cent.

18.   The value of aid is reduced to the extent that British goods are more expensive than those that could be purchased elsewhere, and that the second round costs, such as the purchase of supplies and replacement parts, are increased. Tying may also increase the recipient's administrative costs.

19.   Cmnd. 4687, *Report of the Select Committee on Overseas Aid, Session 1970/71, Observations by the Minister for Overseas Development*, London, HMSO, 1971. The British government has, however, been prepared to untie its aid provided other donors do the same, and has pressed for international agreement to this end.

20.   Aid is calculated on the basis of gross aid disbursements net of interest and amortisation payments.

21.   See *ODI Reviews* 5 and 6, ODI 1972 and 1973 respectively.

22.   *Report on the Economic Mission to Malawi*, led by C. Hill, 1965, ODM internal document, p. 2, author's emphasis.

23.   This objective is implied in the 1965 White Paper, Cmnd. 2736, *op. cit.*, p. 109, and was explicitly stated officially with respect to Malawi elsewhere.

24.   Book value taken from DTI, *Business Monitor M4 Overseas Transactions*, HMSO, 1971, Table 34.

25.   See above, p. 65.

26.   This interest may have waned somewhat with the recent hardening in Dr Banda's régime's attitudes towards expatriates in Malawi.

27.   See Chapter 5 for a discussion of this.

28.   The most celebrated case, but not the only one, was Dr Banda's refusal of the £18m aid offer from China in 1964.

29.   See Table 3.3. British aid receipts recorded by the Malawi government differ from the aid disbursements recorded by Britain. Most of the discrepancy appears to be explained by the exclusion in Malawi's data of (i) the CDC loans and finance made directly to public enterprises in Malawi and (ii) aid received in kind.

30.   More than thirty countries, including a large number of ldcs, have provided non-cash technical aid to Malawi. The main sources have been the UN, USA, UK, West Germany, Canada, Denmark and Taiwan.

31.   Malawi government, Ministry of Finance *Public Sector Financial Statistics 1970*, Zomba, Government Printer, 1970, Table G. 2.

32.   Drawn from Malawi Government *Accountant-Government's Report on Public Accounts*, years 1964 to 1971. The grant payments include some gratuities made to contract officers serving under British aided terms of service and consequently overstate the quantity of 'non-aid.'

33.   The DAC (Development Assistance Committee) has made a variety of recommendations on minimum concessionality for aid. This recommendation is the only one which subjects each transaction within a donor's 'aid' programme to a concessionality test and is therefore most suited for the kind of comparisons required here. See DAC *Review 1972*, OECD, 1972, p. 59.

34.   Using the standard 10 per cent discount rate, the grant element of an interest free loan with a twenty-five year maturity and seven years' grace period is 77 per cent, the concessionality of a six and and eight per cent loan with the same amortisation terms is 42 per cent and 23 per cent respectively.

35.   See the statement on this subject by the Minister of Overseas Development, *Hansard*, 11 March 1970, p. 1344. If one accepts the argument that, while Malawi was in receipt of grants-in-aid, the debt service burden of the compensation and commutation loans was effectively carried by Britain anyway, then the agreement in 1971 was not belated but timely. It came into force when budgetary grants-in-aid had almost been phased out.

36.   Malawi Government *Economic Report 1972*, pp. 80-1.

37.   This figure refers to the annually agreed commitments of budgetary aid. Actual grants-in-aid were less because of budgetary savings. See Chapter 4.

38.   Grace periods are now to be 7 years as against 2 years previously, with reduced repayment terms over the next 5 years. Loans to Malawi are now on the most generous terms offered by Britain. Britain's financial aid commitment for 1975-78 will be more generous still, with £12m in grant form and the remaining £3m in an interest-free loan.

39.   The financing of 90 per cent rather than 100 per cent of development projects has in effect meant a relaxation of British tying restrictions, although it has reduced Malawi's scarce local resources, and thereby increased Britain's potential influence on total government expenditure.

40.   The trainees are often on courses which last less than a year, hence the data given above understate the number of trainees coming to Britain.

41.   Cmnd. 2736, *op. cit.*, pp. 39-40.

42.   The phased reduction of budgetary aid commitments to Malawi could be regarded as another very important instance, but the policy it reflected was jointly decided.

43.   CDC, *Annual Report 1965*, p. 3.

44.   As CDC puts it, 'overseas development projects cannot be managed from Mayfair!' CDC, *Annual Report 1971*, p. 71. The CDC has a number of regional offices responsible for administration.

45.   And indeed the late Sir Andrew Cohen stated that CDC finance was 'as efficient a form of aid as exists in this country or anywhere in the world, a view which I know the World Bank also holds.' Quoted in CDC *Annual Report 1968*, p. 8.

46.   In 1964 and 1965, CDC provided loan finance directly to the Malawi government for a high density housing scheme: the commitment was made before 1964.

47.   Mainly due to the decline in tung oil prices.

48.   Subject to ODM approval, CDC can now receive interest waivers on a limited amount of its borrowings, for particular projects of developmental value which, because of their nature or the risk involved, do not support full capital and interest repayment terms.

4   BUDGETARY ASSISTANCE

The British government has generally regarded budgetary aid as an undesirable form of assistance to independent countries. And although it has been a major feature in Britain's aid programme to Malawi, it has now been completely phased out. This chapter sets out to answer two main questions. First, what did budgetary aid contribute to Malawi's development? Secondly, was the policy of eliminating budgetary aid appropriate to Malawi's case? It begins, however, with a brief factual description of Britain's post-independence provision of budgetary aid to Malawi and its quantitative importance in the Malawi government's expenditure.

Government Finance and Budgetary Aid

The Malawi government's expenditure system is divided into two components: the revenue, or recurrent account and the development fund account. The recurrent account is financed from recurrent revenue receipts, certain items of special, non-recurrent, revenue and some external grants and loans. Expenditure carried on the recurrent account is for the financing of the government's ongoing commitments plus certain relatively insignificant, capital purchases by government departments (mainly equipment and vehicles). Development account receipts are made up of grants and loans from internal and external sources, small quantities of local revenue from miscellaneous sources, and, in principle, savings from the recurrent account. Expenditure carried on the development account is on capital projects and on certain recurrent items deemed as being developmental in character.[1] Except for statutory items, all expenditure is voted and is subject to direct government control. Contributions to, and receipts from, other parts of the public sector are made through both accounts. Apart from local authorities, all other public sector bodies are expected to finance their own ongoing commitments, while the central government makes subventions through the development account towards their capital expenditure requirements. The surpluses of public sector bodies — Treasury Fund[2] and statutory enterprises — could in principle be available for the financing of government expenditure on the recurrent or development accounts. In practice, the possibility of such contributions being made has been slight and the actual contributions small.

Budgetary grants-in-aid were provided for the purpose of financing

Malawi's recurrent account deficit. It should be noted in passing that the size of this deficit reflected in part the accounting conventions adopted by the Malawi government, since these determined which items of income and expenditure should be allocated to the recurrent rather than the development account. These conventions remained virtually unchanged over the period considered. Nevertheless the existence of a *potential* for switching income and expenditure between accounts is of some significance in evaluating the conduct of British policy on budgetary aid, and will be considered below.[3] For the moment, however, budgetary aid will be regarded simply as a contribution to the recurrent budget, as defined by convention.

The amount of budgetary aid to be provided was decided in advance of the financial year, on the basis of recurrent revenue and expenditure estimates, and the aid was then drawn as required during the year. Between 1964 and 1971, the budgetary grants-in-aid amounted to nearly half of Britain's net disbursements to Malawi. The grants, otherwise free foreign exchange for the Malawi government, were subject to two conditions. First, Malawi had to agree to make its recurrent account offshore purchases in Britain whenever possible: this was, of necessity, a 'gentleman's agreement.' Second, Malawi's annual recurrent estimates and accounts had to be subjected to Britain's scrutiny. Thus, Britain could reassure itself that the deficit to be financed was not artificially inflated, and that efforts were being made to control expenditure and increase resources with the aim of removing the need for budgetary aid.

This vetting took the form of annual discussions or negotiations in London between the British and Malawi governments. In 1964 and 1965, the amount of budgetary aid was negotiated on a purely annual basis. Then in 1965, budgetary aid ceilings for three years in advance were announced.[4] The actual amount of aid to be provided was to be negotiated annually within these maxima. In 1966, as an incentive to budgetary savings, Britain allowed that if the *annually* agreed grant-in-aid was not fully drawn, half of the remainder could be added to Britain's development loan commitment to Malawi. In the following year, the budgetary aid ceilings, with successive annual reductions, were agreed up to 1970, again with actual commitment subject to annual negotiation. By 1970, when the next three years of successively reduced aid ceilings were announced, a rough target date of 1975 was adopted for the termination of budgetary aid. The target date compared well with earlier estimates in the mid-sixties that budgetary aid would not be phased out until 1980 or beyond.

In 1969-70,[5] Britain's contribution accounted for only 14 per cent of Malawi's gross recurrent expenditure as compared with 37 per cent in the peak year of 1965 (see Table 4.1). In 1970-1, the budgetary aid contribution dropped to 9 per cent of Malawi's gross recurrent

Table 4.1 UK Budgetary Grant-in-Aid to Malawi 1964-73/4

(1) Year	(2) Agreed maximum grant*	(3) Grant drawn	(4) Malawi Gov't gross recurrent expenditure	(5) Col (3)/Col (4)
	£m	£m	£m	%
1964	4.25	5.00	16.00	31.4
1965	6.25	5.94	16.14	36.8
1966	5.30	4.24	18.92	22.4
1967	4.60	4.16	19.44	21.4
1968	3.30	3.20	20.17	15.9
1969/70**	3.63	3.63	26.22	13.8
1970/1	2.10	2.10	23.47	8.9
1971/2	1.80	0.42	25.23	1.7
1972/3†	1.30	-0.48	28.52	-1.7
1973/4††	0.80	-	30.72	-

*　Up to 1970-1, the maximum represents that agreed at the annual negotiations (see text). The maximum amounts for 1971/2 to 1973/4 were agreed in 1971, and include the British pensions pick-up.

**　Figures relate to the fifteen-month period 1 January 1969 to 31 March 1970.

†　In this year the Malawi government repaid previous excess drawings of budgetary aid.

††　No budgetary aid required: revised rather than actual estimate of government expenditure.

Sources:　M.G. *Budget Statements: Public Accounts Statements*; and *Financial Statements*; 1964 to 1974/5.

expenditure. It was therefore agreed, in 1971, that budgetary aid should be eliminated by the end of 1973-4. Revised ceilings for budgetary aid were set for the three financial years up to and including 1973-4. At the same time, the annual budget talks were discontinued. Britain also agreed to take on an increased share of the responsibility for pensions and other related payments to expatriate officers.[6] The fixed amounts of budgetary aid included these payments, hence the actual fixed amount was subject to downward adjustment – expected to be approximately £0.5m per annum – to take account of the British government's pension payments. The agreement was subject to the understanding that should the Malawi government's revenues be unexpectedly buoyant or there were an unexpected reverse in Malawi's fortunes, the ceilings would be reviewed and adjusted; this meant that the Malawi government could not necessarily expect to be allowed to use half of the budgetary savings for the development account.

Budgetary aid drawings in fact ceased after the fiscal year 1971-2. The final outturn for 1970-1 revealed that, because of revenue buoyancy, budgetary drawings for that year had been in excess of requirements. And after wiping out the accumulated deficit on revenue account and taking account of budgetary aid drawings in 1971-2, Malawi had a surplus of K967,667 to bring forward into the budget for 1972-3. This was revealed in August 1972. At ODM's request Malawi then refunded the budgetary aid drawings, K644,000, made in 1971-2, and later in the fiscal year 1972-3, refunded the rest of the surplus when the continued buoyancy of its revenue seemed assured. It was agreed in August 1972 that Malawi should receive half of its budgetary savings in the form of development aid in future years. During 1972-3 and 1973-4, £594,000 was paid to Malawi as budgetary savings. The precise amounts yet to be paid are complicated by the need to offset the effect of the pension pick-up.

Contribution to Development

A measure of the importance of budgetary aid is given by the large share, albeit declining, of total recurrent expenditure that it financed. To assess its contribution to development more closely, however, it is necessary to consider what would have happened to Malawi's economic performance without such aid. Obviously the Malawi government would have had to solve its financial problems by adopting measures to bring about one or more of the following: a cut in its own expenditure, an increase in its income by taxation, deficit financing or an increase in external borrowing. The developmental consequences of adopting only the first course of action – a reduction in expenditure – will be considered first. Then the government's ability to mobilise other domestic or external resources as a substitute for budgetary aid, and the developmental consequences of using such resources, will be considered. Attention is focused on the initial post-independence period. In later years, the withdrawal of budgetary aid would have posed fewer problems and had less drastic effects on Malawi's economy but this would be so mainly because of the budgetary support provided in earlier years.

An Expenditure Cut

Budgetary aid was given in support of recurrent expenditure. It does not follow, however, that if the government had to cut its expnediture because the aid was unavailable, it would have cut recurrent spending only. In principle, a cut in both development and recurrent expenditure could have been made and resources financing the former diverted to the latter. In practice, such flexibility was limited in the early post-independence years by the nature of the resources channelled to the development account and the smallness of the development budget. Nearly 80 per cent of the development account resources in 1964-5 came from external donors — mainly Britain — as project finance. Leaving that aside, some K3.2m from local sources[7] remained, which was available for switching. But this represented only 5 per cent of the recurrent expenditure that took place in 1964 and 1965. Thus initially, at least, cuts in expenditure would mainly have to be made on the recurrent account. Therefore the following analysis concentrates on the scope for, and developmental implications of, such cuts.

Recurrent expenditure may be regarded as a prerequisite and as a complement to public sector efforts to bring about development. In relation to development, recurrent expenditure may be divided into four categories: statutory, basic government, development overheads and expenditure on the provision of services which may be regarded as directly developmental.

The first two categories do not relate directly to development. On the other hand, if these expenditures are not made, development would be difficult to say the least. In Malawi, the two main items of statutory expenditure have been debt servicing and the payment of pensions and gratuities. Basic government expenditure encompasses the maintenance of law and order, external defence and the provision of general administrative services necessary for the operation of government. If the government had reneged on its mainly external debt obligations its developmental activities could have been jeopardised to the extent that present lenders would have been unwilling to make further outlays in Malawi and potential lenders discouraged. Pension and related payments were largely balanced by external receipts (from Britain) earmarked for such payments: if the latter were cut, the receipts would doubtless also have been cut, leaving Malawi with a minimal budgetary saving and probably fewer expatriate civil servants (to whom some of the payments were made). The developmental necessity for basic government expenditure is obvious (though the precise level required is less so). Without expenditure on law and order, or on general administration, the government in all probability would not exist, and the necessary framework for development would be absent.

In practice the distinction between government services which represent development overheads and 'basic' services is hard to pin down. Some government 'overhead' services may be said to have an almost exclusively developmental function, for instance development planning, while others, for instance customs and excise, are 'overheads' both of development and of the maintenance of basic government. Generally the services provided by most executive ministries and at least part of the services provided by most central ministries or departments, do represent 'development overheads,' in that they provide the framework for economic and social policy making and its execution.

The final category represents expenditure on services which have a direct effect on income levels, e.g. education and health services and road maintenance. Such expenditure is necessary both to maintain existing income levels and to complement development expenditures. Again, the case for the inclusion of expenditure in this category is not clear cut. Expenditure on both education and health, for instance, can result in higher productivity — and as such may be regarded as investment in 'human capital.' But it frequently includes a consumption element, which is developmental only insofar as the current income transfer by government to individuals improves income distribution.[8]

Given these relations between development and recurrent expenditure, what potential was there for cutting back expenditure without adversely affecting development?

In 1964, excluding budgetary grant-in-aid but including other grants and loans made by the UK, and Special Revenue items (mainly arising from the dissolution of Federation), Malawi's recurrent revenue receipts covered less than 70 per cent of its total expenditure. After expenditure on statutory items was financed,[9] these receipts covered only 53 per cent of voted expenditure.[10] But clearly if the Malawi government introduced no tax changes and were to rely only on its revenue receipts to finance expenditure, the actual expenditure cut would have to be considerably greater, since a drop in government expenditure equivalent to budgetary aid would lower total incomes and hence tax receipts.[11] It is difficult to see how the Malawi government could have roughly halved its voted expenditure *and* stayed in business, let alone carried out development.

General government services — broadly fitting into the basic government services category — accounted for 36 per cent of voted expenditure. In absolute terms, the expenditure was modest — less than £4m (see Table 4.3). The law and order expenditure under the justice, police, prisons and defence votes amounted to approximately £1.8m. Even without Malawi's somewhat fragile internal stability and its strained relations with two neighbouring states,[12] this sum would not have appeared excessive. Assuming that any self-respecting nation state,

Table 4.2 Recurrent Account Revenue and Expenditures (Actuals) 1964-73/4 (in £000)

	1964	1965	1966	1967	1968	1969/70*	1970/1	1971/2	1972/3	1973/4†
Revenue receipts										
Taxes and licences	2,661	3,050	3,702	4,649	5,454	7,220	6,771	7,875	9,006	9,769
Customs and excise	2,228	3,198	4,378	4,927	4,974	7,665	7,686	10,161	10,630	11,568
Other	2,612	2,868	3,013	3,765	4,328	3,403	2,993	1,822	2,312	2,237
*Total ordinary revenue*****	7,501	9,116	11,093	13,341	14,756	18,288	17,450	19,858	21,948	23,574
Budgetary grant-in-aid	5,000	5,948	4,244	4,165	3,195	3,625	2,100	644	-	-
Other grants and loans	2,185	1,628	1,477	1,817	2,003	(1,608)	(1,248)	n.a.	n.a.	n.a.
Total UK support	7,185	7,576	5,721	5,928	5,198	(5,233)	(3,348)	n.a.	n.a.	n.a.
Special revenue	1,257	56	400	-	71	274	14	4	-	-
*Total revenue*****	15,943	16,748	17,215	19,323	20,025	22,186	19,564	20,183	21,948	23,574
Expenditure										
Statutory***	/5,230/	/3,968/	3,896	3,930	4,028	4,911	5,347	5,960	(6,173)‡	(6,447)‡
Voted	/10,772/	/12,169/	14,027	15,507	16,142	21,310	18,126	19,541	(21,528)‡	(23,481)‡
Total gross expenditure	16,002	16,137	17,923	19,437	20,170	26,221	23,473	25,231	28,516††	30,722
Appropriations in aid	-	-	-	-	-	3,930	4,505	5,265	6,525	6,498
Total net expenditure	-	-	-	-	-	22,291	18,968	19,965	21,991	24,223
Deficit/surplus (+)**	-59	+611	-708	-114	-145	-105	+596	+218	-43	+363
Gross expenditure minus UK budgetary grant-in-aid	11,002	10,189	13,679	15,272	16,975	22,596	21,373	24,587	28,516	24,223

**** From 1969/70 onwards certain revenue items, including 'other grants and loans' from the UK, were transferred to appropriations-in-aid. Ordinary and total revenue for these years are thus not comparable with earlier years. From 1969/70 approximate estimates for 'other grants and loans' were only available for two years: these estimates are not included in total revenue.

‡ Revised estimates for 1972/3; estimates for 1973/4;

† Revised estimates.

*** Statutory expenditure was voted in 1964 and 1965 and the breakdowns between statutory and voted expenditure for these years are estimates only.

** Gross expenditure minus total revenue 1964-8; net expenditure minus total revenue for subsequent years.

* Fifteen-month financial year January 1969 to March 1970.

†† Includes repayment of previous excess drawings of budgetary figures do not therefore add up to gross expenditures in these years. aid amounting to £0.48m.

Sources: M.G. *Statement of Public Accounts* for 1964-70/1; *Financial Statements* for later years.

particularly a newly independent one, wants an army, Malawi's one battalion with a recurrent cost of just over £0.3m was not an extravagance. The courts and prisons services were in fact over-stretched. A cut in the police vote would have been politically difficult and, in any case, not significant in terms of the total budget shortfall. General administration expenditure was insufficient to finance the level of services required by an independent state. In 1964, the government had to take on new responsibilities and these, together with the strengthening and expansion of existing central government services, would require increased expenditure on this vote. It is worth noting here that there are economies of scale for such expenditure and that Malawi with its small population was accordingly put at a disad-vantage.

Of the remaining expenditure the main items, education, natural resources, health, transport, and communications, together accounted for 43 per cent of voted expenditure. In terms of felt needs, both the health and education services, and particularly the former, were inade-quate. A cut in either would have adversely affected future income levels and reduced the present incomes of those deprived of the services. A cutback, moreover, would have brought widespread resentment, while the skilled manpower needs of development dictated at least an increase in expenditure on secondary and higher education. The deve-lopmental priority attached to communications and natural resources, plus the inadequacy of the services then provided, also suggested more recurrent spending. And the need for increases rather than decreases was generally true of other items.

While there were opportunities for cost paring [13] within the govern-ment service, they were relatively insignificant. To make cuts consistent with the size of the budgetary deficit, the government would have had to have sacrificed large items of expenditure. At the same time, this would have affected the rest of government expenditure possibilities, since the facilities for formulating and executing development projects, the ability to attract funds, and the capacity to maintain the increased level of services permitted by capital expenditure would all have been limited.

On the somewhat unrealistic assumption that, without budgetary aid, the Malawi government could not have financed its deficit by other means, it is clear that the implied cut in its expenditure would have had drastic repercussions on the economy. There would be a fall in national income and a rise in unemployment. Private monetary sector activity would have been depressed while the scope of public-sector-led develop-ment would have been vastly curtailed. And the thwarting of the people's independence aspirations combined with a rise in urban unem-ployment would almost certainly have led to political unrest. Such a scenario points to a future of political instability, repression and economic stagnation. In these circumstances, it would require extreme optimism to imagine that Malawi would have done better -- by, for instance, adopting a self-help style of development -- than it did with budgetary aid.

Financing the Deficit without Budgetary Aid

There were three ways in which the Malawi government could have tried to finance its deficit: by increasing its local revenue, by local borrowing and by external borrowing. All three methods would, in fact, have been subject to severe limitations.

Although in 1964, both the British and the Malawi governments were of the opinion that taxation in Malawi constituted 'a fair and substantial burden,' there was scope for increasing government revenue. At 6.5 per cent of GNP (and 12.9 per cent of monetary GNP), the tax ratio could be raised, even allowing that average incomes were low. Direct taxation on the upper income groups and on companies, for instance, was relatively low,[14] and the same was true of excise taxes on luxury items. That Malawi had untapped tax potential is, moreover, suggested by the fact that, while real incomes per head have increased by 44 per cent since 1964, the government has increased the tax ratio by 68 per cent to 10.9 per cent of GNP.[15] But if the government were to finance its deficit by increasing its revenues, a large transfer of resources from the private to the public sector would have been required in a short period. While a gradual increase in taxation of this magnitude might have been feasible, a sudden increase would have been extremely difficult, if not impossible.

The revenue raising ability of any government depends on popular consent and its administrative capacity to assess and collect what is due. Public resistance to any increase in taxation is a well-known phenomenon -- and the potential for such resistance certainly existed in Malawi in 1964, as witness the widespread resentment which caused Dr Banda to withdraw his attempt to introduce a small flat rate charge for health services. The administrative capacity of the government meanwhile would undoubtedly have been severely strained if a large increase in tax revenue had been sought, particularly since this would inevitably have involved extending the tax base.

Even supposing the government could have overcome these political and administrative problems, the economic consequences would have brought considerable problems. Essentially, the government would be affecting a large reduction in private sector purchasing power in order to maintain its own level of expenditure and to avoid balance of payments difficulties. The precise nature of the consequences would vary according to the revenue raising methods employed. Certain types of taxation, for instance consumption taxes on luxury goods or a land tax based on potential yields, would have had relatively few adverse effects and could have improved income distribution and production. Administrative and political constraints, together with volume of additional revenue required, suggest, however, that the government would have adopted a less beneficial approach. It was more likely to introduce some form of broadly based indirect taxation, such as a sales tax, or to use its virtual monopoly position as a crop purchaser to extract a surplus from the agricultural sector. Output and investment would both have suffered. With the majority of people living at near subsistence levels, any cut in their disposable incomes would lead to a greater fall in savings than in consumption. At the same time, reduced demand in the economy would lead to a fall in production, in investment opportunities and incentives, and probably, unless checked, an outflow of foreign capital.

The effect of increased taxation on agricultural production, and hence exports, would depend on the form it took. Given that a land tax would have been administratively impossible to implement in a short time, the government had three main ways of raising revenue from the agricultural sector: by increasing the existing minimum tax rate (effectively a poll tax), by raising indirect taxes on rural sector purchases and by lowering crop prices to farmers. Political and administrative factors would have weighed heavily against the first and second options respectively. The third, if implemented, by lowering farmers' incentives to produce for the market and thus lowering export earnings, would have had the most serious economic consequences.

Without going into inevitably speculative details, it is reasonable to conclude that political and administrative constraints were such that if the government succeeded in financing its deficit through taxation, the economic effects, in terms of lowering living standards, output and economic incentives, would have seriously damaged Malawi's development potential.

The government, of course, could have financed its deficit by local borrowing or by credit creation. These methods would certainly have been more attractive to politicians and hard-pressed civil servants. Given the rudimentary state of Malawi's financial institutions, deficit financing through credit creation rather than by local borrowing would have been the only feasible course for the government to take. But if such a course had in reality been feasible – and it implied additional deficit financing since the government was already tapping domestic resources in this way in order to finance the much smaller development account deficit [16] – then Malawi would not have needed budgetary aid. It was not feasible because the volume of untapped domestic savings that could be mobilised by deficit financing was likely to be extremely small. Consequently an expansion of the money supply would either have been inflationary or have led to balance of payments difficulties — or both. Assuming that the government had the administrative capacity to avoid the adverse balance of payments effects — a somewhat heroic assumption — deficit financing would simply be another form of taxation: inflation would provide the means of bringing about a decline in living standards and so forcing private sector savings.

So long as Malawi had to rely on its own resources to cope with the central government deficit by reducing government or private sector expenditure, the country would have suffered an economic decline and its development prospects would have diminished. Yet the chances of obtaining external finance of any kind to cover the budget deficit were small. The country would have appeared even less credit worthy than it did in 1964 when it was receiving budgetary aid. Thus potential commercial borrowing, which would anyway have been the least suitable form of finance, would have been negligible. And, as argued in Chapter 1, Malawi was unlikely to attract external donors, whose aid, in any case, was rarely proffered to finance recurrent expenditure. Conceivably, had Malawi been left to its own resources, and had the most probable outcome occurred — economic collapse and political unrest — one or more of the white dominated southern African states might have intervened to prop up the economy and restore law and order, if they feared that Malawi, despite its physical unsuitability in some respects, would become a breeding ground and retreat for guerillas operating in their territories. To some extent also, disinterested donors might have been willing to adapt the conditions of their aid to allow its use for recurrent expenditure. But this would have been a deviation from established practice. Even with budgetary aid, the Malawi government had an incentive to obtain external finance for recurrent expenditure, and the fact that Britain has been the only donor to allow the use of its development finance for essentially recurrent expenditure (except when it was clearly part of the specific project) suggests that this possibility would have been limited.

British Policy on Budgetary Aid

Budgetary aid was clearly crucial to Malawi's development. Yet while Britain recognised both the supportive and the developmental roles of budgetary aid, it was anxious that this form of aid should be phased out. This section considers first why this was so, and why the Malawi government was apparently so willing to go along with British policy. And second, it examines whether the British approach on budgetary aid was justified in Malawi's case or whether the aid was curtailed too quickly. Finally, there is a brief consideration of the effects of the 'gentleman's agreement' on procurement.

The Basis for the Elimination Policy

Grants-in-aid are the oldest and, traditionally, the least preferred forms of British aid. In the past, the British government was opposed to such aid because, as a contribution to general revenue, its use was difficult to control, because it was an open-ended commitment, and because the prevailing doctrine was that the recipients – colonial governments – should be self-financing. Accordingly, the British Treasury sought to ensure that the recipients of grants-in-aid made every effort to end their need for them by imposing a rigorous assessment of their estimates and severe restrictions on their expenditure. Since the colonial governments disliked this interference in their domestic affairs, they sought to avoid recourse to British budgetary support. Grants-in-aid were not regarded as development assistance, and this was borne out by Britain's negative approach to their provision.

The developmental importance of budgetary aid has since been recognised. The 1965 White Paper on aid observed that the elimination of budgetary aid depended on development and that revenue expenditure, and possibly budgetary support, would have to be allowed to rise: 'more money is needed in the short term in order to reduce the need in the long run.'[17] Nevertheless, the impetus to curtail budgetary aid to independent recipients has been greater than it was when such aid was provided to colonies.

Aid to the revenue account meant effectively that Britain was supporting all the recipient's expenditure and policies, since (a) it could not be identified with any particular recurrent expenditure and (b) the level of recurrent expenditure was partly a consequence of policies pursued outside the context of the revenue account. The requirement that the British government account for its use of public funds was, as a result, extremely difficult to meet without close surveillance of the whole of the recipient's public accounts and policies. At the same time, such close surveillance over an independent sovereign state was politically unacceptable. This problem of achieving accountability while not interfering with sovereignty is common to all aid, but is considerably more acute for a donor providing large amounts of budgetary aid. Inevitably, Britain was put in a position of supporting policies and programmes of which it did not approve. It is true that the annual budget negotiations provided Britain with the opportunity of exercising some control over individual items of expenditure and of ensuring that local resources were not diverted from approved revenue expenditure. However, such leverage would have been strongly resented by the Malawi government and was regarded, on the whole, as improper by the British government. The negotiations between the two governments were 'full and frank,' but in the interests of amity and propriety, Britain did not attempt to exercise its full powers. (Even so, the course of the negotiations did not always run smoothly.) Britain made known its disapproval of certain aspects of the estimates and proffered advice in respect of policies, but it was left to the Malawi government to take account of British views. On rare occasions, expenditure items were specifically disallowed,[18] but the UK government's chief means of influence, besides advice, was to provide somewhat less budgetary support than was needed, given the estimated deficit. This practice also served to ensure that continuous efforts were made to reduce the need for budgetary support, and, to some extent, simply took account of the normal and sound budgetary tendency to over-estimate revenue expenditure and under-estimate receipts.

Britain's commitment to provide budgetary aid had a further disadvantage in that it was essentially open-ended. So long as the Malawi government was insolvent, Britain was morally obliged to provide an unspecified amount of budgetary support. Even if accountability were assured, this kind of commitment would have been disliked. The British government had only limited control of the level of future payments, and these might prove difficult to meet, given other demands for public funds. Although Britain did attempt to limit its liability, and with the Malawi government's cooperation was successful in so doing, an escape clause always existed: should Malawi be in real need of a greater subvention from Britain, this would be supplied.

Britain also had objections to budgetary aid, which might be viewed as being held in the best interests of the recipient, but were also closely linked with the fear that such aid was inherently self-perpetuating. First, it was argued that with the availability of grants-in-aid, the recipient government would be discouraged from exercising full financial responsibility for its affairs. In drawing up its estimates for expenditure, the recipient would be tempted to go for what it wanted to spend and not what its financial position dictated. Further, it would have no incentive to improve its revenue position or to curb overspending. Secondly, even if it attempted to exercise full financial responsibility, it would be weakened *vis-à-vis* the spending ministries because of the budgetary aid fall-back.

These two factors increased the case for fixing limits in advance to the level of budgetary aid. But while fixed limits might have encouraged Malawian financial discipline, they would have significantly reduced Britain's control over the use of the aid. Moreover, given the uncertainty as to future budgetary deficits, it would have been difficult to fix annual amounts of budgetary aid in advance without running the risk of encouraging overspending or putting Malawi in financial difficulties. Britain therefore preferred the more flexible approach of setting budgetary ceilings in advance but negotiating the actual amount of aid annually on the basis of Malawi's estimates.

Why Malawi Agreed

In purely financial terms, British budgetary aid was extremely valuable to Malawi, being untied, bar the 'gentleman's agreement,' and in grant form. In addition, it provided considerably more flexibility than project-tied aid. Yet the Malawi government has clearly shared Britain's determination to end budgetary support. To some extent, it could not do otherwise. After 1965, Britain made it clear that any increase in Malawi's recurrent expenditure would have to be financed through an increase in revenue, and after 1968 the budgetary aid ceilings fixed in advance were progressively reduced. The Malawi government was further encouraged by Britain's methods of assessing its budgetary aid needs. There is no doubt that having to go 'cap in hand' to the annual negotiations was regarded by Malawi as undignified. But Malawi appears also genuinely to have believed that *budgetary* aid dependence was undesirable.

This belief stems from the view that budgetary aid more than other forms of aid was a constraint on Malawi's political independence, because the government's ability to govern depended more on being able to meet recurrent expenditure commitments than capital expenditure commitments. To some extent, the distinction between the two forms of expenditure was more a matter of degree than of kind. A shortfall in external receipts for either capital or recurrent expenditure could have adverse, disruptive effects. But in the short term, the Malawi government was more vulnerable to a shortfall or curtailment of budgetary support. This in turn put the Malawi government in a weak bargaining position should it adopt policies or projects of which Britain disapproved. Although in practice Britain generally did not exercise its leverage potential, it was reasonable that the Malawi government should be aware, and wary of, Britain's power. By the seventies, when budgetary aid was relatively small and the annual budgetary scrutiny was stopped, Malawi had little reason to oppose budgetary aid. Indeed Malawi officials are aware of the fairly unmixed blessings accruing from small quantities of external budgetary support. However, budgetary grants-in-aid carry the stigma of colonial dependence and it has been this stigma — as well as the realities of political dependence immediately after 1964 — that underlies the close connection perceived between the ending of budgetary aid and the attainment of full independence. And in any case, the increased palatability of budgetary aid was in large part due to measures taken by Britain precisely because a terminal date for budgetary aid had been agreed: the Malawi government was not then in a position to change its mind.

94

Was the Rate of Elimination Appropriate to Malawi's Needs?

Budgetary aid was, as shown earlier, crucial to Malawi's economic development since independence. At the same time, it was clearly a politically unsatisfactory form of aid for both parties. Accepting that it had to be phased out, the question remains whether Britain reduced the aid too fast or too slowly from a developmental point of view. If anything, given that Britain's dislike for budgetary aid was founded largely on self-interest rather than on a concern for its ill effects on the recipient, the former seems more likely. Nevertheless, it is worth looking at the Malawi government's budgetary performance for any evidence that might suggest budgetary aid was eliminated too slowly. In other words, did budgetary support permit or encourage an unproductive increase in government expenditure, or slow down government efforts to mobilise domestic resources or increase its own efficiency?

Looking simply at Malawi's recurrent account expenditure between 1964 and 1971-2, it would be difficult to argue that budgetary aid had permitted or encouraged unproductive expenditure. Expenditure over the period increased by 58 per cent. Leaving aside statutory items, over which the Malawi government had less control,[19] expenditure increased by 81 per cent with most rapid growth occurring in the first few years after independence.

As can be seen from Table 4.3, between 1964 and 1967 non-statutory expenditure increased by 47 per cent or just under £5m.[20] The fastest growing item was education, followed closely by defence and then health.[21] Education expenditure rose largely in consequence of the expansion of education services. Health expenditure rose to meet some of the staffing requirements of existing services and to purchase drugs and other medical supplies which had been run down in 1964. The restocking of army stores, also run down in 1964, and the recruitment of a fifth company of Malawi Rifles accounted for most of the increase in defence spending (which in absolute terms reflected an increase of only £0.2m). General administrative services increased by 40 per cent, mainly to provide new services required for development and for an independent state, e.g. setting up external missions. During the period the only civil service salary increase which has been allowed since independence took place – 6 per cent on basic salaries – and that increased expenditure by nearly £0.3m, some of which was borne by the general administrative vote. On the whole, the increases in expenditure between 1964 and 1967 were consistent with the needs of development and remedying the deficiencies in basic government services in 1964.

After 1967, there was a marked change in the pattern of expansion. Voted expenditure increased by 22 per cent between 1967 and the

Table 4.3 Malawi Government Revenue Account Expenditure by Function 1964-71/2
(Km)

Function	1964*	1967	1968	1969†		1970/1	1971/2	percentage change 1964 to 1967	1967 to 1971/2	1964 to 1971/2
General services	7.7	10.6	10.3	11.2	(14.6)	11.5	13.2	37.7	24.5	58.3
of which:										
General administration	(4.2)	5.6	5.2	6.0	(8.2)	6.0	7.4	33.3	32.1	76.2
Defence	(0.7)	1.1	1.1	1.2	(1.4)	1.2	1.4	57.1	27.2	113.3
Justice, police & prisons	(3.0)	3.9	4.1	4.0	(4.9)	4.2	4.4	30.0	12.8	46.3
Natural resources	2.2	2.9	2.8	3.1	(3.6)	3.2	3.6	45.0	24.1	61.6
Manpower	6.0	9.8	10.7	11.9	(14.6)	12.4	13.5	63.3	37.8	125.0
of which:										
Education	3.8	6.5	6.9	7.7	(9.5)	8.0	8.5	71.0	30.8	123.7
Health	1.8	2.7	2.7	2.9	(3.7)	3.1	3.3	50.0	22.2	79.8
Community development etc.	0.5	0.6	1.0	1.2	(1.5)	1.3	1.6	20.0	166.7	241.4
Communications	1.3	2.8	2.3	2.2	(2.7)	2.3	2.3	115.4	-17.9	76.9
of which:										
Transport	n.a.	1.3	0.7	1.4	(1.6)	1.3	1.4	-	7.7	-
Posts & telecommunications	n.a.	1.5	1.6	0.8	(1.1)	0.9	1.0	-	-33.3	-
Other services	3.2	4.1	4.1	4.1	(5.1)	4.7	4.5	28.1	9.8	40.6
Public debt	6.5	4.0	4.0	4.9	(6.1)	6.8	8.1	-38.5	102.5	24.6
Unallocable	5.1	4.7	6.0	5.1	(5.6)	6.1	5.3	-7.8	12.8	3.9
Total gross expenditure	32.0	38.9	40.3	42.5	(52.4)	46.9	50.5	21.6	29.8	57.8
Total excluding public debt and unallocable	20.5	30.1	30.3	32.4	(40.7)	34.1	37.1	46.8	23.3	81.0

* 1964 definitions of functions not wholly comparable with other years.
† Estimates for calendar year; actual gross expenditure for fifteen-month financial year running from January 1969 to March 1970 given in brackets. Figures for all other years are actuals covering a twelve-month period.

Sources: Ministry of Finance, *Public Sector Financial Statistics 1970*, Zomba, 1970; NSO *Malawi Statistical Yearbook 1972*, Zomba, 1972; M.G. EPD, *Economic Report 1972*, Zomba, 1972.

financial year 1971-2, while total expenditure rose by 31 per cent, the difference being a consequence of increased public debt expenditure. Of the largest items, expenditure on education and natural resources increased by 37.4 per cent and 22.5 per cent respectively, while that on total general government services, including law and order expenditure, increased more slowly, by 20.8 per cent. To some extent, the shifts in expenditure on these and other smaller items, including a decline in expenditure on transport, ports and communications are illusory. Some items were taken out of voted expenditure, while there was some limited switching from the recurrent to the development account.[22] The main 'switching' was not, however, of existing expenditure, but of new expenditure.[23] The bias towards increasing expenditure of a developmental nature is not, however, illusory. And while one might criticise certain items, for instance the continued increase in expenditure on defence or the subsidies for civil servant housing,[24] it would be difficult to argue that the Malawi government has overspent in general on items which are only indirectly related to development. Indeed, bearing in mind that the government stores price index for vehicles and plant, and other items (financed through the recurrent account) rose by 26 per cent and 24 per cent respectively between 1967 and October 1971, and the retail price index rose to a similar extent, it can be argued that both the government, and its civil servants, have been remarkably restrained. On the whole, the balance of increased spending has been in support of development.

Budgetary aid is not, of course, simply a support for recurrent expenditure but rather a supplement to total government resources. The major part of these other resources — government recurrent revenue and most external finance — were earmarked for recurrent or capital spending respectively. But other local receipts were in principle available for either recurrent or capital expenditure, and were in fact used for the latter to meet the local project cost contribution required by donors and to carry out projects for which no donor finance was available. Inability to make local cost contributions would have involved a high cost to Malawi in terms of aid foregone. Hence budgetary aid cannot be seen as permitting unproductive expenditure in this area, even supposing that, with less budgetary aid, Malawi *would* have sacrificed local cost contributions, rather than recurrent expenditure. On the other hand, some of the local finance used for wholly Malawian financed projects has not always seemed very productive. But the largest of these projects, for instance the presidential palace, appear to have had a high priority. Thus it is by no means clear that a reduction in budgetary aid would have curbed such expenditure.

The Malawi government's restraint on recurrent spending has been matched by considerable efforts to ensure the efficient use of resources within the government service. An important instance is the introduction of the appropriations-in-aid system of expenditure allocation in 1969, which provided individual ministries or departments with an incentive to ensure efficient collection of departmental fees and other receipts, since these constitute a part of their budgetary allocation. At the same time, the introduction of a three year rolling programme for recurrent, as well as development, spending based on voted expenditure, net of appropriations-in-aid, has helped to increase this incentive as well as improving the basis for the allocation of total government resources. And notwithstanding the difficulties of objective assessment, the general view that the Malawi government service is, and has been, efficiently run is borne out by the existing evidence.

As indicated earlier, the level of domestic resource mobilisation by the government has increased rapidly since independence. Both ordinary revenue and total government receipts from the domestic sector more than tripled between 1964 and 1971-2. Over the same period the tax ratio has risen from 12.9 per cent to 17.3 per cent of monetary GNP and 6.5 per cent to 10.9 per cent of total GNP. To a considerable extent these increases are due to the buoyancy of revenues resulting from economic expansion. But they also reflect a significant tax effort by the government. The rates of both direct and indirect taxation have increased and a major new indirect tax, called a surtax but effectively a sales tax, on both domestic and imported consumer goods was introduced in 1970. While the government *might* have done more in the way of resource mobilisation, it would be hard to argue that it was lax in the matter. Its efforts in this direction as well as in restraining expenditure and improving efficiency do not, of course, prove that British fears of slack financial discipline and inefficiency were ill founded. They were closely related to Malawi's continuing tight financial situation, and the annual budget scrutinies, both designed by Britain to prevent any slackening of effort.

The evidence thus points to restraint bordering on austerity in government consumption and private sector spending. There is little to suggest that the rate at which budgetary aid was phased out was too slow. But was it too fast? If it were, one might expect to find three possible adverse effects on development. First, the restraint on recurrent spending may have led to inappropriate capital spending. Second, it may have led to the neglect of existing capital stock. Third, the need for rapid domestic resource mobilisation for the public sector may have militated against development.

The third possibility may be virtually discounted as a consequence of budgetary aid policy. Any feasible slowdown in the elimination of budgetary aid could have been most unlikely to diminish the government's tax effort, given that the pressures were for an increase in recurrent spending. The fact that the Malawi government imposed no new taxation in 1972-3 and 1973-4, when the elimination of budgetary aid was in sight, is attributable more to the size of the existing tax burden and the buoyancy of revenue than to a relaxation of effort. It is, however, recognised that any future increase in the tax ratio will have to be limited over the next decade.[25]

Capital expenditure that is appropriate to the limitation of recurrent spending, viz. projects which are self-financing or which have low running costs, is not necessarily appropriate to the needs of development or to Malawi's factor endowments: the kind of projects required by three out of four of its development priorities — agriculture, education and, to a lesser extent, transport and communications — have relatively high recurrent costs. At the same time, expenditure on such projects would be wasted if the necessary running costs were not met: there is little to be gained from having schools without teachers,[26] while the neglect of running costs and maintenance could increase development costs to the extent that the regular maintenance of plant, buildings and roads yields higher returns than periods of neglect remedied by capital expenditure.

Malawi's government development programme will be examined in the next chapter. Broadly, the problems posed by the necessity for restraint on recurrent expenditure have not biased project selection away from priority areas. More than half of total development account expenditure until 1967 was in the three priority areas, agriculture, transport and natural resources, and this share has since risen to over two-thirds of total expenditure. Until 1967, the other largest single heads of expenditure were water supplies and sanitation (1964), works organisation (1964), power (1965), government buildings (1966 and 1967), finance, commerce and industry (1965-7) and housing (1967). These expenditures did not represent a distortion of Malawi's development strategy. After 1967, a number of items have been included in the development programme which might be regarded as a distortion created by the shortage of recurrent funds. For instance, between 1967 and 1970-1, approximately K1m (£0.5m) has been spent on part of the construction of a presidential palace, over K4m (£2m) has been spent on the new capital — essentially on government buildings. It is unlikely, however, that all such items would have been foregone had more recurrent funds been available.

On the other hand, certain areas — specifically health and primary education — have been virtually left out of the development programme. It might be argued that the expansion of either service was a luxury that Malawi could ill afford. But these services would have had a greater effect on mass living standards than, for instance, spending on urban housing. Moreover, both health and primary education facilities do, in fact, contribute to future income. Primary education does so not only because it enhances the productive capacity of the consumer but also because, since it is not free, it provides a production incentive to potential consumers.[27] And in a country where debilitating diseases such as bilharzia and malaria are widespread and where nutritional standards are generally low, preventive medicine and health education could clearly enhance individual well-being and hence productivity.

In deciding the extent to which budgetary restraint led to the neglect of these two areas, account has to be taken of the fact that more rapid expansion (as also in agricultural development) was limited also by the shortage of trained teachers and health personnel (and agricultural extension workers). In respect of education and agriculture, for which local training programmes were instituted, personnel problems were probably at least as important as the lack of recurrent funds in determining the level of development expenditure. In health, although considerably fewer local efforts were made until recently to relieve staff shortages, the shortage of recurrent funds was probably the main factor. The administrative weakness of the health ministry *vis-à-vis* other spending ministries and the unwillingness of donors to finance health projects have also been cited as factors limiting government expenditure. But the former can be regarded as an effect rather than a cause, while one cannot accept the latter without also accepting that health had a low priority as compared with other locally-financed projects. Thus since the Malawi government financed one or two projects which were neither very productive nor in support of government administration out of local resources, which potentially could have been directed partly to capital and partly to recurrent development expenditure, it is not budgetary restraint that should be blamed but rather the government's priorities. This is doubtless partially true but two points have to be borne in mind. First, until 1971, a switching of local resources raised for the development account to finance recurrent spending might have led Britain to reduce budgetary aid, even though the increase in revenue would have been matched by an increase in expenditure. Second and somewhat less cogent, the amount of additional resources that could be made available in this way was relatively small.

In short, even if the government had attached priority to increasing health and primary education spending, lack of recurrent resources would have been a constraint. The need to increase spending – both development and recurrent – on health and education is recognised by the government and has recently been given a fairly high priority.[28] If more recurrent funds were available, spending in these areas would probably increase. But obviously since all recurrent spending has been restrained, although to differing degrees, it is unlikely that an increase in recurrent resources would be wholly devoted to improving and expanding health and primary educational facilities. The policy of holding down government wage and salary rates, frozen since 1966, would, for instance, be difficult to maintain if recurrent resources were increased.

If additional priorities might have been desirable, on the whole, the decline in budgetary aid does not appear to have caused bias away from Malawi's stated priorities. But did the shortage of recurrent funds limit the effectiveness of such expenditure?

In education, it apparently did not: recurrent expenditure has generally expanded to keep pace with capital expenditure — which in some years has included elements of recurrent spending. At first sight, natural resource recurrent spending has not kept up with the increase in development account expenditure: it has increased by only 45 per cent as compared with a nearly 500 per cent increase between 1964 and 1970-1. However, much of the latter has been of an essentially recurrent nature, supporting both the direct costs of the extension service and training and some of the recurrent overheads of the natural resources development programme.

The observable discrepancy between the shifts in recurrent expenditure on transport and in development expenditure has been real, however: it is widely recognised and financially and physically obvious that road and railway maintenance has been neglected. To some extent, Malawi's development programme has included an element of transport maintenance, while certain major road reconstruction projects have reduced the need for road maintenance expenditure in the short term, e.g. the Zomba-Lilongwe road. However, maintenance expenditure has been considerably below the estimated requirements of Malawi's transport system with the result that user costs and the costs of development projects in this field, other than new road/rail projects, have probably increased. Unless the government finds increased recurrent finance for such maintenance, even assuming that some external support will be forthcoming for 'reconstruction', 'rehabilitation' and 'upgrading' projects, much of the development expenditure on the transport system will not yield the expected returns, while the existing system will deteriorate.

This probable outcome would seem evidence of too much capital finance, as much as too little recurrent finance. The priorities attached to the major road and rail projects undertaken — which account for the greater part of all expenditure on transport — have been high. Had all finance for transport been available for either recurrent or capital expenditure, the government might not have chosen very differently. On the other hand, additional finance might have been spent on maintenance, and the costs of certain reconstruction projects would have been less.

The Gentleman's Agreement

One last aspect of British policy on budgetary aid needs to be considered — namely the 'gentleman's agreement' that Malawi should make its recurrent account offshore purchases in Britain wherever possible. This could have had adverse effects, to the extent that Malawi actually switched to the use of British supplies and that such source switching raised total recurrent account costs. There are no details of the Malawi government's offshore recurrent expenditure nor of such purchases from Britain but a variety of considerations suggest that any adverse effects were small.

The actual portion of recurrent expenditure from which offshore purchases might have been made was relatively small — K7.7m in 1964 and K15.1m in 1970-1, roughly 23 per cent and 32 per cent respectively of total gross expenditure.[29] The major part of this expenditure would have been on local goods and services, e.g. public utilities, uniforms, office and school furniture, equipment and other sundries. And certain offshore items, for instance petrol, could not be purchased from Britain. Thus even if the Malawi government did seek to keep the agreement — and it was such that it need not — any resultant excess costs would have been small relative to total recurrent spending.

There were, as it happened, a number of factors which increased the likelihood of the government buying British goods and services even without the moral obligation of the agreement. Britain has been a traditional import source for Malawi and tariffs favour British suppliers: British expatriates predominate in the government service and there is a close aid connection. Moreover, the devaluation of sterling in 1967 and its more recent downward float increased Britain's attractiveness as an import source.

If there were any — small — excess costs, then as long as Malawi was receiving budgetary aid, these would have been borne in effect by Britain. The implicit subsidy to British exporters through the aid programme can be criticised but Malawi cannot be regarded as bearing any burden because of this subsidy. If the gentleman's agreement has any adverse effects, these will occur now that budgetary aid has stopped and the agreement ended. Their extent depends on how far Malawi now relies on more costly British supplies as a result of the agreement and whether this reliance can be reversed. From the foregoing, it can be concluded that such additional costs are likely to be small.

NOTES

1.   In practice, mainly those recurrent items which donors would finance.
2.   Treasury Funds have been set up for those government enterprises which are operated on commercial lines, yet over which the government has wished to retain a greater degree of financial control than that it has with respect to statutory public enterprises. Examples are the Post Office, the Government Print and the Forestry Department sawmilling enterprises.
3.   See p. 97.
4.   Malawi government *Budget Statement*, 1966.
5.   A fifteen-month period because of the change in the financial year from a calendar year to one running from 1 April to end March.
6.   See Chapter 3.
7.   Including K0.5m raised from the sale of external assets.
8.   To some extent such expenditure also assists in assuring the development prerequisite of popular support and consent for government policies.
9.   As stated earlier, some of Malawi's statutory expenditure was balanced by external receipts specifically for statutory items.
10.   See Table 4.2. If local resources from the development account were added to Malawi's receipts, 57 per cent of voted expenditure would have been covered.
11.   A rough and conservative calculation illustrates this: budgetary aid was equivalent to 12.6 per cent of monetary GDP in 1964; assuming that monetary GDP fell by this amount and that tax revenues fell proportionately – at least – government tax receipts would have dropped to £6.6m, and so total receipts would have been equivalent to 44 per cent rather than 53 per cent of voted expenditure.
12.   Zambia and Tanzania harboured some of Malawi's dissidents, including some rebel ex-ministers (see Chapter 2). Differences over policy towards the white dominated states to the south and, to a minor extent, Dr Banda's territorial ambitions (dreams) in respect of parts of these states, also contributed to the poor state of diplomatic relations.
13.   Mainly by improving the efficiency of the government machine.
14.   The maximum personal tax rate was 60 per cent while the standard company rate was 37½ per cent.
15.   Over the period 1964 to 1971-2.
16.   If the government had restricted the local resource contribution to development account expenditure, it would have been unable to use fully the funds for development supplied by aid donors.
17.   Cmnd. 2736, *op. cit.*, p. 109.
18.   Malawi Government *AGR 1968* stated that Britain disallowed certain unspecified items of expenditure made during 1967 and 1968.
19.   It should be noted, however, that statutory expenditure, which comprises the heads 'public debt' wholly and most of 'unallocable' in Table 4.3, has shifted somewhat throughout the period: public debt payments declined after the exceptional post-federal debt payments in 1964, but have steadily increased their share of total RA expenditures while compensation and pension payments have begun to fall. Obviously the government had control over debt service liabilities incurred after independence.
20.   Non-statutory expenditure is defined here as all expenditure excluding the heads 'public debt' and 'unallocable.' There was some switching of this expenditure between the recurrent and development accounts between 1964 and 1967

but only small amounts were involved and the switches were in both directions, e.g. in 1965 localisation training expenditure (£100,000) was transferred to the development account, in 1967 it was returned to the recurrent account.

21.   The analysis by function is not strictly comparable between years, but may be taken as a broadly accurate indicator of the changes that occurred.

22.   For instance, the Post Office and the Plant and Vehicle Hire Organisation accounts were taken out of the voted expenditure in 1969 and 1971 respectively and consequently reduced total and changed relative expenditure. In 1971 also, the works and supplies recurrent account vote was reduced by a transfer of 'development overhead costs' of K0.28m to the development account.

23.   See below.

24.   These were, however, reduced in 1966 (to compensate for the civil service pay increase!) and while civil service wage levels are pegged, it would be politically difficult to change this policy.

25.   See Malawi Government, *Statement of Development Policies 1971-1980*, Zomba, 1971 p. 114.

26.   As the government was well aware: 'it is no use our planning and executing new projects if we cannot maintain the services the government already possesses.' *Budget Statement, 1965* .

27.   There is some concern in Malawi that the lack of social services, together with the inadequacy of rural trading agreements, is acting as a brake on agricultural development. Supporting evidence is impressionistic, but see, for instance, a recent small-scale survey, Ministry of Agriculture and National Resources, *Agro-Economic Survey of Hara*, mimeo, 1972, p. 9.

28.   See *Budget Statement 1973*, Zomba, 1973, p. 10.

29.   These figures exclude salaries, grants and subsidies, loans and capital transfers and debt service payments. They are based on an economic analysis of the Malawi government's total recurrent and development expenditure and relate only to government consumption of goods and services. Since it is apparent (from the data for years in which separate breakdowns are available) that recurrent account gross fixed capital formation was roughly equivalent to development account purchases of other goods and services, the figures given in the text are approximately correct.

5   AID TO MALAWI'S DEVELOPMENT ACCOUNT

Britain has, until recent years, been Malawi's main single source of finance for its development account spending. Yet, just as the contribution of budgetary aid cannot be seen simply in terms of the specific items which were financed (even if these could be identified), so the contribution of British development aid cannot be evaluated in these terms. Further, the effects of such aid cannot be judged merely in terms of what it permitted, since the very fact of Malawi's reliance on British aid for the execution of its development programme, together with the terms and conditions attached to such aid, inevitably meant that Britain was in the position of influencing, directly and indirectly, the kind of development programme chosen. This chapter considers first, the extent to which British policy led to changes in Malawi's development programme; second, the direct effects of the aid provided; and finally what would have happened without British aid. A brief, initial description of Malawi's development programme and of British aid in its support provides a background to this discussion.

Malawi's Development Programme

Malawi's development strategy has remained virtually unchanged since independence. The elimination of the budget deficit through the rapid expansion of the economy has been a dominant objective. Top priority was accorded in public sector expenditure to agricultural development: a priority dictated by the economic importance of agriculture at independence and by the natural resource endowments of the country. Increased agricultural output was crucial to expanding exports in which, given its small domestic market, Malawi's main growth potential lay. This priority was endorsed in 1967, when the importance of increasing foreign exchange earnings was more fully recognised. The improvement of transport and communications was seen mainly as a corollary to agricultural development, and had second priority. The shortage of skilled manpower dictated the third priority: expenditure on secondary and higher education. Finally, industrial development was to be promoted to exploit the import-substitution opportunities, which emerged with the dissolution of Federation and with economic expansion. The virtue, expediency and efficacy of self-help and private initiative have been stressed, and the role of the public sector has been seen as that of providing the preconditions for private enterprises and acting as a catalyst to it. Nevertheless, the government's approach has not been doctrinaire: it has been prepared to take on private sector activities if it considered that existing opportunities were not being fully exploited. Considerable importance has been attached to domestic efforts, partly to reduce the trade deficit, but also because a degree of self-reliance has been thought important in itself and a means of attracting foreign aid.

While Malawi's overall long-term strategy has been clearly stated, no attempt has been made, until recently, to show in detail how public sector policies conform with long-term goals, and Malawi's development planning has tended to proceed on an *ad hoc*, short-term basis. It has, nevertheless, considerably improved since independence.

The focus of the Malawi government's development efforts has been and remains its development programme. This consists of investment in public sector enterprises, and central government expenditure out of the development account. The latter has included mainly — but not only — non-recurrent investment expenditure. Not all such expenditure has been closely related to economic development (in the sense that it has not been intended to increase the productive capacity of the economy or otherwise to permit an increase in material living standards, e.g. through the provision of social service infrastructure), since the account covers virtually all government capital expenditure. The investment expenditure of public enterprises has been financed from external borrowing, directly or via the government, domestic borrowing and their own resources. Development account expenditure has been financed mainly by external and domestic borrowing and, to a small extent, from miscellaneous revenue and the sale of Malawi's assets.

Initially, Malawi's development programme was put together annually, despite the existence of a five-year 'development plan.'[1] Estimates were made of the financial resources available in the coming year and, provided that they could be financed, projects were included if they were broadly consistent with established priorities and/or if Dr Banda had proposed them or if they met some self-evident need outside the priority areas. There was little attempt at detailed appraisal of individual projects — and, given the lack of expertise and data, little possibility of such. The annual development account budget estimates provided virtually the only guide to Malawi's annual development expenditure proposals.

Between 1966 and 1967, an expatriate-staffed Economic Planning Unit (EPU) [later named the Economic Planning Division (EPD)] was established. It was responsible for drawing up a long-term development plan to replace the largely irrelevant 1965-9 'plan,' produced at independence. Its main efforts were, however, concentrated on the preparation of projects for, and the compilation of, the annual development programme. In 1967, the terse financial statements of annual development expenditure were supplemented by a document, entitled *The Development Programme*, mainly the work of the EPU. The *Programme* provided a brief statement of the government's development policy, but the main part of the document was devoted to a description and justification (including in some cases, rudimentary cost-benefit analyses) of projects included in the annual development estimates. For the first time, forward projections of expenditure were made, covering the succeeding two years.

This document formed the basis for Malawi's three-year rolling programme introduced in 1968, for development expenditure. The major difference between the 1967 *Programme* and that produced in 1968 [2] was that the latter covered not only future expenditure on existing projects but also expenditure on projects due to start in 1969 and 1970. The *Programme* was to be revised annually in the light of new requirements and conditions and, after each year, a further year's expenditure was to be added, so that the total programme always covered three years. This approach to public sector expenditure planning continues, and, in 1971, a similar procedure was adopted for revenue account expenditure. The rolling programme is a flexible device and well suited to Malawi's conditions, given the heavy reliance on external aid, which tends to be committed for relatively short periods (two to three years) and the uncertainties on the availability of domestic resources and the country's short-term economic needs.

The introduction of the rolling programme marked not only a more forward looking approach to the planning of development expenditure but also an increased realisation that the total size of the programme should not cause financial difficulties. By 1966-7, the close connection between domestic credit creation and the level of foreign exchange reserves was recognised. Similarly the choice, in allocating domestic resources, between wholly locally financed and partly donor financed expenditure, was made explicit. The rolling programme allowed development expenditure to be brought forward or pushed back according to the economic situation and provided a framework for the choice of projects according to the availability of domestic and foreign resources. Given this framework, choices were made on the basis of individual project appraisal and according to the broadly stated sectoral priorities. Efforts were made to improve project appraisal methods — although these were largely irrelevant to the choice of certain major projects, included because of Dr Banda's unswerving and virtually unchallengeable conviction that they were needed.

Malawi's somewhat *ad hoc* approach to project selection was adequate to its needs. And to have done more would have severely taxed those few civil servants with planning expertise. The acute shortage of such personnel after independence — the Minister of Development and

Planning remarked in 1965 that his ministry contained 'only four officers and none of them . . . an expert in planning'[3] — was eased with the establishment of the EPU, the increase in local expertise and the use of advisory technical assistance. However, the increase in personnel was accompanied by an expansion of the total size of the development programme and greater demands by donors for carefully prepared project submissions. Consequently, would-be planners have been mainly occupied with the preparation of suitably justified projects for submission to donors.

Increasingly, however, it was felt, among donors and within Malawi, that resource allocation would be improved if there were a more detailed and explicit statement of the government's developmental strategy. Although the Malawi government's expenditure pattern conformed with its sectoral priorities (see Table 5.1), many of the more obvious projects had already been undertaken. Therefore, after some delay, the *Statement of Development Policies 1971-80* — known as Devpol — was produced in 1971.

Devpol is basically a perspective plan; setting out in detail Malawi's various development objectives and attempting to reconcile means with ends over the ten year period. It is not intended as a substitute for the rolling programme but rather as a framework for their compilation. Indeed, although Devpol makes some fairly detailed projections for production and investment in Malawi until 1980, it explicitly recognised that 'events are bound to change this evaluation in the future.' The actual policy statements do not on the whole diverge from those that have been made — in less detail — in various places and at different times since independence. Their inclusion in one document, however, clarifies the nature of Malawi's development strategy and increases the possibility of consistent short- and long-term policy decisions — even if the document itself does not provide a wholly coherent, or complete, statement of policies.[4] It remains to be seen whether Devpol will improve Malawi's planning. But it is undoubtedly valuable window dressing for those external donors, including Britain, who have pressed for a greater measure of forward planning.

The government's concern for the efficient implementation of its development programmes is reflected in institutional changes — occurring mainly between 1966 and 1968 — and the development of an organisational structure for monitoring implementation. Malawi's implementation record in financial terms is good. Only in one year, 1967, did actual expenditure fall below 70 per cent of planned expenditure, and in most years Malawi has achieved a rate of over 80 per cent. And since the annual estimates include 'reserved items,' to be implemented only if financial resources became available, the spending rate is even better: in 1967, for instance, actual expenditure was 77 per cent

Table 5.1 Malawi Government Development Expenditure by Head (in %)

	1964	1965	1966	1967	1968	1969/70	1970/1	1971/2	1972/3	1973/4*
Natural resources	21.8	18.1	19.8	24.7	28.3	30.5	19.4	28.5	29.5	29.3
Natural resources) Agriculture)	4.2	7.0	10.7	12.8	19.0	23.5	15.1	22.4	21.9	21.4
Fisheries)			0.4	1.2	0.5	0.3	0.1	0.3	0.5	0.9
Forestry & game	7.7	7.4	5.8	8.0	5.8	4.1	2.1	2.5	2.4	3.3
Vetinary services	1.4	1.1	0.7	0.9	1.4	1.6	1.1	2.2	3.8	2.9
Surveys & lands	8.5	2.5	1.3	1.9	1.5	0.9	0.5	1.1	0.9	0.8
Education	21.0	14.0	8.0	7.4	7.5	11.9	8.1	5.9	6.0	4.7
Transport	7.6	23.2	28.6	22.2	31.4	29.5	50.0	20.4	19.6	20.7
Finance, commerce & industry	1.4	10.4	9.3	6.5	6.6	2.0	1.6	4.3	1.4	2.1
Posts & telecommunications	2.2	2.8	3.5	4.8	3.7	2.9	2.5	2.7	4.0	5.3
Housing	3.7	3.0	4.4	6.4	5.1	2.8	1.0	1.8	2.4	2.3
Government buildings	3.6	7.6	11.2	11.0	3.6	2.5	1.9	3.7	7.5	12.4
Power	-	9.2	4.4	5.8	0.4	-	2.1	10.3	9.6	1.5
Water supplies & sanitation	13.3	3.4	4.4	3.7	2.7	2.4	1.0	2.1	2.3	1.2
Health	-	1.0	1.6	1.7	1.4	0.9	0.3	1.1	1.1	4.4
Community development	0.5	0.9	0.4	0.4	4.2	0.2	0.3	-	0.2	0.2
Works organisation	10.4	4.3	2.3	4.0	3.4	6.0	4.6	6.7	0.1	1.2
Miscellaneous	8.8	3.8	2.3	0.5	0.5	0.4	0.5	1.5	0.9	2.5
New capital	-	0.5	0.4	1.0	1.5	7.5	7.5	10.9	14.4	11.9
1964 development plan	4.9	-	-	-	-	-	-	-	-	-
Total Km	5.4	9.1	12.8	10.1	14.0	21.3	35.2	31.2	26.7	34.4
% estimated expenditure	78	84	84	69	85	n.a.	91	103	85	n.a.

* Revised estimates only.

Sources: Malawi government *Estimates of Expenditure on Development Account 1971-72 and 1972-73*, Zomba, 1971 and 1972, and *Financial Statements 1972-73 and 1974-75*;

'actual' planned expenditure, compared with 69 per cent of the total expenditure estimate.

There are a number of reasons for the shortfalls — for example internal constraints such as cement shortages, design and supervisory staff shortages. And, since a large part of the development programme has consisted of construction projects — on which work is effectively confined to the dry season — delays in these cases cannot easily be made good. There are also external factors. Unforeseen procedural delays in obtaining final approval for projects to be financed from 'general' and 'specific' aid finance have held back expenditure in some years. Procurement regulations have resulted in delays in obtaining necessary equipment for individual projects. A further factor has been delays in reimbursement. The external finance for aided projects (with the exception of British aided projects between 1965 and 1967 and the South African aided new capital scheme) has been provided only after the donor has received proof of expenditure. Any extensions of the 'normal' (six to eight weeks)[5] time for reimbursements to be made entailed the use of local resources as 'bridging finance' — thus limiting their use for those locally financed projects included in the programme.[6] Moreover, since most aid has been project-tied and reimbursable, under-expenditure on an approved project did not allow Malawi to switch aid resources to others: the only resources freed by such under-expenditure were the local cost contribution and the short-term bridging finance which would otherwise have been tied to that specific project.

British Aid

The terms and conditions of British aid to Malawi's development account are set out in Chapter 3. To recap briefly, Britain has agreed to provide over £33m[7] for this account since 1964, of which Malawi had received over £26m by 1972-3. Grants accounted for over a fifth of the aid receipts, the remainder being soft loans. The details of these aid commitments and receipts[8] are set out in Table 5.2. Since 1967 Britain's annual aid commitments from the agreed loans have included an element of overcommitment to facilitate expenditure up to the agreed portion of the loan available for any given year. With the exception of a £1m grant towards the construction costs of the University of Malawi in 1965 and a £0.5m soft loan offer — later withdrawn[9] — for locomotives, British aid has been committed before the individual projects to be financed by it have been approved. The aid has been available for either local or British procurement and, until 1969, financed total project costs. Since then, a local contribution of 10 per cent of the cost of British aided projects has been required.

Table 5.2 British Development Account Aid to Malawi

£m

Year	Commitments*			Malawi's gross receipts from Britain***		
	Grants	Loans	Total	Grants	Loans	Total
1964	3.00	-	3.00	1.34	0.36	1.70
1965	2.50	-	2.50	3.40	-	3.40
1966	0.25	7.00	7.25	0.28	1.70	1.98
1967	-	-	-	-	2.20	2.20
1968	-	0.15**	0.15	-	2.30	2.30
1969	-	5.00	5.00	-	3.06	3.06
1970	-	-	-	n.a.	n.a.	n.a.
1970/1	-	0.50**	0.50	0.11	3.29	3.40
1971/2	-	3.35†	3.35	0.45	4.30	4.75
1972/3	-	11.00	11.00††	n.a.	3.35	3.35‡
Total	5.75	27.00	32.75	5.58	21.10	26.14

* 1966 commitment of £7m is for three years, 1969 commitment of £5m two years, 1971/2 commitment fifteen months and the 1972/3 commitment three years.

** Estimates of supplementary loans arising from budgetary savings and UK aid under expenditure respectively.

*** 1970/1 receipts cover a fifteen month period. 1971/2 and 1972/3 receipts based on revised estimate. Receipts exclude UK aid to the recurrent account.

† Includes £0.5m specifically for diesel locomotives, later withdrawn when the locomotives were financed by Canada.

†† Represents a commitment of £3m in the first year and £4m in the remaining two years. It excludes commitments arising from budgetary aid savings: some £0.3m was disbursed in this account in 1972/3.

‡ Excludes grant disbursements for the university.

Sources: Commitments: Malawi government Budget Statements, and internal ODM/ODA documents.

Receipts: See Table 3.3

Table 5.3 British Project Aid Commitments by Sector, 1966-73/4*

Sector	1966	1967	1968	1969	1970/1	1971/2	1972/3	1973/4
Natural resources	41.3	42.8	45.4	40.8	42.7	34.0	52.1	48.4
of which:								
Agriculture	16.4	17.3	24.4	23.0	24.6	18.8	28.6	25.1
Fisheries	1.0	2.4	1.2	0.5	0.6	1.0	0.4	1.6
Forestry	17.0	17.1	12.7	9.7	8.1	6.5	10.4	10.6
Vetinary	2.5	2.8	4.2	5.2	6.4	6.0	7.3	6.5
General**	3.9	3.2	2.7	2.4	2.5	1.7	5.4	4.6
Education	8.5	11.3	11.7	12.9	5.9	6.9	5.9	2.6
Transport	18.9	11.7	12.0	11.9	12.7	22.2	23.8	30.7
of which:								
Roads	10.4	10.8	5.4	3.9	10.7	14.3	15.4	25.0
Rail	-	-	-	-	-	5.8	6.1	5.4
Air	8.4	0.9	6.6	8.0	2.1	2.0	2.3	0.3
Industry etc.	5.6	7.4	6.7	0.9	1.3	0.1	-	-
Posts & telecom- munications	8.0	8.0	10.1	7.8	11.8	7.2	7.0	8.6
Public housing	2.7	4.8	4.8	4.7	3.3	3.0	5.9	4.7
Government buildings	-	1.2	0.9	0.5	0.3	0.3	0.1	0.3
Power & public utilities	5.4	11.3	5.1	7.0	5.2	2.4	4.4	2.1
Health	-	-	-	-	-	0.7	-	0.8
Miscellaneous***	9.5	1.6	3.3	14.4	17.3	23.2	0.6	1.8
Total	100.0	100.0	100.0	100.0	100.0	100.0	100.0	100.0
Total £m	2.1	2.3	3.1	3.2	4.6	4.9	3.2	4.0
Total number of projects supported in a year †	50	55	71	47	57	62	54	57

* Apart from commitments for 1972/3, annual commitments include a 'carry-over' of finance from previous years. Hence the total annual commitment in any one year is inflated and the relative allocation of aid commitments between sectors may be somewhat distorted.

** 'General' includes aid for geological surveys and game reserves.

*** Includes such 'projects' as a population census and a works training scheme, general equipment spares and vehicles.

† Includes many projects which have been in operation over most of the period. For instance, nearly half of the 1972/3 projects had been receiving finance in 1966.

Sources: ODM/ODA. Project lists, internal documents.

British development aid has been provided in support of more than a hundred projects since Malawi's independence. The majority of projects – or more properly expenditure items – have been small, having an annual expenditure of less than £50,000. Very few have had a *total* estimated cost above £250,000 – at which level the project used to be subject to detailed British appraisal and approval by ODM's Projects Committee. A considerable proportion of British project aid – over a quarter in 1974-5 and more in earlier years – is provided to finance essentially recurrent expenditure in the development account, mainly in the natural resources sector.

Table 5.3 sets out British aid commitments to specific projects by sector between 1966 and 1973-4. Because of carry-overs between one financial year and the next, and an element of over-commitment this breakdown provides only a rough guide to sectoral commitment – and an even rougher guide to actual disbursements for which consistent data are lacking. Nevertheless, the orders of magnitude are correct. In most years well over 60 per cent of Britain's commitments – rising to over 80 per cent from 1972-3 on – has been in Malawi's priority areas: natural resources, transport and education. The wide range of projects financed by Britain, as well as their total number, contrasts with the practice of other donors, whose aid tends to be confined to a few projects in a few sectors.

A sectoral breakdown of British aided projects in 1964 and 1965 is not available. In these two years, British aid financed most of Malawi's development account spending (63.5 per cent and 72.7 per cent in 1964 and 1965 respectively). Aid was not provided for government buildings, community development or health projects and, in general, it supported a range of projects similar to that in later years. Many of the British financed projects in 1964-5 had been started prior to independence.

British Influence on Malawi's Development Choices

It was only after ODM was established that Britain began to take a close *and* active interest in Malawi's development strategy – or, indeed, that it clearly formulated its objectives[10] in providing development assistance. Thus, initially, development aid was largely permissive in that it was provided in such a way as to allow Malawi to use it according to its own view of how development should be engineered. To satisfy the accountability requirement, the aid was to finance approved projects but, in practice, British approval was little more than a rubber stamp procedure. And any other approach would have been inhibited by the ignorance of both donor and recipient as to Malawi's precise requirements.

The establishment of ODM did not result in any major change in the terms and conditions of development aid to Malawi, apart from the replacement of grant aid, provided in advance of expenditure by reimbursable soft development loans. However it did represent a marked change in Britain's general approach to the aid relationship. Essentially Britain was to move from a position of passive response to the aid requests of independent ldcs to one of active 'partnership' in the development process. Efforts were to be made to assess ldc requirements and to ensure that aid was provided accordingly, and if it appeared desirable, Britain was prepared to take the initiative in providing aid for particular purposes. Understandably, given that it was receiving the much disliked budgetary aid, and British aid of all kinds, Malawi was one of the first countries to feel the effects of this change.

ODM was set up in October 1964. In December 1964, it was decided to send an economic advisory mission (known as the Hill Mission) to assess Malawi's economic policies and aid requirements in the light of the need for economic expansion and the limitation of budgetary aid. The mission reported in August 1965 and, from that time on, Britain sought to ensure not only that aid was provided according to Malawi's requirements, but also that Malawi's development strategy accorded with the twin objectives stated above. In principle, however, Britain has seen its role as a 'partner in development,' and has tended to fight shy of any overt attempts to force Malawi to adopt particular policies.

On the whole, Britain and Malawi have been agreed as to the type of development strategy to adopt, and the particular projects to undertake. To a certain extent the broad agreement reflects the fact that even without the budget deficit Malawi's economic position would have virtually dictated the strategy to be pursued. Nevertheless, it must also be attributable — in part at least — to the indirect influence exerted by Britain, as Malawi's main aid source.

It is obviously difficult to pin down the extent of this kind of influence. There can be little doubt that its reliance on external aid — and on British aid in particular — has affected the Malawi government's approach to development. Having little to offer to potential donors but the assurance that aid would be well used, Malawi has taken steps to demonstrate its commitment to development through its efforts in mobilising local resources via taxation, the encouragement of local savings and investment, and popular involvement in development activities, and in ensuring administrative efficiency and the absence of corruption. And Malawi's choice of projects has, to some extent, been affected by what donors were prepared to finance. Thus, although it is possible to find instances of specific project initiatives by Britain, much of the time Britain has appeared to respond fairly passively to Malawi's requests for project aid. Yet this passivity is deceptive since Britain, through continuous contacts, has let the Malawi government know what kind of projects it would support, and has put forward its views on broader policy issues.

The Malawi government has not, however, always acted in accordance with Britain's views, nor has the aid relationship between them been conducted solely in this somewhat oblique way. Britain has attached a high priority to the strengthening of Malawi's planning procedures and the avoidance of projects and policies which would not contribute to the rapid expansion of Malawi's economy, and the promotion of those that would — including specifically those projects which would be eligible for other donors' aid. To these ends, Britain has engaged in a 'developmental dialogue' with Malawi on issues both directly and indirectly related to the British aid programme, and has tried to adapt the terms and conditions of its aid accordingly.

Britain's failures of influence have been more conspicuous than its successes, which is not to say that the latter have been unimportant, but rather that they are more difficult to identify and are certainly less dramatic. It is instructive to consider these failures, for they illustrate the constraints on British influence.

Throughout most of the period. Britain has strongly opposed two major projects to which Malawi attached high priority — the new capital and the Nacala rail link — and has been concerned over Malawi's refusal to adopt any policies to limit population growth. The World Bank (IDA), also a major donor to Malawi, has shared Britain's views. Yet neither have prevailed.

Britain's opposition to the two projects was mainly on economic grounds: that they would not contribute to Malawi's short- to medium-term economic expansion and could have a high opportunity cost in terms of projects foregone. Since both projects involved large capital outlays — the cost of the new capital was estimated initially to be £15-20m, the Nacala link around £5m — Britain's opposition to these projects was correspondingly greater than it was to other less costly but, in Britain's view, similarly 'non-economic' projects that Malawi wished to undertake. It was also thought that the implementation of such 'prestige' projects would reduce Malawi's ability to attract external support.[11]

Malawi's, or more accurately Dr Banda's, case for the two projects has stemmed from the belief that both would radically change the country's economic potential. The new capital would provide a 'growth point' for the central region, stimulating agricultural and industrial development and redressing the regional economic imbalance that had occurred during the colonial era. The re-siting of the capital would counteract the migration of population to the south, where land pressure was greatest. Further, administrative efficiency would increase from the location of the government machine — partly based in Zomba and partly in Blantyre — in one place. A final and unconvincing point made in favour of the site was that Lilongwe, situated in line with the flight path between Nairobi and Johannesburg, would be the ideal setting for an international airport! The Malawi argument for the Nacala rail link was that it would reduce transportation costs of agricultural exports grown in the central and northern regions and thus stimulate development there. It would form the first link in a trans-Malawi-Zambia railway, and end Malawi's reliance on only one outlet — prone to disruption — the congested port of Beira.[12] Finally, Nacala was physically better suited as a port than Beira. Both projects had and have a certain visionary appeal both economically and politically. There was, however, no attempt to assess in detail the returns to such projects or to consider alternative means of achieving similar ends. The former would have been difficult given Malawi's lack of expertise but the latter would not have been beyond the country's means. In the event Malawi's case for the projects did not allay British fears that they represented a gross misuse of resources.

Britain employed several means to forestall the two projects. It refused to aid them and since, initially, no other donor was prepared to provide support for the projects — and Malawi's own resources were inadequate — this refusal held up implementation. Britain also made it clear to Malawi that it considered the projects undesirable. However, it went beyond this 'development dialogue' by 'warnings' to Malawi, mainly on the new capital project, to the effect that if Malawi went ahead with 'certain projects,' Britain would have to 'reconsider' the extent of its aid commitment.

Dr Banda characteristically ignored the warnings and discounted British objections as stemming from a 'too narrow a view, too short-sighted a view of economic development in [Malawi].'[3] By 1967, after shopping around for possible donors, some external support for the projects began to emerge. A somewhat rudimentary report, produced in 1967 by a South African mission, was considered to reinforce the case for the new capital project,[14] while Danish loan funds financed an engineering consultancy on the Nacala rail link. By 1968 the South African government had agreed to provide a loan for the commencement of the new capital project and, having rejected a near-commercial loan from the Japanese, Malawi accepted a loan from the Industrial Development Corporation of South Africa for the construction of the Nacala rail link. Neither credit was soft by normal donor standards. The £5m Nacala rail link loan was virtually on commercial terms with a grant element of 8 per cent,[15] while the £4.7m new capital loan had a grant element of about 60 per cent. An important concessional element in the latter loan, however, was that payments were to be made annually in advance of expenditure.[16]

Britain's threats of reconsidering its aid commitments had thus failed. Indeed, since South Africa financed the two projects, Britain's political, as well as developmental, interests in Malawi were harmed. With the benefit of hindsight, it seems that Britain, while not wholly underestimating Dr Banda's commitment to the projects, failed to take account of the possibility that others could be willing to provide support or that Malawi would be prepared to flout Britain's wishes, and to accept finance on fairly onerous terms. It is not clear whether Dr Banda saw his moves as calling the British bluff. However, given Britain's moral obligation to provide budgetary support, and its knowledge that, without its support for the development programme, the economic expansion required for the elimination of budgetary aid would be slowed, it was not in a particularly strong position to carry out its threat. Britain's strategy seems to have been mistaken. It served to antagonise rather than influence and reduced the possibility of any further involvement in these two projects and of exerting influence in other spheres. Had Britain not acted as it did but rather recognised the virtual inevitability of the projects concerned, it might have been able to exert a beneficial influence on them, to the extent of improving their cost effectiveness and perhaps even delaying their implementation further.[17] However, a conciliatory approach would have been difficult in the mid-sixties, when Malawi's actions in other directions were causing irritation: for instance, after British architects had spent two years planning the University, Dr Banda decided to change the site, while Malawi had embarked on a number of smaller non-economic projects at the cost of its foreign exchange reserves, both moves earning the strong disapproval of Britain. Further, Britain did manage to delay the two projects for some time by its refusal to provide aid for them.

The population policy question was different. Although the issue of limiting population growth is something of a political hot potato, it is partly so because of other outside attempts to influence Malawi's activities. Dr Banda has resolutely opposed any official population control measures. From his public pronouncements, for instance that Malawi is 'large, rich and underpopulated,' one might deduce that he sees no need to limit population growth. But he has not opposed the use of contraceptive techniques by Malawians. And other sources suggest that his main argument against official efforts to limit population growth is that, while Malawi cannot afford to provide its people with basic medical services and while infant mortality rates are high, it would be politically difficult — and possibly inhumane — to attempt to limit family size. The arguments *for* a population policy were, however, strong, being based on the reasonable proposition that Malawi's growth depended on an increase in agricultural output for export, which depended on the availability of land, which in turn depended on the amount of land not pre-empted for subsistence needs.

Britain's attempts to influence Malawi on this issue have been confined to a statement of its concern. Given that popular acceptance of family planning probably does depend on the availability of other health services, Britain could have helped Malawi to develop rural health services so as to bring forward the time when a population policy could be implemented. Instead, given Dr Banda's objections, British policy has tended to discourage the adoption of a population policy. In favouring projects with fairly rapid returns, it has avoided aiding the health sector, while its policy of encouraging the rapid elimination of budgetary aid has inhibited local expenditure on the improvement of the health services, which would have resulted in a considerable recurrent cost burden on the budget.

A combination of British policy and British impotence in the face of Dr Banda's determination and the existence of other donors willing to help him, has limited British — and IDA — influence in these important areas. But Britain has certainly not been without influence in other areas, particularly where its own aid has been directly involved and in Malawi's development planning procedures.

Indirectly, through its insistence that aid be attached to specific projects, which should be well prepared and efficiently implemented, Britain created an incentive for improved planning procedures. More directly, British initiative has both promoted and permitted such improvements. The Economic Planning Unit was formed largely at Britain's instigation. Similarly it provided the initiative for some of the early data collection, which helped to provide the framework for general economic policy making and for specific project preparation.

In the process of vetting projects for the eligibility for British aid and monitoring their implementation, Britain has suggested various modifications to individual projects. It has also offered advice on the desirability of particular projects and policies besides those related to Malawi's planning activities. Because of the relative importance of the British aid contribution, Britain could have exerted considerable influence on the composition of Malawi's development programme by rejecting proposed projects of which it disapproved. However, instances of the outright rejection, as against modification, of a project submitted for approval are rare — as are instances of largely British inspired projects. There are three main reasons. First, much of British aid has been allocated at the start of any one year because many British aided projects have been continuation projects. Second, fresh project submissions to Britain have often been informally discussed beforehand. Third, Malawi has attempted to anticipate the kind of projects that Britain might support. Thus, while some projects may be traced to British initiatives, for instance, the British Irrigated Rice Project, and others have been referred back or rejected, e.g. the Northern Extension Railway Project, on the whole, Britain's choice of projects generally appears to be a response to Malawi's requests. And even though there has been an element of direction underlying the apparent permissiveness of Britain's aid provisions, Britain has been exceptionally responsive to Malawi's needs: it has been prepared to back small projects, despite its general preference for large ones, in a wide range of sectors, despite its stated preference for two or three particular sectors in Malawi.

Outside those areas directly related to British development aid, and leaving aside the issues already touched upon, Britain has not attempted to exert direct leverage on the Malawi government even where its aid has been concerned. The chief impression is that Britain has acted as a 'development partner,' proposing or opposing but not imposing particular policies or projects, although obviously, while the acceptance of Britain's views was not generally explicitly required, a certain concurrence on Malawi's part was politic, given that it wanted aid to continue.

Indirectly, some of the terms and conditions of British aid have affected Malawi's development programme. The policy of eliminating budgetary aid has clearly had an impact on the shape of the development programme. Projects with a high recurrent cost which could not be expected to generate a rapid increase in national income — for instance in the health sector — have been relatively neglected. And certain projects perhaps would not have been undertaken had more recurrent finance been available.[18] But Britain's purpose was to ensure that the general need for the elimination of the deficit was not disregarded, rather than to achieve any specific end.

Britain's most liberal form of procurement tying applies to its project aid to Malawi, allowing Malawi to use the aid for local or British goods and services as it wishes. It is difficult to see that the procurement regulations *per se* have had a significant effect on Malawi's development choices. There has, however, been a tacit agreement that Malawi should offer Britain some projects with a high import content (or as Malawian officials put it, that 'some fat' should be included in projects submitted to Britain). But the bulk of British aided projects have had a relatively low import content.[19] Indeed, Britain has made it a matter of policy that the object of directly generating British export orders through the provision of aid should not be allowed to interfere with that of assisting Malawi's development. And Malawian officials argue that, in recent years, they have increasingly been able to parcel projects to various donors in such a way as to maintain Malawi's priorities and to satisfy the predilections, terms and conditions of its donors. Obviously, the requirement that offshore purchases from British project aid be made in Britain can reduce the nominal value of the aid received but this aspect of tying, particularly in Malawi, is relatively unimportant.[20]

British development aid policy, however, has had two other indirectly compulsive elements. The first has been the policy of reimbursement, adopted in 1966 in place of providing aid in advance of expenditure. As stated earlier,[21] while the policy was designed to prevent the misappropriation of aid, it had the side effect of limiting local finance available for development account spending. The second element of policy – the 1969 change from 100 per cent to 90 per cent project financing – was intended to have the latter effect. Since 1967, ODM has been openly averse to certain wholly locally financed projects executed by Malawi, for instance, expenditure on presidential residences. The 90 per cent ruling has significantly reduced the availability of local resources for locally financed projects – in 1969 by over 40 per cent, subsequently by roughly a quarter.[22] The pattern of wholly locally financed expenditure does not appear to have changed but the rate of spending must have been less than it would have been. Malawian officials, however, stress that the policy change helped by easing the difficulties of meeting procurement regulations since not all offshore expenditure associated with British aided projects could be made in Britain.

Direct Effects of British Project Aid

This section considers the direct contribution of British development aid to the achievement of Malawi's development objectives. Two problems are raised: identifying Malawi's use of the additional resources supplied by Britain and assessing their impact.

Shunting

The first problem occurs because of the possibility of 'shunting.' While aid is provided for specific uses, its effect may be to free the recipient's existing resources for other uses – in which case, the effect of aid is not to be measured by what is ostensibly financed, but by the use to which the freed resources are put. In order to show whether shunting occurred as a result of British project aid, one has to ascertain whether – if the aid were not provided – the projects which it nominally financed would have been undertaken or not. If the former is the case, then shunting has taken place; if the latter, then it has not.

In Malawi's case, British aid has financed a large portion of total development expenditure. Obviously, one cannot assume that the relative priorities attached to individual projects, and to expenditure in different sectors, would have remained the same without that aid. Further, one cannot assume that Malawi would have had the same quantity of aid from other donors or of local resources for its development programme that it had *with* British aid.[23] However, taking British sided projects individually and assuming that other development resources were unchanged, it is possible to estimate the extent to which shunting occurred. It could have taken place in two ways. First British project aid could have permitted the Malawi government to relax its efforts to raise local resources, thereby freeing private sector resources for other uses. Second, it could have allowed the government to carry out projects that it would not otherwise have implemented.

That Malawi relaxed its domestic resource mobilisation as a consequence of British project aid seems unlikely. Since savings from the current account were not a possible source of local development finance, the Malawi government has had to obtain local finance mainly through borrowing, both inside and outside the banking system. Local revenue on development accounts amounted to only £0.1m or less a year. Over the period 1964 to 1971-2, local resources have financed some 17 per cent of total central government development expenditure. If the government had not attached importance to encouraging the private sector or maintaining an open economy, it could have mobilised more bank credit for its own use or raised the level of credit creation. But given these limitations, it would be difficult to argue that the government could have mobilised more local resources. Certainly, even with British and other donors' aid, there has been a considerable incentive to maximise local resource mobilisation, because of the number of desirable projects which were for one reason or another ineligible for donor aid.

To determine whether British aid permitted Malawi's other development account resources to be shunted to other projects, it is necessary to establish the relative priority of projects. For 1964 and 1965, it is impossible to identify the projects which British aid nominally financed with any precision, and the priorities on individual projects are far from clear. It is highly probable that the availability of British aid allowed Malawi to use local resources for projects that would not otherwise have been executed. On the other hand, some locally financed projects would have been carried out anyway; for instance, some of the expenditure on government buildings. Since British aid accounted for roughly 70 per cent of total expenditure in these two years, it is likely that more than half of the projects thus financed could not have been implemented, even if all had a higher priority than those financed locally.[24]

From 1966 onwards other sources of external finance began to make a significant contribution to development expenditure. From this time on, a distinction should be made between local resources used as counterpart contributions to external aid or as bridging finance for externally aided projects and those used for wholly locally financed projects. The first two uses of local resources have tended to receive priority, so that it is the relative priorities of the wholly locally financed projects (virtually by definition those that are considered unsuitable for donor finance) compared with British aided projects that is significant. The amount of expenditure on, and the number of, wholly locally financed projects have been small. The budget estimates indicate that they account for not more than 6 per cent of total development expenditure.[25] Most of these projects have had a relatively high priority for administrative, political, as well as economic reasons. Some local expenditure has been on essential development overheads, viz. works organisation, project planning. Some has been on government buildings providing the basic infrastructure for law and order and administration, e.g. police and army housing/barracks, immigration posts. Presidential residences have taken a large slice of available local resources for reasons of national prestige, as well as personal aggrandisement.[26] Finally social amenities — community and health services — have received local finance. If there has been *no* British aid, some of these projects would probably have been dropped or considerably curtailed: many British aided projects have had, in principle, a higher priority than, for instance, the locally financed Blantyre sports stadium costing more than £300,000. However, it is less likely that such projects would have been abandoned if, other things being equal, British aid had been reduced by an amount equivalent to that spent on locally financed projects: more probably there would have been a reduction in spending on the British projects as well as on some local projects.

The scope for shunting between British aid and other donor's aid appears to be greater simply because, since 1966, the latter has been larger than non-counterpart local resources. In practice, however, it was limited, not because British aided projects have had relatively low priorities but because many such projects would not have been undertaken by Malawi's other donors.[27] A large portion of British aided projects have not been amenable to a full economic appraisal, have had a large element of local costs, including some recurrent costs, and have involved a relatively small total outlay. Three of Malawi's six major donors — the ADB, the United States and Denmark — have imposed fairly stringent offshore procurement regulations on their aid; so it could only be used for projects with low import content if Malawi could have contributed the local costs — which was not the case. Moreover, the US, the IDA and Germany have shown a marked preference for identifiable, economically justifiable projects, and the IDA, for administrative reasons, prefers large projects. Besides the fact that many British aided projects would have been ineligible for other donors' aid, a significant proportion of non-British aid has certainly been used for projects which have had a higher priority from Malawi's point of view than British aided projects. South Africa's financial aid (32 per cent of

Malawi's gross receipts of non-British external finance on development account between 1964 and 1971-2) has been used for two top priority projects: the new capital and the Nacala rail link. The bulk of US financial aid and over £1m of German aid have been allocated to the construction of sections of the high priority lakeshore road. Since both the major road transport projects assisted by Britain (one of which was another section of the lakeshore road) were started after these two transport projects, it is reasonable to assume that they had a lower priority.

It is possible that shunting occurred over a small range of aid, viz. as between some British, ADB, Danish and German aid. Most of the projects involved fall into four categories: power, posts and telecommunications, water supplies and sanitation, and industrial promotion. The priorities of such projects are, however, hard to establish and, consequently, the extent of shunting is unknown. Fortunately, the amount of aid concerned is relatively small.

On the whole, it is reasonable to assume that shunting is not a significant problem. This is not because Britain has provided aid only for low priority projects — the usual assumption when it is claimed that project aid actually finances what it is intended to finance. Rather it is a consequence of Malawi's lack of domestic resources and the terms and conditions of other donors' aid. Nevertheless the direct impact of British development finance cannot be considered simply in terms of the individual projects which it financed.

Assessment of British Project Aid

An assessment of the impact of British aid, even though its use may, on the whole, be identified, is virtually impossible because of the nature of the British programme. Many British aided 'projects' are in fact part of a broader programme or project. Some items of expenditure or projects have not been directly developmental in purpose, being designed to improve the framework for development planning and for the administration and implementation of development activities. Finally those, relatively few, projects which are clearly identifiable and potentially amenable to cost-benefit analysis are on the whole incomplete and their outcome uncertain. Given that time anyway did not permit a detailed project-by-project consideration, the approach adopted here is to consider briefly British aid to Malawi's main priority sectors, natural resources, transport and education (which together account for between 60 and 80 per cent of Britain's annual aid commitments), and then to make a general and inevitably impressionistic assessment of the remaining British aided projects.

Natural Resources   Malawi's development efforts, and British aid, have largely been concentrated on renewable natural resources: in agriculture, livestock, fisheries and forestry. Agricultural development has been the key element and Malawi's strategy has had two objectives: first, the maintenance of self-sufficiency in maize production (to avoid imports and costly over-production); and second, the expansion of cash crop production for export. In order to contain the encroachment of subsistence farming onto marginal or cash crop land, to maintain soil fertility and to ensure competitive export prices, great importance has been attached to increasing agricultural productivity. The focus of government efforts has been on the customary land farmers (i.e. African smallholders) rather than private estate farmers.

Besides investment in the transportation network, the agricultural strategy has involved a combination of intensive schemes and broadly-based development efforts. The latter have essentially consisted of maintaining and expanding the pre-independence countrywide and/or crop based system of agricultural research, extension and technical services, and marketing facilities,[28] and the use of input and crop prices as production incentives to farmers. Britain's aid has been mainly in support of these activities. The more intensive approach was evolved in the mid-sixties, partly in response to the need to increase development spending in agriculture and partly to obtain external support from donors who had a preference for large-scale development schemes. It has consisted of a concentration of extension and technical manpower, farm inputs and investment in the institutional and physical infrastructure of specific areas of the country, and has taken two forms – major development schemes involving relatively large areas of land and significant proportions of the total population, and settlement schemes involving few people and small acreages. Britain has not been directly involved in the four major schemes now underway, but with other donors, notably Taiwan, has supported the small-scale settlement schemes. The intensive approach now accounts directly for roughly half total development spending in agriculture.

British aid financed the majority of central government development spending on agriculture until 1968 and, after large-scale integrated projects were begun, the major part of the expenditure – much of it of a recurrent nature – outside those schemes. As such it has played a crucial role in the government's agricultural development programme. It has not only permitted the government to maintain and expand its countrywide development but has also helped provide the basis for attracting additional aid funds to the agricultural sector.

The Malawi government's ability to attract other donors' aid to agriculture has depended largely on the submission of feasible, integrated schemes. Britain has assisted Malawi in the identification and appraisal of such schemes, and continues to do so, through its aid to specific data collection projects (for instance, the National Sample Survey of Agriculture, the Agro-Economic Surveys), to pilot schemes (for instance, that which formed the basis for the major agricultural project in Lilongwe), and to Malawi's agricultural research institutions.[29] Meanwhile, British support to agricultural extension and technical services has helped to maintain a reasonably efficient organisational framework which, in turn, has lent credibility to project submissions made to other donors.

The move towards a more intensive approach to agricultural development, aided and abetted if not directly financed by the British government, is open to some criticism on the grounds that it is inequitable. A relatively small proportion of the farming population has benefited from a large proportion of government spending on agriculture. Further since the areas chosen for the intensive approach have, understandably, generally been those with the best endowments, it has often been the case that farmers' incomes were, at the start, relatively high.[30] However the criticism applies most to the small-scale settlement schemes for which Britain has provided direct support rather than the large integrated schemes. Whereas the latter tend to accentuate regional inequalities but provide similar opportunities to all farmers within the region, the small-scale schemes accentuate individual income inequalities, creating a privileged elite.

While there is an element of political favouritism in the settlement schemes – the main beneficiaries have been the Malawi Young Pioneers (MYP)[31] – Malawi's choice of this approach and Britain's support for it are defensible. The concentration of resources entailed by the schemes can be justified since the schemes have been expected to raise output substantially (although the irrigated settlement schemes have yet to produce the expected returns). Some of the schemes have been essentially experimental, e.g. the non-MYP smallholder tea and tobacco schemes. Further, the schemes have ensured a spread of development effort throughout the country. It could be argued that many of the local inhabitants gain little as a result of this 'spread,' except a certain *kudos* from having a scheme in their area. But since visible evidence of development taking place does generate local pride and maintain popular support for the government, the developmental value of the political returns to such projects should not be underestimated. And it is likely that the schemes do have some 'spread' effect on neighbouring areas.

Despite the shift to a more intensive approach, and within the constraints of skilled manpower, financial resources, and donor preferences, and the objective of increasing output, the main intention of the Malawi government has been, and continues to be, the creation of a prosperous farming community throughout the country – while not discouraging the emergence of a farming elite. Its efforts to identify the production possibilities for all regions, including those with an apparently low potential (because of transportation difficulties or poor natural resource endowments or both), support this contention – as does the policy of uniform crop pricing. British aid, which has financed the major part of Malawi's countrywide agricultural support services and its efforts to evolve suitable production schemes for the poorer areas, was an important factor in Malawi's ability to involve most rural inhabitants in the development effort.

At first sight Malawi's agricultural strategy has not been conspicuously successful. Export earnings from smallholder production have certainly risen – from K12.2m in 1964 to K28.8m in 1973, a growth rate of some 10 per cent a year – but in volume terms, the marketed surplus from smallholders has shown no distinct trend.[32] On the other hand, despite population growth, and the extension of cultivation to less productive land, smallholders have maintained surplus cash sales over the years, and maize output has in most years met domestic needs. This in itself is a considerable achievement, which has, moreover, been evident throughout the country and not merely in the areas singled out for intensive investment activities. In part this reflects the price responsiveness of smallholder farmers. It is, however, unlikely that cash sales would have been maintained without the widespread development efforts, supported by British aid, of the central government – the extension service, the building up of the physical infrastructure, (e.g. crop extraction roads, boreholes) and the provision of subsidised farm inputs (e.g. fertiliser, improved seed, crop sprayers).

In the three other main areas of the natural resources sector, fisheries, livestock and forestry, the government's chief object has been import substitution. The Vipya forestry plantation, eventually intended to provide the raw material for a kraft pulp mill, is a major exception in that this project, on which over £1m British aid has been spent since independence, is primarily export oriented. In all three areas the maintenance of the existing stock has been an important item of government expenditure, involving extension and research inputs, mainly financed by Britain, in addition to spending to improve and expand marketing and processing facilities for animal, fish and wood products. Malawi is still a substantial importer of these products but local output has risen rapidly, for instance fish landings doubled between 1966 and 1971, cattle slaughterings increased by approximately a half, and production of sawn timber from government sawmills[33] more than trebled as have sales of other wood products by government departments. The increase in forestry output is directly attributable to the government development effort, largely financed by Britain. And government measures to conserve and expand output of animal and fish products, again supported by Britain, have been indirectly responsible for increases.

Transport   Britain has given considerable financial support to Malawi's development spending on transport. This aid has generally been for identifiable projects and has constituted only a part of Malawi's total aid receipts for projects in this sector. Malawi transport policy has had four main aims: to reduce transport costs to facilitate internal and external trade, to open up underdeveloped areas, to promote transit traffic and – more recently – to promote tourism. In pursuit of these objectives, Malawi has carried out a series of *ad hoc* projects, concentrating mainly on the development of the arterial road network. There has been no integrated plan for the transportation system, taking into account the relative advantages and interdependence of the three chief modes – road, rail and lake. Thus the projects supported by Britain have to be considered – and appraised by ODM – chiefly on their own merits. Recently ODM attempted to encourage the consideration of alternatives in the appraisal of projects, and offered to undertake two feasibility studies for this purpose. In the first case – related to the Northern Extension railway – the offer was declined. In the second – the Lilongwe airport – it was accepted. In neither case does Malawi's original view as to the need for the projects appear to have changed.

The main part of British aid has been for Malawi's arterial road network and, with one exception,[34] all of this aid has been devoted to upgrading and reconstruction. Until 1969, road projects did not receive full economic appraisal. One, at least, was considered to be fully justified by all parties concerned (including a USAID advisory mission).[35] Two other roads on which British aid money was spent were in fact ones where the Hill Economic Mission had advised against expenditure (however the Mission's objections were to a level of proposed expenditure and construction standards that were much higher than actually occurred). The two latest road projects[36] have received economic appraisal by the Malawi government in conjunction with ODM officials and advisors. Both have been justified at an 8 per cent discount rate, although one of the projects, in which considerably more British aid is involved, was not subject to a rigorous appraisal: data were inadequate, and a delay until further data were available was thought politically undesirable. While ODM was reasonably convinced of the returns to most of the road's length, the construction of one section was considered to be marginal. Unhappily, after implementation was delayed for over a year mainly because of difficulties in obtaining a realistic tender from any contractor, construction work has begun first on this section.

Britain has also provided aid for the construction of bridges, the maintenance and improvement of main and secondary roads and the construction and improvement of feeder roads. These items have involved relatively small amounts of money [37] but meet important needs. In 1964, many roads were poorly aligned, bridges were inadequate, there were too few feeder/crop extraction roads and the whole road network was in poor repair. Major road reconstruction removed some of these deficiencies, but many major and minor roads have been relatively neglected mainly because of the shortage of recurrent finance. British aid in these areas, while only a small proportion of the total expenditure that *ought* to take place,[38] has consequently been important. Efforts have been made to ensure that priority be given to road improvement and construction in areas where agricultural development potential was greatest and/or where projects were under way.

Other British aid in this sector has been for rehabilitation of the southern section of Malawi's railway and the development of airport facilities. While the former allocation was made after some qualitative economic appraisal,[39] the latter, involving a number of separate projects, does not appear to have been examined in detail by Britain, but, insofar as can be judged, has been consistent with Malawi's needs.

Education   Malawi's policy has been to expand opportunities for secondary and higher education and for technical and vocational education. The quality of primary education was to be improved but no corresponding expansion was planned.[40] Nevertheless, a policy of equalising opportunities for primary education at the district level exists, which entails some expansion — district enrolment rates are to be raised to the national average of 35 per cent of school age population (rates above the average are to be maintained).

This policy followed broadly from Malawi's development requirements but was not until recently based on any attempt at a coherent assessment of manpower needs. 'Plan' targets have consequently been somewhat arbitrary, e.g. for a day secondary school per district,[41] but within this context, plans have generally been consistent. British aid — both project finance and technical assistance — has been extended in support of secondary education, the development of university education and vocational training, while technical assistance personnel have been provided to assess manpower and training needs, both in general and for specific kinds of education. By 1973, an educational plan related to manpower need emerged. This plan has, however, a number of major weaknesses limiting its usefulness.[42]

While most items to which Britain has provided support appear to make sense, despite the absence of an overall plan and the importance of political factors,[43] the setting up of the University requires some explanation. At first sight, it would seem that such a project should be included in the very short list of low developmental priority projects receiving British aid.[44] This would certainly be true if the University were planned in imitation of British institutions: if it were intended to meet all Malawi's needs for academically trained graduate manpower, the costs would be very high, while if such costs were spread over a large number of students, Malawi would fairly soon face the problem of graduate unemployment. However Dr Banda originally envisaged the University of Malawi,[45] it was decided in 1964, on the recommendations of an expert planning team, that the University should be an umbrella institution with facilities for academic, technical, professional and vocational training and providing various degree and diploma courses for school certificate entrants. Without detracting from the standards of education provided, one might best describe the University as a comprehensive. It has five constituent colleges: the secondary school teacher training Soche College, the further education, degree-giving Chancellor College, the agricultural diploma − and now degree-giving − Bunda College, the Polytechnic, and the Institute of Public Administration (IPA). Malawi has generally followed a policy − not always, it would appear, from choice[46] − of not providing the costly facilities for top level manpower training: such training has been sought abroad.[47]

Four of the five colleges were situated in Blantyre, as geographically separate establishments, while the fifth is at Bunda in the central region. To benefit from the umbrella, viz. flexibility between courses for students and in educational planning and the interchange of staff and equipment, and in the interests of economy and efficiency, it was early proposed to move the University to one campus in Zomba. It was for this purpose that Britain agreed in 1965 to provide finance for the capital construction of the University, which was to accommodate three colleges: Chancellor, Soche and the IPA. The vacated facilities were and are in no danger of being redundant, although plans for their use are still incomplete. The University, meanwhile, was to use some of the facilities, including housing, vacated by the removal of the administration to Lilongwe. In the event, implementation has been slow, and it was not until 1970-1 that construction of the University began. The delays, involving some cost,[48] were caused by a variety of factors, mainly on Malawi's side. Initially, Dr Banda changed his mind about the proposed site in Zomba (it was too close to State House) but not before consultants had drawn up plans for the campus. These then had to be modified for the new site, and were later altered in the light of revised capital costs, manpower requirements, available recurrent finance and the phasing of the move to the new capital.

Other Aided Projects   Most of Britain's aid commitments outside the above three sectors have related to the expansion of the modern urban sector of the economy, involving projects in housing, posts and telecommunications, power, water and sanitation, and industry (the last consisting of financial assistance to the Malawi Development Corporation and the construction of an industrial site). Smaller quantities of aid have been provided for miscellaneous projects, e.g. the Population Census, a Ministry of Works training scheme, a government vehicle supply and maintenance scheme.

As with British aided projects in the three areas already considered, implementation has been generally efficient and few projects appear to have little justification in terms of their direct impact on development or their contribution to development overheads. Indeed, in general terms, the rapid expansion of Malawi's industrial sector can be taken as a measure of the effectiveness of the government's industrial policy, and hence of the British aid provided in support. Although one may have reservations about Malawi's urban, industrial development — for instance, the failure of employment opportunities to keep pace with output growth, the continued bias of both private and public sector investment in the south — it remains true that Malawi has, as yet, avoided some of the major pitfalls of industrialisation, such as urban unemployment or excessively protectionist policies encouraging uncompetitive industries.

Certain specific reservations have, however, to be made. Over the years 1966 to 1971-2, Britain has committed between 7 per cent to 11 per cent of its annual development aid provisions to Malawi's posts and telecommunications. It is a criticism of both ODM and Malawi that there has been no detailed appraisal of this expenditure — which has come under several different project heads. Project submissions do not provide economic justification, and it may well be that Malawi is developing a communications system which is, in some respects, expensive and over-sophisticated. Britain's apparent lack of interest in the economic justification of such expenditure has perhaps not been unconnected with the export earnings thereby generated[49]: virtually all expenditure financed by British aid has been on British exports. This is not to suggest that all British financed expenditure in this sector has a dubious economic value: clearly a communications system is required for administrative, commercial and social purposes. However, it would seem that the exporters and the engineers, rather than the economists, have dominated in deciding what constitutes an adequate system. A similar criticism might be applied to Britain's somewhat ready accession to requests for vehicles, although recently Britain has been closely involved in a scheme to improve the utilisation and maintenance of government vehicles by the creation of a self-financing centrally based supply and maintenance organisation.[50]

ODM support − along with that of CDC and the Barclays and Standard Banks − for public housing development also raises some doubts. The Malawi Housing Corporation is providing a subsidy to the tenants of its houses. Both the existence and the extent of a subsidy have been disputed[51] but ODM's grounds for arguing for the former seem reasonable, although the latter is open to question. This subsidy has two potential effects: it may harm the efficient operation and growth of the housing market, and involve an inequitable transfer of resources to individuals. The former result is disputed by MHC on the fairly convincing grounds that there is no evidence that the private sector would have filled the gap. No convincing evidence exists to suggest that the latter does not occur.[52] It should be noted, however, that Britain has used its involvement in the housing schemes to introduce incentives to MHC to move further towards an economic rental policy.

NOTES

1. *1965/69 Development Plan*, Zomba, 1964. The plan, essentially a shopping list, was put together in a hurry and was scrapped very early on.
2. Malawi Government, *Development Programme 1968-70*, Zomba, 1968.
3. J. Tembo, *Malawi Hansard*, 1965.
4. For instance, although the new capital project is heralded in Devpol as the government's 'most imaginiative' instrument of regional policy and is expected to involve a total expenditure of K50 (£25m) over the ten years (13.4 per cent of planned public sector investment) there is no detailed account of Malawi's regional policy.
5. Malawi Government, *Budget Statement 1969*, p. 6.
6. This problem was considerable in 1968, when total external aid receipts amounted to £3.8m while expenditure on covered external aid amounted to £5.3m: thus, at the end of the year, the government had to find 'bridging finance' for 28 per cent of aid-financed expenditure. *AGR 1968*.
7. Including budgetary aid savings from 1971-2 onwards which are not included in Table 5.2.
8. Malawian statistics are used for receipts since available British data include various non-developmental loans and grants − as well as the budgetary grants-in-aid.
9. See Table 5.2.
10. See Chapter 3.
11. A number of Malawian officials also held this view: the fact that the presidential palace and the new capital would occupy a dominant position in any detailed plan has been a point against the preparation of such a plan, because of its likely effect on potential donors.
12. Malawi's vulnerability − and the usefulness of the Nacala link − was demonstrated in 1971 when the Beira rail line was closed for three weeks because of washaways.

13.   Dr H.A. Banda, *Malawi Hansard*, January 1968, p.232.
14.   The report of a technical assistance mission led by Rautenbach, the Chairman of the South African resources and Planning Advisory Council. It was concerned with physical rather than economic planning and, while promoting the idea of regional development via 'growth points,' did not make a detailed appraisal of the project.
15.   Officially the loan was £6.3m with 6 per cent interest, but the capital sum includes £1m finance charges in addition to the 6 per cent interest charge on the unpaid balance which reduces the concessionality.
16.   Devaluation of the South Africa rand relative to the kwacha has further reduced the cost of this aid.
17.   The Nacala rail link, for instance, is widely considered to have been an 'engineer's project,' the standards of construction being in excess of what was required or what could be afforded. It is interesting that Britain has since carried out a feasibility survey for the new international airport at Lilongwe – a move which may be construed as diplomatic but appears to be in accordance with the strategy suggested above to the extent that the survey considered alternatives to the new airport (itself something of a prestige project). The main drawback in adopting this approach is that the donor may find it more difficult to refuse aid for the project, having become involved in it.
18.   See Chapter 4.
19.   In 1970, British officials estimated that the total import content of British development assistance was roughly 40 per cent with an increase in recent years. The latest estimate puts the import content at 45 per cent. A breakdown of the import content of individual projects in the development programme carried out by the Malawi government in 1969 indicated that the majority (by value) of British projects had an import content of 40 per cent or less. Only a few projects involved expenditure on imports of more than 50 per cent. These were in telecommunications, water supplies and sanitation, works and transport.
20.   See Chapter 4. There are a number of factors in addition to tying which tend to make Malawi favour Britain as a source of imports.
21.   See p. 110.
22.   These figures relate to *estimated* development expenditure by source of finance.
23.   See p. 124.
24.   Other external aid was relatively insignificant, financing 3.4 per cent and 6 per cent of total development spending in 1964 and 1965 respectively.
25.   Since 1969, roughly 70 per cent of local resources have been allocated as counterpart contributions, of which about a third were allocated to British aided projects.
26.   By the end of 1971-2, K1.9m had been spent on presidential residences (and as much again was scheduled to be spent). This amounts to about 8 per cent of total local resources but over a fifth of those local resources not tied to donor financed projects.
27.   If project A has a higher priority than project B and both cost the same amount, then donor A, who finances project A, effectively finances project B *only* if donor B would, in the absence of donor A, finance project A; if he would not, then project A is the project actually, as well as nominally, financed by donor A.
28.   Initially cooperatives were considered an important means of developing the institutional framework for rural development but these were abandoned shortly after independence, following fairly widespread mismanagement and fraud.

29.   Some of this aid has been provided via British funded technical assistance personnel, and by grants (on the recurrent account) specifically for agricultural research, rather than from the development loans.

30.   This was not the case in respect of the German aided Salima Development Project, according to the *National Sample Survey of Agriculture 1968-69*.

31.   Local farmers as well as Young Pioneers usually drawn from outside the area do, however, participate.

32.   See Table 2.9.

33.   These account for the bulk of total output.

34.   A section of the lakeshore road.

35.   The upgrading of the Zomba-Blantyre road.

36.   The lakeshore road section and the Monkey Bay road.

37.   Leaving aside bridge construction, the improvement of main and secondary roads has received c. £30,000 p.a. and the construction and improvement of feeder roads c. £30-40,000 p.a. of British aid.

38.   In 1971-2, for instance, Malawi spent an average of K313, K335 and K158 per mile on the maintenance of bitument, gravel and earth roads respectively: the minimum maintenance expenditure actually required was estimated by the Ministry of Works and Supplies to be K746, K801 and K403 respectively.

39.   It would seem that Britain is footing a bill that would not have been presented had it not been for the construction of the Nacala rail link and the financial burden that this imposed on Malawi Railways: without the latter the Malawi government could probably have financed most of its rehabilitation programme. In this event, it might still have sought aid, however, since the programme – with its high import costs – was more attractive to donors than other projects which might have been financed from the Railway's surplus.

40.   Indeed primary school enrolments actually fell as a result of the closure of some primary schools shortly after independence.

41.   Population per district varies widely as does primary school enrolment: Dedza, for instance, has a population of over 230,000 and primary school enrolment in state assisted schools of c. 13,500 (1972) while Ntchisi, also in the central region, has a population of c. 70,000 and a primary school enrolment of c. 7,000 (1972), but both are allowed only one day secondary school.

42.   The most serious are that it deals with only primary and secondary schooling, and teacher training, and is in part based on the EPD manpower plan, itself having several major shortcomings (see Chapter 6).

43.   The distribution of educational institutions, which determines the catchment areas of primary and day secondary schools, reflects political demands at the regional and district level, which could not easily be ignored: although the quality of the secondary school intakes might have been enhanced in the short-term if the day secondary schools had been located mainly in areas where primary schooling was well established, clearly such a policy would have been inequitable and widely resented.

44.   An example has been the £100,000 Mineral Exploration Unit project, which allows members of Malawi's Geological Department to carry out prospecting work. Arguably this should be carried out by private firms, and would be if Malawi's mineral resources, as revealed by the British financed Geological Survey, were commercially attractive. The project appears to be a diplomatic concession to Dr Banda, who has insisted, in the face of known facts and informed opinion, that there are 'large quantities' of commercially valuable minerals in Malawi.

45.   It was part of his Gwelo Plan, but the actual form that the University should take was unclear. Originally it was to be situated in the northern region – a tribute to the early missionaries and a means of redressing regional imbalance.

46.   A £1m teaching hospital at Zomba, for instance, was proposed but had to be dropped for lack of external support.

47.   See Chapter 6.

48.   The expenditure of c. £150,000 on the first architectural plan, for instance, was largely wasted. Further, the original commitment of a £1m grant is now worth considerably less than it was in 1965 as a result of inflation.

49.   In 1967, an ODM appraisal team expressed doubts as to the justification of the expansion of the telex system and remarked that the export gains to Britain were a factor in any decisions regarding aid allocation to this sector.

50.   The Plant and Vehicle Hire Organisation set up in 1970-1. It has not been without teething troubles but should, in the view of user government departments improve on the previous system. And it certainly provides a sounder basis for costing projects.

51.   For instance, with two different valuations (ODM's and MHC's) of MHC's housing stock, its rate of return was estimated to be, respectively, 5½ per cent or c. 8½ per cent, given MHC's intended rental charges. Whether or not a subsidy is involved also depends on the opportunity cost of capital in Malawi: the Malawi government uses a somewhat arbitrary 12 per cent cut-off rate for projects, ODM uses 8 per cent. If the ODM rate is chosen but MHC's valuation of stock is accepted, no subsidy is involved. Further, it may be, as MHC argues, that the financial returns do not fully measure the benefits.

52.   Although MHC 'site and service' traditional housing schemes which Britain now aids do counter this effect to some extent.

6   BRITAIN'S TECHNICAL ASSISTANCE TO MALAWI

Under the British aid programme, technical assistance (TA) covers the provision of training for recipient country personnel, of expatriate personnel in executive or advisory capacities, of consultancies, and of equipment for training, demonstration, pilot schemes or surveys in the recipient country. Unlike financial aid, it is usually wholly tied to British goods and services and is often provided in kind, although most of the technical assistance to Malawi has been in cash. But the distinction between the two is blurred. Some technical assistance, for instance the supply of equipment and finance towards the upkeep of ldc-based research institutions, might equally be termed financial aid, while some projects supported by financial aid are similar to those supported via the technical assistance programme, for instance pilot schemes. Further, there is often an element of technical assistance in both the procedures for providing financial aid and the projects thereby financed.

British technical assistance disbursements to Malawi, all in tied, grant form, have increased relative to the total aid programme from 11.4 per cent of total net aid disbursements in 1964 to 40.2 per cent in 1972. Actual disbursements rose by roughly 40 per cent between 1964 and 1968, from £1.2m to £1.7m, since when they remained fairly stable until 1972 (see Table 6.1). Approximately 80 per cent of this aid has been reimbursements[1] to the Malawi government for some of the payments, made in addition to the local salary, to British personnel serving in established posts. Until 1968 a significant proportion of these reimbursements[2] — and hence total technical assistance — were to cover half the cost of compensating permanent and pensionable ex-colonial officers for loss of career. As argued earlier[3] these payments do not constitute aid. Since 1968, however, they have been a relatively minor element in total TA disbursements.[4] In all, the financing of Malawian students and trainees in Britain and of British personnel working in Malawi accounts for 90 per cent or more of Britain's technical assistance to Malawi, with equipment and surveys the remainder. In terms both of expenditure and of the total numbers of personnel involved, the salary supplementation schemes[5] have been most significant (see Tables 6.1 and 6.2). There has, however, been a small shift away from these schemes towards the provision of wholly aid financed personnel and training and tuition for Malawians.

Since supplementation schemes have been the most important element in Britain's TA, the main focus of attention will be on them.

Table 6.1 British Technical Assistance Disbursements to Malawi by Category of Expenditure 1964-72 (in £000)

Type of Expenditure	1964	1965	1966	1967	1968	1969	1970	1971	1972
Students and trainees	n.a.	10	59	89	102	165	176	189	159
% Total		(0.9)	(4.6)	(6.5)	(6.1)	(9.5)	(10.5)	(10.9)	(5.6)
Wholly financed experts	n.a.				48	45	63	129	173
% Total		956	1107	1174	(2.9)	(2.6)	(3.7)	(7.4)	(6.1)
Assisted experts and volunteers		(85.9)	(86.3)	(85.7)	1452	1448	1337	1306	2343
% Total					(86.6)	(83.5)	(79.4)	(75.0)	(83.0)
of which:									
OSAS	1052	924	1063	1092	1306	1309	1191	1121	1498
% Total	(88.0)	(83.0)	(82.9)	(79.7)	(77.9)	(75.5)	(70.7)	(64.4)	(53.0)
Equipment	n.a.	-	-	3	2	21	22	80	96
% Total				(0.2)	(0.1)	(1.2)	(1.3)	(4.6)	(3.4)
Surveys	n.a.	58	52	73	66	52	61	-	-
% Total		(5.2)	(4.1)	(5.3)	(3.9)	(3.0)	(3.6)		
Other	n.a.	88	64	30	8	4	27	37	50
% Total		(7.9)	(5.0)	(2.2)	(0.5)	(0.2)	(1.6)	(2.1)	(1.8)
Total	1195	1113	1283	1370	1677	1734	1685	1742	2822
Total as % net British aid to Malawi	11.4	10.7	15.4	17.5	24.1	28.4	25.5	36.8	40.2

Source: ODM, *British Aid Statistics.*

Table 6.2 Persons financed under British Technical Assistance to Malawi: 1964-72*

Type of Personnel	1964	1965	1966	1967	1968	1969	1970	1971	1972
Students & trainees	n.a.	37	52	85	106	123	149	118	104
of which:									
students	n.a.	18	25	69	92	96	122	104	56
trainees**	n.a.	19	27	16	14	27	27	14	48
Experts & volunteers	824	716	766	1010	998	974	989	920	855
of which:									
Wholly funded**	16	18	24	21	22	16	29	42	40
Assisted	780	650	669	916	894	874	861	794	736
Volunteers	28	48	73	73	82	84	99	84	79

* Refers to numbers of personnel in Malawi at end of each year except in the case of volunteers where data for 1965 to 1970 refers to numbers of volunteers serving under the 1965-6, 1966-7 programmes, etc.

** Unlike students, and other personnel working in Malawi, trainees and wholly-funded personnel are frequently financed for periods of less than a year. Consequently the figures here understate the total number of trainees or wholly-funded personnel involved in any one year, but are a reasonable guide to the relative importance of these types of technical assistance.

Source: ODM, *British Aid Statistics.*

Brief consideration will be given to the complement to supplementation schemes — the overseas training of Malawians — and the volunteer
programme. Other types of technical assistance — consultancy and
advisory services, equipment, and research support — supplied on a
largely *ad hoc* basis to meet particular needs usually arising in the context of the development programme will be ignored. They are best
regarded as forming part of Britain's development programme support,
considered in the previous chapter.

Supplementation Schemes

In most years since independence, there have been around 800 or more
British personnel working in established posts within Malawi's public
service under British supplementation schemes. Three schemes have
operated in Malawi. The oldest and most important is the Overseas
Service Aid Scheme (OSAS) introduced prior to Malawi's independence,
in 1961. The other two schemes were introduced in 1966 to extend
the coverage of OSAS-type arrangements to British personnel in public
service who were not eligible for inclusion in OSAS.[6] The British Aided
Conditions of Service (BACS) scheme extended supplementation
arrangements to expatriates who had previously been federal government employees, while the British Expatriate Supplementation Scheme
(BESS) extended the arrangements to British personnel working in
public but not government service (for instance, those working in the
University of Malawi).[7]

Under these schemes,[8] Britain has made various payments towards
the cost to Malawi of employing expatriate personnel, viz. inducement
allowances, which essentially 'top up' the local salaries to bring them
roughly in line with British salary levels, educational and passage allowances, gratuities (in the case of contract officers); and pensions and
compensation payments (in the case of permanent and pensionable
officers). Malawi's contribution has generally consisted of half the cost
of the passage allowances and the compensation payments, and the
whole cost of gratuities and pensions accruing to officers as a result of
their local salary payments. In addition, supplemented personnel have
longer leave entitlements and enjoy larger housing subsidies than their
Malawian counterparts; the latter cost being borne solely by the Malawi
government.

The object of the schemes has been to enable ldcs to retain and
recruit the services of expatriate officers. OSAS, the first, was designed
to meet the deficiencies that were thought to exist in the old colonial
service system, whereby officers were recruited in Britain but remune-
rated locally: these arrangements were thought to 'offer insufficient
inducement to troubled [sic] officers to continue to serve so long as

their services are needed, and they offer insufficient assistance to those territories . . . who wish to retain the services of expatriate officers in the interests of economic and social progress and stable administration until such time as they can build up their own local Public Service.'[9]

In Malawi's case, it was of crucial importance to retain and recruit expatriate personnel. Although in 1960 the Malawi Congress Party called for the Africanisation of the civil service 'at the greatest possible speed,' it was clear that this process would be incomplete some years after independence. In 1962, there were only five Malawians in the administrative service, and, in all, Malawians held only 13.5 per cent of the 1,271 filled posts in the upper classes of the government service.[10] In considering Malawi's post-independence needs, British policy makers dwelt on the need not only to provide sufficient inducements to expatriate officers through aid schemes but also to secure a social and political climate that would not deter expatriates. This latter concern was met — insofar as was possible — by constitutional measures, and by the assurances of Dr Banda.[11]

The OSAS agreement with Malawi was designed to assist the country meet its manpower needs 'for some time' but, like budgetary aid, the scheme was not seen as permanent. Nevertheless, although termination dates for the schemes were set,[12] there were no built-in arrangements for their run down. In accordance with the OSAS agreement, the Malawi government was required each year to furnish Britain with 'such information, including any variation in the numbers of designated officers (i.e. officers approved within the schemes) which results from the establishment requirements . . . as the Government of the United Kingdom may require to calculate the amount payable . . . during the ensuing year.' Further, the Malawi government was to 'consult the Government of the United Kingdom before effecting any changes in policy which might affect the recruitment, terms of service and numbers of designated officers so as to vary the amounts reimbursable by the Government of the UK.'[13] Similar requirements existed for the other schemes, the main concern being to ensure accountability and smooth operation. Within the limitations of recruitment possibilities and finance, Malawi generally received supplementation for officers as requested.

The permissiveness of British policy in this respect contrasts with the budgetary aid policy yet OSAS-type arrangements might encourage the very complacency and dependence that it was feared budgetary aid would engender. On the other hand, there were two countervailing factors. Unlike budgetary aid, OSAS-type aid involved the provision of counterpart local finance. Second, and more important, since the localisation of the civil service was generally viewed by ldcs as a key indication of 'real' independence (more so than the achievement of a balanced budget), there was a strong political incentive to curtail this form of aid. Certainly, when the OSAS agreement was reached with Malawi, this was the case. It is also true, however, that Britain viewed such aid more positively. The developmental importance of an efficient civil service and the possible adverse effects of rapid localisation were appreciated: while expatriates could not be forced upon Malawi, their services should remain on offer. And there was the factor that the supplementation schemes would also benefit British nationals previously in the employment of the colonial government.[14]

Recently, there has been some hardening in Britain's attitude to OSAS-type aid. Signs of the change came with the publication in 1969 of the White Paper *Public Service Overseas*, which reviewed the existing supplementation schemes due to expire by 1971. It concluded that:

> 'Although most of the new countries remain in need of the professional help that supplementation schemes can foster, they have made considerable progress in recent years in identifying their manpower need more accurately, in setting priorities for economic and social growth, and in increasing and diversifying their supplies of skilled manpower. HMG consider that, in negotiation of supplementation schemes for the period up to 1976, account should be taken of this changing situation, with the aim of beginning a more selective and flexible approach to the operation of the schemes.'[15]

In Malawi's case, this shift towards paying greater attention to the persons to be recruited and designated under the supplementation schemes is reflected in the 1971 agreement,[16] replacing the expiring BACS and OSAS agreements. The scope of the annual review was broadened from considering the financial obligations arising from the operation of the agreement, to determining the types and numbers of officers designated. To this end ODM set up an annual Manpower Review procedure. The first ODM team visited Malawi in 1973 and a second visit is scheduled for autumn 1974. Although the first team concentrated on establishing the needs for supplemented personnel, it is hoped that the procedure will also permit a better assessment of other aid requirements, specifically those for overseas study and training and for Malawi's domestic educational and training facilities.

One of the problems that currently faces Britain in considering Malawi's future technical assistance requirements — and would have faced it had it adopted a more selective and forward looking policy earlier — is that Malawi has been slow to produce a coherent assessment of its manpower needs and its policy on localisation has been obscure. Britain has for some time pressed Malawi to make such an assessment. This pressure stems from a desire to see how the educational programme for which it was providing financial and technical assistance fitted in with Malawi's manpower needs, as well as from the more recent policies regarding supplementation schemes.

Initially, manpower planning in Malawi was hampered by the same deficiencies which affected general economic planning — lack of data and of personnel. Although an attempt was made in 1962 to assess the existing stock and future requirements for skilled manpower,[17] the results would have been a wholly inadequate basis for policy making had they been used, which they were not. A second attempt was made in 1966-7 by a British technical assistance expert.[18] The data base had improved and the coverage of the stock of manpower was far more complete than the earlier survey. However, the classification of this stock was suspect, and no data were collected on the educational requirements for specific occupations. In the absence of macroeconomic projections, the forecasts were based on individual employers' views of future demand. The report of this exercise was accepted 'in principle' but largely disregarded as a basis for educational planning, although it was used as a guide to Malawi's technical education and training requirements by a team of British experts in 1969. Its deficiencies were recognised within Malawi, but several years passed before another forecast was attempted. This latest exercise,[19] executed by the EPD partly in response to external pressure, is considerably more thorough and reliable than its predecessors. It has, however, two main shortcomings — no data were collected on the link between occupations and educational training requirements; and its forecasts on the demand for skilled manpower are likely to be considerable over-estimates.[20] As in the case of previous surveys, the question of localisation and expatriate manpower requirements is not considered in detail.

Malawi's Localisation Policy

Since independence, Malawi's localisation policy in the public sector has only been stated in outline, and that outline leaves plenty of scope for individual interpretation. Malawi was, of course, unable to produce an unambiguous and detailed statement of its localisation plans without an adequate manpower plan. Nevertheless, it is reasonable to suppose that the neglect of manpower planning stems at least in part from Malawi's reluctance to make specific commitments on localisation.

Ldcs usually attach political importance to the rapid localisation of government services, and Malawi was no exception *before* independence. But since then the issue has been muted.[21]

Policy statements have only been made in general pragmatic terms: there should be no 'Africanisation for the sake of Africanisation.' Posts should be localised as and when Malawians had sufficient training and experience to take over European-held posts. Efficiency and honesty were required, and there was to be no lowering of public service standards through over-hasty promotion. Although government departments have made some plans for localisation, no specific, or explicit, guidelines existed, and the pace of localisation has largely depended on the somewhat subjective broadly stated criteria of 'sufficient training, efficiency and experience.'

In some ways the pattern of localisation in Malawi's public service conforms with expectations. The fastest growth of posts held by Malawians has occurred in those grades where Malawians were least represented before independence. Thus in the upper grades —superscale, administrative and professional — Malawian-held posts increased from 2 per cent of the total in 1962 to 44.2 per cent in 1970 as compared with an increase in the lower grades from 17.7 per cent to 73.3 per cent. As is evident from Table 6.3, however, it is in the grades in which Malawians were least represented — with the exception of the administrative grade — that the proportions of posts still to be localised is greatest, the largest shortfalls being in the superscale, professional and technical grades.[22] This pattern reflects the traditional arts base of Malawi's educational structure, the greater flexibility in training administrative and executive staff than professional and technical staff, the longer training periods for the latter two grades, and the rapid increase in the demand for such personnel with the expansion of development activities.[23] What is surprising, however, is that the upper levels of the government administrative, police and army services have remained in expatriate control until recently, despite the fact that there was considerable potential for localisation in these areas of government service. Until 1968, there were no Malawian Permanent Secretaries and in 1972 29 per cent of the posts in the administration service at the Under-Secretary level and above were occupied by expatriates.[24] The top post in the police force was not localised until 1971, that in the army not until 1972.

There can obviously be no hard and fast statement of what localisation was possible, given the general policy criteria. But it is widely thought that localisation in Malawi has lagged behind other African countries. Certainly, the fact that the number of British supplemented personnel in Malawi has remained fairly static while numbers elsewhere in Commonwealth Africa have declined since the mid-sixties supports this view.[25] There does appear to be a case for asking whether efforts to localise in certain areas were as strenuous as they might have been. It might appear that Britain's willingness to ensure a supply of expatriate manpower for the public service has in fact served to encourage a certain degree of complacency, as well as to permit Malawi to carry out a basically sensible, if vague, localisation policy. This issue is discussed

Table 6.3 Localisation in the Senior Classes of Malawi's Public Service 1962-70*

Class	1962 All filled posts	1962 % localised	1964 All filled posts	1964 % localised	1966 All filled posts	1966 % localised	1968 All filled posts	1968 % localised	1970 All filled posts	1970 % localised	Absolute increase in filled posts 1962-70	Absolute increase localised posts 1962-70	Posts localised since 1962 as % of 1970 filled posts
Superscale	117		201	6.5	216	12.0	281	23.1	304	33.2	187	101	33.1
Administrative	88	5.7	57	66.7	100	80.0	79	87.3	90	88.9	2	75	83.4
Professional	141	1.4	120	12.5	156	25.6	232	35.8	234	41.0	93	94	40.2
Total	356	2.0	378	17.4	472	30.0	592	30.0	628	44.2	282	270	43.0
Executive	204	54.4	379	73.4	476	82.8	623	87.0	751	89.9	547	565	75.2
Technical	367	8.7	337	32.9	416	45.7	469	55.0	712	62.5	345	413	58.0
Other**	286	7.9	454	41.0	561	46.7	630	62.4	560	72.9	274	386	68.9
Stenographers	68	-	34	-	54	16.7	79	29.1	121	37.2	53	45	37.2
Total	925	17.7	1204	47.0	1507	50.0	1801	60.0	2144	73.3	1219	1409	65.6
VSO	-	n.a.	45	n.a.	75	n.a.	75	n.a.	85	n.a.	85	n.a.	n.a.
Temporary†	-	-	75	-	100	10.0	122	32.8	142	56.3	142	80	56.3
Total	1271	13.5	1702	37.7	2154	46.9	2590	56.9	2999	64.4	1728	1759	58.6
Total number of Malawians in post	171		641		1011		1473		1930				

* These data are not considered reliable by the Economic Planning Division of Malawi. However, they are the only available indicators of the rate of localisation.

** Includes police, immigration, education, health, transport and communications personnel not classified under any other head.

† Temporary personnel occupying established posts.

Source: Personnel Division, Zomba.

in the next sections but there is little doubt that the policy and the speed of localisation of the upper grades of the politically important services — the administrative and security services — were also influenced by the political events of 1964-5.

As recounted earlier, Dr Banda faced a cabinet revolt shortly after independence.[26] One of the points in conflict was the appropriate rate of Africanisation, which the rebels thought should be faster. The rebels' most significant backing came from the educated urban élite, including a large number of African civil servants. Up to the defeat of Chipembere, the most powerful of the rebel ministers, in early 1965, Dr Banda's position was insecure. Although he had the support of the Young Pioneers and considerable popular backing, he was heavily reliant on the expatriate public servants. It was they who carried on the administration and acted as a moderating force *vis-à-vis* the African civil servants, who, if not openly in revolt, were decidedly sullen. It was they who organised the enforcement of the security regulations. Despite Dr Banda's scathing remarks on the foolish aspirations of 'yelping intellectuals' and the 'ambitious and parasitic clerks in the offices of Zomba and Blantyre,' he was clearly shaken by the disloyalty of his ministers and Malawi's African public servants and the gravity of the threat to his own position, and he appreciated the crucial role played by the expatriates during the crisis.

While no direct connection may be observed between these events and the subsequent localisation policy, there is little doubt that they influenced Dr Banda's approach to the issue. Certainly, there was some shift in policy. Before independence there had been two schools of thought on Africanisation, expressed in the MCP call for immediate Africanisation of the Civil Service, and in the moderate and officially accepted proposals of the 1960 Localisation Committee, which set out a programme for Africanisation 'at the greatest possible speed': with the exception of a few sensitive posts, this would be achieved through replacing expatriates on their retirement. It was thought that localisation should, and would have to, be most rapid in the case of the administrative service. After the crisis, when Dr Banda assumed direct responsibility for training and localisation, it is significant that no pronouncements were then made on the future rate of localisation, that the less tangible requirements of competence and efficiency were stressed as opposed to basic training, and that the urgency of the issue was played down: the declared policy was one of 'eventual Africanisation.'[27] And the rebels' demand for more rapid localisation could not have been met without damaging the efficiency of the government machine.[28]

In the late sixties, the pace of localisation speeded up. This reflects not only that there were more Malawians with training and experience, but also — probably — the greater security felt by Dr Banda. It also indicates that internal pressures for localisation at the higher levels were becoming more difficult to resist without incurring political problems.

The Effects of the Supplementation Schemes

The contribution of British aided manpower[29] to Malawi's economic development is difficult to gauge with any accuracy. Much depends on the weight attached to such factors as job experience and formal training, and on the intangible costs of employing expatriates rather than nationals. However, it is possible to analyse their impact in terms of Malawi's alternative without such technical assistance. This section considers the developmental impact of doing without British aided expatriate manpower in the public service, assuming that the government could have obtained expatriate services only through the supplementation schemes and could not have added to its stock of skilled manpower more quickly; the possibilities of attracting expatriates without aid or of obtaining manpower aid from other external sources; and the possibility of Malawi reducing its dependence on expatriates more speedily.

Without Expatriates in the Public Service

The need for the type of skills supplied by expatriates is difficult to establish. Expatriates have generally occupied posts in the upper levels of the civil service. Obviously there is some scope for substituting lower level skills for high level skills: a doctor's functions may to some extent be carried out by medical auxiliaries, and so on.[30] However, this scope was limited at the upper levels, and it will be assumed here that Malawi did need approximately the same number of administrative, professional, technical, and executive personnel as were actually employed. The evidence suggests that the establishment was not over-staffed. Vacancy rates in the upper level of the civil service have been fairly high — in 1964, nearly 18 per cent of authorised posts, and in 1970, nearly 21 per cent. The expansion of the actual establishment has broadly kept in line with that of government activities,[31] while the increase in different grades at the upper levels indicates that this was in response to the needs of government actively engaged in development rather than the mere multiplication of red tape: between 1964 and 1971, filled posts in the professional and technical grades increased by 95 per cent and 111 per cent respectively, and by 79 per cent in the superscale (which includes some professional posts), administrative and executive grades combined.

In 1964, while almost all posts in the clerical and technical assistance classes and below were held by Malawians, 62 per cent or just over one

Table 6.4   British Technical Assistance Personnel (other than Volunteers) in Post in Malawi by Field of Activity 1964-72 (year-end)

	1964*	1965*	1966*	1967	1968	1969	1970	1971	1972
Education	91	99	121	174	199	175	193	194	175
% total	(11.4)	(14.8)	(17.5)	(18.6)	(21.7)	(19.7)	(21.7)	(23.2)	(22.6)
Development planning	-	2	7	23	29	25	23	24	22
% total	-	(0.3)	(1.0)	(2.5)	(3.2)	(2.8)	(2.6)	(2.9)	(2.8)
Public administration	115	207	171	230	203	187	168	136	185
% total	(14.5)	(31.0)	(24.7)	(24.6)	(22.2)	(21.0)	(18.9)	(16.3)	(23.8)
Works & communications	2	36	44	228	216	229	233	218	210
% total	(0.3)	(5.4)	(6.4)	(24.3)	(23.6)	(25.7)	(26.2)	(26.1)	(27.1)
Mining, manufacturing, commerce & allied sciences	40	-	3	4	17	15	17	14	23
% total	(5.0)	-	(0.4)	(0.4)	(1.9)	(1.7)	(1.9)	(1.7)	(3.0)
Agriculture/renewable natural resources	68	36	39	135	115	112	114	113	115
% total	(8.5)	(5.4)	(5.6)	(14.4)	(12.6)	(12.6)	(12.8)	(13.5)	(14.8)
Health	5	40	51	55	41	41	36	31	28
% total	(0.6)	(6.0)	(7.4)	(5.9)	(4.5)	(4.6)	(4.0)	(3.7)	(3.6)
Social services	190	14	13	14	10	12	11	14	13
% total	(23.9)	(2.1)	(1.9)	(1.5)	(1.1)	(1.3)	(1.2)	(1.7)	(1.7)
Other	285	234	244	74	86	94	95	92	85
% total	(35.8)	(35.0)	(35.2)	(7.9)	(9.4)	(10.6)	(10.7)	(11.0)	(11.0)
Total	796	668	693	937	916	890	890	836	776
of which:									
Assisted personnel	780	650†	669	916	894	874	861	794	736

* Not directly comparable with data for succeeding years because of changes in classification.

† Estimate.

Source: ODM, *British Aid Statistics.*

thousand of the posts above this level were held by expatriates. By 1971, their numbers had not diminished to any great extent, but it was only at the superscale and professional grade that they were in the majority,[32] and more than half of all expatriates in post were in the professional and technical grades.[33] This shift in the role of expatriates is reflected to some extent in the distribution of British aided expatriates by field of activity: as can be seen from Table 6.4, the most significant feature has been the decline in numbers engaged in public administration while in areas where specialised skills are required, e.g. in natural resources, education, and works and communications, the numbers have remained high or increased.

If Malawians were to replace these expatriates, they would need to have been recruited from the public service or directly from the labour market. The skill requirement of any job cannot be specified exactly, being a mix of education or vocational training and job experience. In professional and technical occupations, it is reasonable to assume that job experience is not a satisfactory substitute for formal training, while for expatriate-held jobs in general the minimum educational requirement would be a school leaving certificate — acquired after at least twelve years education.

In the administrative and executive grades of the civil service, Malawi has operated a flexible system of local in-service recruitment since independence. Job experience and proven ability at lower levels have been a basis for promotion and the post-secondary school formal educational qualification has not always been required. Using this approach, of which an important element has been short in-service training courses at the Staff Training College set up in 1962, Malawi has localised this side of the civil service at a faster rate than would otherwise have been possible, and without any significant change in administrative efficiency.

However, in the early years the potential for this approach, on either the technical or non-technical side, was limited. Between 1962 and 1964, the number of Malawians in the upper levels of the civil service increased from 171 to 641. At the same time, the total stock of Malawians with a school leaving certificate was approximately 1,000.[34] About two-thirds of these Malawians had received their school certificates between 1962 and 1964, and were consequently young and inexperienced. Between 100 and 200 could be reckoned to be undergoing long courses of further education within Malawi or outside, and these Malawians were probably amongst the more able of the school certificate holders, roughly half of whom had passes in the third and lowest division. Thus, the total number of Malawians in the upper grades of the civil service represented nearly the whole stock of *available* Malawians with the basic educational requirements. They had only recently been appointed to their current posts, were thus inexperienced and, on average, young. There was little scope for in-service recruitment or from the labour market, without having the civil service run by personnel with neither the basic educational requirements nor the compensatory job experience. This was particularly true on the professional and technical side. The educational system was arts based, so raw recruits would need considerable job experience before they could be effective even at the lower levels. There were few Malawians with post-secondary school technical education or professional training and most of these were already in public sector employment. Without the expatriates, Malawi would have had virtually no experienced or trained personnel at the professional or technical levels.

Given this situation, complete localisation − or indeed much more localisation than actually occurred − in 1964 would have undermined the competence and efficiency of the public sector. Since the ability to use aid effectively has been a major determinant of Malawi's aid receipts, it can be assumed that, leaving aside the political consequences for Dr Banda, Malawi would have not been able to attract or use the same amount of aid it actually received − with obvious adverse consequences for its economic development.

As the stock of skilled Malawians has increased − the increase itself owing much to the presence of expatriates in the educational system − the number of Malawians in the upper grades of the public service has risen, trebling between 1964 and 1970. But the same basic obstacles to complete localisation existed later as existed at independence: there was still only a relatively small number of Malawians with either job experience or educational, vocational, or professional qualifications, or both. Even without distinguishing between different categories of skill, Malawi's stock of skilled manpower falls short of demand. The 1971 Manpower Survey indicated that Malawians in both private and public sector employment constituted 83.2 per cent of the estimated stock of skilled manpower − persons in jobs assumed to require at least two years of secondary education or its equivalent. That particular assumption is open to question, given that the survey found that the total number of Malawians in jobs in the skilled manpower category exceeded the estimated number of Malawians with the assumed basic educational requirements by about 15,000 or 37 per cent − a finding which reinforces the view that there is no rigid connection between education and ability to perform a particular job. Nevertheless, it is unlikely that there is at present, or has been since independence, much scope for meeting additional demands from the existing local stock of manpower. So, even if expatriates at the higher levels of government service could have been replaced, i.e. if the kind of skills were locally available either at lower levels in the public service or in the private sector, gaps would have been created elsewhere, to be filled by relatively unskilled manpower and, in the case of the private sector, by expatriates as well.

The Malawi government could not even have localised professional and technical grades by drawing on existing local skills from inside or outside the civil service, without reducing efficiency. The estimated number of professional and technical jobs (in both public and private sector) was 1,053 and 12,137 respectively in 1971, and Malawians held 20.3 per cent and 88 per cent of these posts respectively. In the professional sphere, the number of expatriates in public service considerably exceeded the number of Malawians in the private sector — by some 240 (see Table 6.5). And this figure does not represent the minimum public sector expatriate requirement for professionals, for not all Malawians employed in the private sector had the right qualifications for the public sector. In the technical sphere, the number of expatriates in the public sector was considerably exceeded by the number of Malawians employed in the private sector, but once again, expatriates in the public sector are employed in categories where the total number of available Malawians in the private sector is less than the demand. Thus, some, but not all, expatriate held posts could have been filled by persons with the appropriate job experience or qualifications from the private sector. Others would have had to be filled by personnel without such attributes, drawn from within or outside the civil service, and some left vacant for want of suitable personnel. In either case, efficiency and implementation of the development programme would have suffered.

On the administrative and executive side, there was more scope for localising in this way. Some further in-service recruitment could have been carried out, and presumably those Malawians occupying managerial posts in the private sector, whose numbers in 1971 far exceeded the expatriates in administrative or executive posts, would have had appropriate job experience for the latter. At the top policy making levels, however, there is a case for civil servants to be experienced. Since most Malawians currently employed in the administrative service have not had long experience in the service, let alone in its higher levels,[35] the quality of decision making would probably be adversely affected if all top posts were localised. Similarly, complete localisation at the lower levels might have been costly, since it would almost certainly have brought in less well-qualified and less able personnel.

In addition, the security, prestige, and promotion prospects on the non-technical side of government service compare favourably with those in the private sector, so that the government tends to get the first pick of new entrants to the labour market. To be set against these costs are certain benefits to the extent that it is politically desirable to have a

Table 6.5 High and Intermediate Skilled Manpower in Malawi, 1971

	Public sector		Private sector		All	
	Malawians	Non-Malawians	Malawians	Non-Malawians	Malawians	Non-Malawians
Top management	90	78	78	407	168	485
Middle and junior management and administration	905	238	807	771	1712	1009
Professional	142	311	72	528	214	839
Technical & sub-professional	9622	386	1058	1071	10680	1457
Skilled craftsmen & artisans	6635	14	7879	2344	14514	2358
Office workers	3381	56	3743	1459	7124	1515
Other n.e.s.	3827	115	1497	236	5324	351
Total	24602	1198	15134	6816	39736	8014

Source: Malawi Government, *Manpower Survey*, Zomba, 1971, p. 80.

Malawian-run civil service, and that expatriates are more costly to retain and that their presence incurs other less tangible costs. But these benefits would have been small.

In the first place, while there are political pressures for localisation — and these are, obviously, stronger in respect of the public sector (particularly the non-technical side) — there were certain direct political advantages in retaining expatriates. And, indirectly, since ultimately the government's popularity depended on its ability to achieve its development goals, and this in turn partly depended on the presence of expatriates, the political cost of removing expatriates could have been greater than the gains.

Secondly, while one expatriate is more costly to employ than one national, it does not necessarily follow that the government would save by not employing expatriates. Indeed, it has been argued that the replacement of experienced expatriates may entail the employment of a large number of nationals.[36] But there remains the cost to the economy of increased expatriate employment in the private sector. Since the full wage/salary differential between expatriate and local employees is borne by private employers, the financial cost of expatriate employment in the private sector is greater.[37] Further, there are certain fixed costs in employing expatriates, e.g. those payments made irrespective of occupational status to attract expatriates (for instance, passage and educational allowances), so that it is even more expensive to employ expatriates in lieu of nationals at the lower skill levels. Public sector localisation would thus leave gaps at the lower skill levels in the private sector. Where private firms recruited expatriates to fill these gaps – and they have shown a greater tendency to employ them even at the lower levels[38] – the cost to the economy would be greater than if top-level civil service posts were filled by expatriates at full cost to the Malawi government. Given these factors, it is likely that the government's reduced wage bill would not offset the additional costs borne by the private sector.

Finally, given that expatriate employment would have continued and probably increased in the private sector, some of the intangible costs supposed to be incurred by expatriates would continue: for instance, the 'demonstration effect', whereby the expatriates' life-style reinforces the aspirations of urban, educated Africans to Western living standards. This effect is, however, probably small: the aspirations of the élite were well established at independence,[39] and, if not as numerous as expatriates, there are Africans whose life-styles provide a similar example to those who yet aspire. On the other hand, it may be that localisation would have increased self-reliance to the extent that the presence of expatriates perpetuates the 'bwana mentality' – an unwillingness to accept responsibility while it may be passed to the expatriate. This attitude does exist and is encouraged, not so much by a neo-colonialist assumption by expatriates that they have a monopoly of the ability to make decisions and carry responsibility, but rather by the expatriates' desire to get things done.[40] On the other hand, complete self-reliance would probably be costly. Some of the observed reluctance to carry responsibility stems not from unwarranted lack of confidence or laziness, but from incompetence. A further 'gain' from complete localisation might be avoidance of inappropriate policy making based on experience of Western, rather than Malawian, conditions. Many of the expatriates in top policy making posts, however, have had long experience – not simply confined to central offices – of Malawi or neighbouring countries. At the same time, most of their African colleagues share a similar type of educational background, whether educated in Malawi or abroad.[41]

Given that Malawi required a civil service establishment of the size and structure that it has maintained since independence and given that the local output of skilled manpower had remained the same, it would have needed some expatriates for public service standards to be maintained, and private sector production not to be adversely affected.

Obtaining Expatriate Public Servants without British Aid

But did the Malawi government need to rely on British expatriates — or indeed on aid to finance its expatriate manpower requirements? It is clear that British expatriates working in the Malawi government service are preferable to other foreign nationals: they speak the official language and are familiar with the British-based government system. In addition, many have considerable experience of Malawi or countries in the region, which is shared by few other expatriates. The association of colonialism might be a disadvantage, but the good race relations in Malawi, and the fact that few colonial officers in Malawi had to be retired compulsorily at independence, suggest that this is not very important. Only other English-speaking Commonwealth nationals would share the general advantages of the British.

Malawi, moreover, would have faced difficulties on obtaining the services of non-British expatriates. Commonwealth countries, whose nationals would have been the best substitutes for Britons, do not have technical assistance programmes for operational personnel on a comparable scale. Australia is an exception but its programme is geared mainly to nearby territories. Most other donors' programmes are, and were, small or, like France and Britain, geared to the needs of countries with which there are special ties. It is unlikely, therefore, that Malawi would be able to meet its considerable manpower requirements from such sources. And this conclusion is supported by the fact that the Malawi government is not able to recruit all the technical assistance personnel it deems necessary at present.

It is therefore likely that the Malawi government would have had to recruit a substantial number of expatriates and — very probably — cover recruitment costs and salaries at its own expense, since donors tend to avoid recurrent financial aid, particularly when it is to be used for the purchase of services from other countries. Moreover, the cost of employing expatriates would probably have been higher than the cost jointly borne by the British and Malawi governments under the supplementation schemes. Many of the skills Malawi sought were on the whole only to be found in public service. Without some agreement with the government concerned to protect the career of the potential recruit, Malawi would have had to offer financial inducements. Such an additional burden on its recurrent budget would clearly have restricted developmental potential. It would also undoubtedly have led to greater efforts to localise the public service. As argued earlier, without a change in the pattern of public sector employment or in the rate at which skills were acquired, such efforts would probably have lowered efficiency in both the government service and the private sector. But could Malawi have adopted a different approach to localisation?

Alternative Approaches to Localisation

Various ways of reducing its reliance on expatriate manpower were in fact open to Malawi. It could have substituted lower level local skills for high level expatriate skills; or increased the local supply of higher skills by increased local or overseas training; or modified the training requirements for certain jobs.

The substitution of lower for higher level skills is an attractive proposition in a country where salary structures have a huge differential in favour of the traditionally expatriate-held posts,[42] and there is a scarcity of high level skills and a relative abundance of semiskilled manpower. However, the potential for substitution at any one level is limited by the availability of manpower at the level below; nurses, for instance, may carry out part of a doctor's job but ward orderlies cannot be expected to, although they, in turn, may carry out part of the nurses' job. Within these limitations, Malawi has made some moves towards such skill substitution, for instance through the training of field level workers for the agricultural extension service and of medical assistants in the health service. But outside the agricultural sector, Malawi's educational and training programme has focused on formal secondary and higher education. The latter has been vocationally oriented[43] but has been geared largely to increasing the output of middle level skills to fit into the traditional employment structure. Now, however, greater attention is to be paid to skill substitution, particularly between the relatively scarce middle level skills and those below.[44] Had Malawi been under more pressure to reduce its expatriate manpower requirements, it would probably have moved towards this kind of policy earlier.

There were a number of problems in increasing the supply of higher level skills by raising the output from local or overseas training facilities. In areas where the demand for highly trained manpower is unlikely to be large, local training would be very expensive. Recognising this, Malawi has opted for overseas training in such cases. But two factors impeded this policy. First, entrance requirements for overseas institutions tend to be restrictive: few Malawians possess the appropriate school leaving qualifications. Second, overseas training often took a long time. Malawi could have increased its output of sixth form school leavers, but probably at the cost of a cutback elsewhere. But if the choice was between producing students for local training/education, or for overseas, it made sense to opt for the former, since the skills developed from a secondary school base were scarce and local training tended to be shorter than overseas training, while expatriate employment at the middle skill levels is relatively more expensive than at the higher levels. Malawi's continuing shortage of middle level skills in the public service might indicate that it should have intensified its efforts in these areas. A major reason for not doing so is the danger – which may not be avoided even now – that once the medium-term need to replace expatriates is met, the country could find itself with an over-supply of such manpower. On the other hand, informal training at this level could have been boosted in the private sector, if the government had gone in for more in-service training.

The Malawi government has been very flexible on the educational requirements for non-technical jobs in the public service. However, on the technical side – despite the scarcity of local skills – the government has been reluctant to relax the formal and fairly lengthy training required at the various levels of the service.[45] Obviously there is a danger of lowering standards and the reluctance of the government is, to this extent, understandable. But it appears to have underestimated the value of on-the-job experience combined with short in-service training, as a means of upgrading local skills. And this rigidity is, in turn, a disincentive to potential civil service entrants on the technical side, since good promotion prospects do not offset a relatively low starting salary.

Even if the government had pursued this option more actively, it is unlikely that the country's manpower situation would have changed substantially in the period since independence. The conclusion holds that expatriates have been meeting needs which were crucial to the efficiency of Malawi's public and private sectors, the growth of the local supply of skilled manpower and the country's ability to attract aid and use it effectively. On the other hand, the potential for localisation would probably have improved if the Malawi government had more actively considered manpower needs and policies. Britain's permissive approach to supplementation aid was a factor in the relative absence of such efforts: the recent shift in British policy could provide the stimulus that was previously lacking, and the greater attention being paid to manpower issues in Malawi must be partly attributable to this change.

Volunteers

The British Volunteer Programme is not an integral part of the British aid programme. Volunteers are recruited and trained by voluntary organisations, and it is the British Council staff, rather than ODM representatives, that liaise with the recipient country and supervise the implementation of the programme. Nevertheless, the programme itself is

Table 6.6 British Volunteers in Malawi 1965/5-71/2

Type of volunteer	1964/5	1965/6	1966/7	1967/8	1968/9	1969/70	1970/1	1971/2*
Qualified	16	34	63	60	71	71	89	78
% total	(57.1)	(70.8)	(86.3)	(82.2)	(86.6)	(84.5)	(89.9)	(98.6)
of which: teachers	n.a.	19	34	25	42	43	52	40
Cadet	12	14	10	13	11	13	10	1
% total	(42.9)	(29.2)	(13.7)	(17.8)	(13.4)	(15.5)	(10.1)	(1.4)
of which: teachers	n.a.	12	7	10	8	10	8	1
Total volunteers	28	48	73	73	82	84	99	79
percentage of which: teachers	(n.a.)	(68.8)	(56.2)	(48.0)	(61.0)	(63.1)	(60.6)	(51.9)

* Number of volunteers in post on 31 December 1972.

Source: ODM, *British Aid Statistics.*

largely financed by subventions from the aid budget.

The number of British volunteers to Malawi increased from less than 30 in 1964-5 to nearly 100 in 1970-1,[46] since when the number has fallen to under 30 again. Until 1973, the majority were employed as teachers in Malawi's secondary school system; in October 1972, for instance, of the seventy-seven volunteers in post, forty-one were employed as teachers — thirty-seven in secondary schools, two in teacher training colleges and two in university colleges — and of the rest, ten were employed in the Ministry of Works, ten in agriculture, fourteen in health, and one each in the Government Print and a parastatal trading organisation.[47] All but one of the volunteers were graduates and/or professionally qualified, since untrained or 'cadet' volunteers, usually school leavers with 'A'-levels, were being completely phased out of the Malawi programme.[48] Since 1973, however, recruiting of teachers for the Malawi volunteer programme has stopped, mainly because of difficulties recently experienced by teaching volunteers, linked with changes in Malawi's educational policy — most markedly a move back to traditional and authoritarian methods of teaching.

There is a basic similarity between the volunteer programme and the supplementation schemes, in that volunteers have been recruited to meet specific operational manpower gaps although, being young and usually inexperienced, they normally went to posts at lower levels. The most striking difference between the two schemes is in their costs, both to Britain and to Malawi. As the term suggests, the volunteer programme provides a relatively cheap source of technical assistance. Britain finances the volunteer's passage and some other expenses — including, in the case of qualified volunteers, a resettlement grant — while Malawi has to provide board and lodging, transport and pocket money. The low financial reward that volunteers receive underlines the dual object of the programme in helping meet manpower needs in a developing country, while giving British youth the opportunity to serve overseas for their own benefit.

Since volunteers have little, if any, work experience prior to their appointment, and some possess only academic qualifications, they might seem to be less needed than more experienced and better qualified expatriates. But Malawi lacked skilled personnel at most levels, and the volunteers have helped to meet this shortfall. Only in the case of cadet volunteers, who have been mostly engaged in teaching (and whose numbers, even before 1970-1, never exceeded fourteen) could it be argued that Malawi could equally have employed local manpower. Certainly, Malawi now holds this view, with the result that cadets are no longer recruited. The British Council representatives think otherwise, and there is a case for saying that, since there are not enough secondary school leavers for local manpower requirements, the cadet volunteers whose calibre is generally high, may be replaced by local manpower only at some cost in competence. But the issue is marginal: that cost has to be set against the job experience gained by Malawians, and the political difficulty of resisting localisation of posts held by relatively unqualified, if also low paid, expatriates.

There has been some political pressure for the complete removal of volunteers. Volunteers, both British and American, have been labelled decadent and subversive, their life-style (usually meaning their dress and hairstyles) being regarded as a threat to the four cornerstones of the MCP's national development effort — loyalty, unity, obedience and discipline. The American Peace Corps has borne the main brunt of political disapproval — in 1969, the MCP passed a resolution calling for their withdrawal[49] — but the British volunteers have also been the subject of hostile comment from Dr Banda.[50] Although there were also diplomatic grounds for caution, the fact that the British volunteers were not banned, and that the Peace Corps programme was revamped rather than withdrawn, does suggest that Malawi considers that they could not easily be replaced. Local manpower shortages, budgetary restraint, and problems of expatriate recruitment in some fields where volunteers work, (e.g. architects and surveyors) support that conclusion. And indeed, Malawi still requests teaching volunteers from Britain despite the decision to suspend their recruitment for Malawi.

Overseas Training and Education

Expenditure on training and education for Malawians in Britain has risen relatively rapidly since 1964, although it fell back in 1972 and at its peak accounted for only 11 per cent of total British TA disbursements to Malawi. The number of Malawian students and trainees[51] on aid-financed courses in Britain has risen from less than 40 in 1965 to 118 at the end of 1971. The main fields of study have been education, social sciences, engineering and medical science, and training in public administration (including police training), works and communications and health (see Table 6.7). The main purpose of the overseas training[52] programme is to supplement Malawi's own facilities and thus increase the stock of skilled manpower. The object of promoting a cultural exchange is very minor. Almost all the British scholarships and fellowships provided to Malawi have been intended to provide vocational training, broadly defined, usually for those already in public sector employment.

Overseas training is an inadequate substitute for local training for two main reasons. First, while there may be intangible benefits to the individual students, there may be a tangible cost to the recipient if the student fails to return after his period abroad, and somewhat less tang-

Table 6.7 Malawian Students and Trainees Financed by British Technical Assistance 1965-72*

	1965	1966	1967	1968	1969	1970	1971	1972
Field of Study								
Education	6	16	20	27	19	27	13	12
Law	3	3	3	4	4	1	1	-
Social sciences	7	1	11	18	15	11	7	7
Economics	1	2	2	5	2	1	7	2
Natural science	1	-	-	1	1	4	3	5
Engineering	-	1	19	18	24	37	29	8
Medical science	-	2	11	13	16	22	25	13
Agriculture	-	-	3	4	6	8	6	2
Humanities	-	-	-	-	1	2	1	4
Fine arts	-	-	-	2	8	8	11	3
Other	-	-	-	-	-	1	1	-
Total students	18	25	69	92	96	122	104	56
Field of Training								
Education	5	-	1	1	-	-	-	-
Development planning	-	1	2	2	1	-	1	-
Public administration	7	15	8	6	3	11	4	4
Social services	1	1	1	-	3	-	-	6
Works & Communications	2	4	4	2	4	8	4	19
Industry & Commerce	1	5	-	1	2	1	-	5
Renewable natural resources	1	-	-	-	-	-	2	2
Health	1	1	-	2	13	6	3	11
Other	1	-	-	-	1	1	-	1
Total trainees	19	27	16	14	27	27	14	48
Total students & trainees	37	52	85	106	123	149	118	104

* Refers to number of students and trainees in Britain at end of each year.

Source: ODM, *British Aid Statistics.*

gible costs if the student fails to make use of his newly acquired skills on his return home because of difficulties in readjustment. It is claimed by British and Malawian officials that the wastage rate (for overseas trainees) through non-return is low; the fact that most are effectively on leave of absence and go often for short periods supports this claim. Problems of resettlement are also likely to be less after short courses. Since there is no systematic follow-up of returning students or trainees, it is difficult to know whether these problems are in fact negligible in Malawi. The tightening up of security checks on Malawians going abroad and the banning of certain 'subversive' study locations suggest that some such costs have been incurred. Second, the standard and content of courses overseas may not be wholly relevant to the needs of the recipient country — a factor which may exacerbate the wastage and resettlement problems — although this is clearly not true of all overseas training, some of which is specifically geared to the needs of ldcs.

Overseas training should therefore be seen as supplementing local training. Where the demand for particular skills is small or is likely to be short-term, and where the capital and recurrent costs of establishing institutions to develop such skills would be relatively high, there is a case for overseas training; similarly, when local facilities, although feasible, have yet to be developed. Since Malawi has a shortage of skills at all levels and, at independence, had relatively few facilities for further training, overseas training was potentially an important means of increasing the stock of skilled personnel. The criteria that local facilities do not exist, and that the particular skills that could be acquired overseas are in local demand have apparently guided Malawi's acceptance of overseas training opportunities and Britain's offers of such training.

Aside from these two general criteria, the selection of students and trainees has depended largely on their individual suitability to overseas training rather than on the need for some scarce skills more than others. The pattern of training and education thus provided is clearly somewhat *ad hoc*. Although in general the fields in which students and trainees have undergone courses are ones of skill shortage,[53] better use could probably have been made of overseas training had there been a coherent basis for assessing Malawi's needs, i.e. a manpower plan. On the other hand, the entrance requirements of basic educational or work experience and linguistic ability limited both the numbers that could be sent abroad and, to some extent, the type of training or education that could be accepted. Lack of basic educational qualifications has limited the number undergoing high level professional courses, despite the arrangements for allowing Malawians to enter some British universities without the usual minimum entrance qualifications. Poor linguistic ability, despite crash courses in English, has restricted the numbers receiving training at some lower levels, e.g. craft teacher training courses.

In contrast with other forms of British aid to Malawi, it is unlikely that, without British overseas training assistance, the extent and type of overseas training received by Malawians would have been wholly foregone or that Malawi's ability to attract other forms of aid would have been affected. At the same time, without the access to British facilities provided through the aid programme, Malawi would probably have been unable to use overseas training to the same extent. The fact that the Malawi government itself finances some overseas training suggests that Malawi is unable to attract all the technical assistance it considers necessary for this purpose. Further, Britain has provided between one-quarter and one-fifth of all overseas training places held by Malawians and few donors, other than the USA, could have offered the same number or range of opportunities, still less in English-speaking institutions.

This British-financed training has allowed Malawi to increase its stock of skilled manpower at a faster rate than could otherwise have been possible, both diminishing reliance on expensive expatriate employment and meeting shortages where expatriate recruitment would have been difficult. And besides the financial advantages of expatriate replacement, there are, and were, clear political gains from the use of overseas training for the higher level skills, for which formal training in local institutions was not economically feasible. Dependence on expatriates in these areas is a considerable obstacle to self-reliance, given Malawi's vulnerability should their services be withdrawn. The desire to limit this vulnerability in turn justifies Malawi's recourse to overseas training, which entails relatively long absences of scarce educated manpower, who might otherwise have undergone shorter overseas courses – or, in the later years, lower level local training courses – thereby permitting more rapid localisation at the lower skills levels, where expatriates are relatively costly to employ.

NOTES

1.   Since April 1971, Britain has been making some of these payments directly to the personnel involved.
2.   Around £400,000 a year: just under a third of TA disbursements over the period 1964-8.
3.   See Chapter 3.
4.   And in 1971, Britain took on an increased share of pensions and selected payments to expatriate officers and cancelled all past compensation and commutation loans.
5.   OSAS, BACS and BESS, see p. 138.
6.   OSAS was restricted to members of HMOCS or to persons who had been appointed on contract in the same way as HMOCS officers.

7.   BACS related only to Malawi and Zambia; BESS has a considerably wider coverage, as has OSAS.
8.   Apart from their different coverage, the terms and conditions are broadly similar.
9.   Cmnd. 1193, *Service with Overseas Governments*, October 1960. The terms of the agreements were changed somewhat in 1971, the main change being that some items were paid direct to supplemented personnel by Britain rather than via the Malawi government.
10.   See Table 6.3
11.   It was of course in keeping with British decolonisation policy in Africa to seek to establish a democratic constitution which would ensure the protection of racial minorities in the post-independence period. But the need to do so in order that expatriate public servants would be encouraged to stay and that they per-form in their duties 'without fear or favour' was particularly stressed, see Cmnd. 1887, *Report of the Nyasaland Constitutional Conference*, 1962, especially paras. 11, 15-7.
12.   OSAS and BACS were to end in 1971.
13.   Cmnd. 3533, *Agreement concerning the Employment of Certain Officers in the Public Service of Nyasaland 1962*, HMSO, 1968, p. 5.
14.   It is significant that the BACS scheme for ex-federal officers was less generous than the OSAS scheme. This is thought to have reduced the numbers of such officers willing to remain in government employment.
15.   Cmnd. 3994, p. 7.
16.   Cmnd. 5113.
17.   By Dr Seltzor under the direction of R.J. Harbisen – he was not officially engaged to do so.
18.   The 'Brown' Survey.
19.   *Malawi Government Manpower Survey 1971*, Zomba, 1972.
20.   See G.S. MacKerron, 'A Technical Evaluation of Manpower Plans in Malawi,' mimeo 1972, Sussex University. MacKerron argues that the assumptions regarding future output, the elasticity of demand for skilled manpower, and the wastage rate lead to over-estimates of future demand.
21.   See below.
22.   There is also a large shortfall in the stenographer grade, which is somewhat remarkable since stenographers do not require long training. Partly this slow localisation is due to the preferences of both expatriate and Malawian top civil servants for expatriate secretaries and to lack of effort to localise at this grade. But stenographers are something of a special case in that the basic educational requirements for a potential stenographer are similar to those required for higher grade scarce skills for which remuneration was greater. Every effort to train steno-graphers failed because of the poor quality of recruits.
23.   Authorised posts for technical staff increased by 103 per cent between 1967 and 1971, for professional staff by 75 per cent, whereas executive posts increased by 49 per cent. The position is less clear in the administrative and superscale grades, since the latter includes many professional posts. Reliable data for the private sector do not exist.
24.   C.A. Baker, 'The Administrative Service in Malawi,' *Modern Journal of African Studies*, Vol. 10, No. 4, 1972.
25.   In 1965, Malawi accounted for 8.1 per cent of total supplemented per-sonnel in Commonwealth Africa, 8.9 per cent in 1969 and 10.5 per cent in 1972.
26.   See Chapter 2.
27.   H.K. Banda, *Malawi Hansard*, 7 July 1966.
28.   See below, p. 145ff.

29.   British aided expatriates constitute some 80 per cent or more of all expatriates in government service, and because of the data problems of distinguishing the British aided expatriate group from the others, the two groups will be treated as one.

30.   See below, p. 153.

31.   Filled posts in the upper levels of the civil service increased by 76 per cent between 1964 and 1970; government net expenditure – a crude indicator of government activities – increased by 73 per cent at constant prices between 1964 and 1970-1.

32.   Whereas, in 1964, it was only at the executive and lower levels of the administrative (excluding superscale posts) grade that Malawians were in the majority.

33.   Including superscale posts.

34.   A generous estimate based on the number of school certificate holders emerging from the school system between 1953 and 1964.

35.   Most have less than eight years experience in the administrative service, while their experience in their particular grade within the service has been considerably shorter – in 1972 the average length of service of Permanent Secretaries, as such, was 2.6 years; for Deputy Secretaries, 3.4 years; and Under-Secretaries and Principal Administrative Officers, 3.5 years; and the averages are inflated by the inclusion of expatriates, who accounted for fourteen of the sixty-three posts held at these levels, see C.A. Baker, *op. cit.*

36.   See *Economic Report 1972*, p. 63. But Baker's findings on the localisation of the Administrative Service suggest that a one-to-one substitution has occurred.

37.   Assuming that the Malawi government could get aid towards the cost of expatriate manpower in public service.

38.   Partly a result of the Malawi government's lax policy on employment permits for foreigners.

39.   One major cause of Civil Service discontent in 1964 was the proposal that the salary structure be revised along lines appropriate to local rather than British conditions.

40.   Expatriates generally tend to be better placed to cut bureaucratic corners than Malawians, since, at worst, they have to go home while a Malawian risks loss of promotion or his job. Their willingness to do so effectively takes the initiative away from their Malawian colleagues.

41.   Although, from the University of Malawi downwards, efforts are being made to reform curricula so that they have greater relevance to the Malawian situation.

42.   For instance, the starting salary of an administrative or professional officer is seven times that of a clerical or technical officer. And if Malawi had had to pay still higher salaries to expatriates recruited at its own expense, this option would have been more attractive.

43.   See Chapter 5, p. 129 for a description of the constituent colleges of the University of Malawi.

44.   According to Devpol, *op. cit.*, pp. 99-101. A Manpower Assessment and Utilisation project under UNDP aid was recently set up to examine such possibilities.

45.   Nor, it seems, does it encourage its officers to make efforts to upgrade their skills. MacKerron, in a study of a group of Malawians holding engineering (and business) studies diplomas, found that, despite their willingness to undertake correspondence courses to obtain full professional qualifications, they received little or no encouragement from either public or private sector employers.

46.   See Table 6.6.

47.   Information supplied by the British Council.

48.   See below.

49.   It did so because of 'complaints by the people against the influence of the volunteers over their children, and because of their bad conduct and behaviour and slovenliness'; quoted in UNDP Resident Representative's Annual Report for 1969.

50.   Dr Banda is reported to have gone so far as to state in public that he was not having VSOs in the country, but this remark was expurgated from the printed text of his speech.

51.   Students are defined as persons on systematic courses of instruction in British institutions of higher education; trainees are persons at any level receiving mainly non-academic, practical and vocational training, or training through visiting tours or attending *ad hoc* seminars and courses.

52.   Unless otherwise stated, includes student *and* trainee-type training.

53.   But, in 1969, the number of returning nurses appeared to exceed the effective demand and, given the numbers in medical training abroad, unless recurrent expenditure on health services is stepped up, an over-supply situation in respect of other personnel could emerge.

7   CONCLUSIONS

This book has chronicled Malawi's remarkable economic performance since independence and the impact of different types of British aid. This final chapter assesses the role of British aid in Malawi's development, and draws some lessons for future British aid policy in general and for Malawi in particular.

Aid and Development

Malawi's achievement of political independence in 1964 was precipitated by the break up of the Federation of Rhodesia and Nyasaland. The constitutional form, however, was inconsistent with economic reality: Malawi was scarcely a viable state. Its government was insolvent and it apparently lacked the domestic resources, human, physical or financial, with which it might survive, let alone develop. Since then, Malawi has experienced rapid economic growth, with average income per head increasing in real terms by 4 per cent a year. The gains from the expansion of Malawi's productive capacity have not been evenly spread between regions or between income groups. Nevertheless, they have been widespread and Malawi has gone some way towards removing those features which prompted its pre-independence description as Britain's 'imperial slum.'

During the post-independence period the Malawi government has received substantial external support, with gross financial inflows amounting to over £100m, equivalent to 5 per cent to 15 per cent of GDP and between a third and a half of total government expenditure in any one year. More than two-thirds of these inflows were aid. How far have these inflows – and in particular the British aid component – contributed to Malawi's economic development? Does the evidence provide any support for the various contentions that aid has little or no impact on development or actually does harm; that it reduces the recipient's domestic development efforts and encourages external dependence; that it permits or even encourages policies inappropriate to economic development?

There is plenty of evidence to show that Malawi has not been lax in efforts to mobilise resources for development while in receipt of aid. The rise in gross domestic savings from an average of 2 per cent GDP in 1964-6 to 8 per cent in 1971-3 is wholly inconsistent with the view that aid, in supplementing domestic resources, acts as a substitute for not an addition to, domestic savings. In the monetary sector of the economy where domestic savings were negative at independence, such savings covered nearly half of domestic investment expenditure in 1973, and this investment spending was equivalent to 20 per cent of GDP as compared with 9 per cent in 1964. These achievements owe much to government efforts to restrain its consumption spending and to mobilise domestic resources through taxation, and to a lesser extent through deficit financing: while government consumption barely increased in real terms, the tax ratio rose from 12.9 per cent of monetary GNP in 1964 to 16.4 per cent in 1972-3. But private savings, facilitated by Malawi's expanded financial sector, have also increased, and private sector investment spending has risen faster than public sector.

None of this, of course, proves that Malawi's domestic efforts would not have been greater without aid. But the analysis of different forms of British aid in preceding chapters suggests that, while efforts might have been greater, Malawi's capacity to develop would have been severely undermined without the aid.

Conventionally, aid has been regarded as an addition to the recipient's investment resources. While the distinction between investment and consumption spending is blurred, it is quite clear that Malawi's aid receipts cannot be so regarded. In the early post-independence years, the major part of Malawi's aid (which then came almost exclusively from Britain) was intended to support the day-to-day expenditure of the government. Budgetary grants-in-aid, finance under technical assistance arrangements towards the salaries of expatriate public servants, together with a portion of aid to Malawi's 'development' account from Britain were provided for this purpose. Malawi's recurrent expenditure was not and is not solely of a consumption nature (for example, spending of education, health and agricultural extension services) and it was needed to maintain and expand the framework for development. But even allowing for the recognition of the investment role of recurrent spending which directly enhances individual productivity, much of it would not be regarded as investment. It is, and was, crucial to Malawi's subsequent development, however, that such expenditure was supported by aid.

At independence, the Malawi government (previously in receipt of federal subsidies) was spending at a level well above that which domestic resources could support. It faced a recurrent budget deficit of over £7m, and was almost wholly dependent on external resources for spending on its development account.[1] However, had the government tackled its deficit problems in the absence of aid, economic decline would have been inevitable, and would probably have been accompanied by political unrest. Assuming that Malawi received no other external support, its prospects thereafter would have been poor. Other things being equal, the rate of domestic savings would undoubtedly have dropped as GDP declined. And although the government could and probably would have sought to mobilise additional resources from the private sector, this would probably have lowered the country's total domestic savings rate still further. A reduction in private sector disposable income would have resulted in a proportionally greater cut in investment than in consumption spending there. Meanwhile, since government recurrent expenditure is more difficult to cut than planned government investment, any increase in government income would have been used to meet its recurrent deficit. Thus, total domestic savings (defined as income minus consumption) and the rate of investment would have dropped.

Initially, the economy would probably have moved into a period of stagnation, at a considerably lower level of output than that in 1964. Government spending, beyond that needed to maintain law and order, would have been too low and its skilled manpower inadequate to be a significant stimulus to development. The organised monetary sector would have been in a depressed state, with low domestic incomes and political uncertainties inhibiting new investment and particularly deterring foreign private investors who have been important contributors to Malawi's rapid economic growth. Without development efforts in the rural areas, population pressures would have added to Malawi's problems. Foreign exchange earnings from cash crop exports would have been reduced as more land was taken up for subsistence production. With increasing population pressure on the land, emigration would have increased. Since it is unlikely that this could have occurred on the scale required, urban unemployment would probably have become a major social and political problem.

Eventually Malawi *might* have shaped a self-help development strategy which would have brough widespread institutional change and a faster growth in economic welfare than that promised by the present development path. But it is at least equally possible that the educated urban élite or the armed forces, or both, would have seized power and sought to exploit Malawi's limited resources at the cost of neglecting and probably repressing the poorer sections of the population.

But it is unlikely that Malawi would have been left to its own devices. Located between the white racist régimes of southern Africa and the emergent black states to the north, it was of obvious interest to those seeking to end or support white rule. Thus although Malawi would have been unattractive to donors who did not have political and economic interests allied to these objectives, or to commercial investors and lenders, it would probably have attained some external support. The options *with* such support range from eventual annexation by southern, most probably South, Africa to Chinese-aided self-help development. An option involving southern African support seems the most likely, despite evidence of Chinese interest in Malawi at independence. In any case, the support that Malawi would have received would probably have been weaker, and less appropriate to development, than that it actually received. Only with extreme optimism is it possible to imagine that its development prospects would have been improved by the absence of aid, in particular the absence of British aid. And although aid financed both consumption and investment spending in Malawi, it is probable that the conventional indicator of effort, the rate of domestic savings, would have dropped despite an increase in tax.

In later years, the withdrawal of aid would have had less dire consequences than those outlined above but it is extremely unlikely that, at any time since independence, it would have enhanced Malawi's development prospects. Indeed, it is probably only by attaching more importance to such factors as self-reliance and domestic effort than to economic stability and growth that a case may be made for the developmental value of withdrawing aid to Malawi. But, even then, it is hard to show that autonomy and effort were severely eroded by the presence of aid or that its autonomy — at least — would have been significantly increased by the absence of aid. And only those with puritanical inclinations could demand significantly more domestic effort in a country where average private consumption expenditure per head (its growth having been held down by government policy) was only £35 in 1973.

Malawi's achievements in respect of domestic resource mobilisation have been noted earlier. Much credit is due to the efforts of the Malawi government, which attached considerable importance to reducing the extent of Malawi's reliance on external aid, particularly budgetary aid. Nevertheless, these achievements could not have occurred without the inflow of aid which has helped to maintain and raise output and incomes, both directly and by expanding income earning possibilities, thus enlarging the total resource base to be tapped for development. But aid was not simply a permissive agent in resource mobilisation. A major incentive to the latter was provided by Britain's policy of phasing out budgetary grants-in-aid; and also, to a lesser extent, Britain's and other donors' requirements that Malawi contribute to the costs of the projects they financed and of the technical assistance they provided. Moreover, Malawi was well aware that Britain's, and most of its other major donors', willingness to supply aid depended in part on its own domestic resource mobilisation, and that certain forms of expenditure were ineligible for aid finance.

The area in which the Malawi government is most open to charges of laxity and undue reliance on external aid is in relation to the British supplemented manpower assistance. That is not to say that Malawi could easily have dispensed with the services of all British-aided expatriates or of the aid with which they were financed: without the latter Malawi could not have attracted expatriates in sufficient numbers and its development potential would have been harmed both by reduced competence in the public sector and by skilled labour problems in the private sector; and, given the importance of expatriates in Malawi's educational sector manpower problems in the future would have been exacerbated. Nevertheless, the Malawi government has been somewhat slow in formulating detailed manpower plans and in considering ways of changing the structure of public service employment so as to economise on the use of scarce skills, and of encouraging localisation in the private sector. This slowness is explained in part by Malawi's lack of planning expertise, particularly in the earlier years, and by its political problems immediately after independence. But British aid policy in this sphere — its *ad hoc* response to demands for supplemented personnel within certain financial limits — also created conditions for a lax manpower policy. Although a more positive approach would probably not have significantly reduced Malawi's need for expatriate manpower in the period considered here, it would have reduced needs in the future. The more recent British policy of actively assessing demand for expatriate skills will probably encourage the Malawi government in its own — also recent — efforts to improve its manpower policies.

Nevertheless, aid has generally not inhibited Malawi's efforts to help itself and, by preventing economic decline and by providing resources for development, has had an overwhelmingly beneficial effect. But it is possible that — as aid critics predict — it may have permitted or encouraged Malawi to pursue policies which have or will have harmful effects on its development. Bauer,[2] for instance, argues that aid tends to increase the level of public sector spending which reduces economic efficiency and growth, since in his view the public sector is inherently inefficient. And this latter effect is encouraged, he maintains, by the concessionality of aid since the recipient government does not bear the costs of its spending and so has no incentive to ensure adequate returns. He and others[3] argue that the predilections of donor or recipient governments, or both, will cause an inappropriate development strategy to be adopted: over-investment in physical infrastructure, capital-intensive investment and a neglect of agriculture, resulting in an inegalitarian distribution of income, itself fostering further misallocation of resources in both the private and public sectors. Donors are more frequently considered to encourage rather than simply permit such distortions. The critics attribute to donors the belief that capital, and particularly physical overhead capital such as roads and railways, is all that is lacking for development to occur and accuse donors of encouraging over-investment in such capital. Consequently, returns are low, if

168

not zero, and the need for strengthening and changing institutions disregarded. Donors' preference for projects which provide visible evidence of their aid and are easier to administer encourage the observed tendency for ldc politicians to favour prestige projects, often resulting in lowered productivty. And the adoption of costly and inappropriate production techniques and patterns of expenditure is encouraged by the practice of tying aid to the purchase of goods and services from the donor country.

Despite Malawi's heavy reliance on external support, its pattern of development does not bear out the critics' predictions. The government's top priority was to promote agricultural production, its development programme for this sector being backed by investment in the transportation system. Although government spending to provide the infrastructure for urban, industrial development has been high relative to the proportion of the population in towns, the main focus of its policies and spending has been on the rural sector. The development of secondary and higher educational and training facilities to increase the domestic output of skilled manpower has also had an important place in the government's programme. Private entrepreneurial activity in both the urban and rural sectors has been encouraged through government policy. Malawi has had its share of large aid-financed projects but few could be regarded simply as prestige or as unproductive. Most have been related to the development of the country's productive capacity, although some, e.g. the new capital, less obviously than others. And although the Malawi government has undertaken a few projects with its own resources (which were expanded indirectly by aid) that bear little relationship to development, such expenditure, with the exception of the £2m on the presidential palace, has been small. On the whole, the rapid growth of agricultural and industrial output and foreign exchange earnings and the avoidance of such problems as large-scale urban unemployment and balance of payments difficulties in Malawi belie the critics. Certainly, exogenous factors — world price movements, Rhodesian UDI and the white southern African labour market — have been favourable. Nevertheless, its aid donors, particularly Britain, must take substantial credit for the country's performance.

In important ways, the majority of Malawi's chief aid donors did not conform with the critics' caricatures of them. Most notably, Britain's aid programme had a number of features which were very different from what the critics might expect. The major part of the aid was provided not for capital spending, narrowly defined, but for recurrent spending. Thus, rather than encouraging capital-intensive investment, it allowed the Malawi government to maintain and expand important development services which would otherwise of necessity have been neglected. British aid was, moreover, free from restrictive procurement conditions, which would undoubtedly have biased the Malawi government's development spending pattern. The budgetary grants-in-aid were subject only to the requirement that the Malawi government should buy British 'wherever possible' when making offshore purchases from its recurrent account, while the 'development' loans and grants could be used either for local costs or for the purchase of British goods and services. Further Britain adopted a procedure on project finance whereby a lump sum was agreed in advance of the projects to be aided and it was willing to accept small, and often diffuse, projects as part of its aid programme. This approach, together with the other terms of British aid already stated, in no way encouraged a development strategy inappropriate to Malawi's needs.

Not all Malawi's main donors have been so liberal in their provision of aid. None have contributed to Malawi's recurrent expenditure except as part of technical assistance or where such expenditure constituted an integral part of the costs of aided projects. Apart from Denmark, all donors have provided aid on the basis of individual project requests and have shown a marked preference for large projects. And donors' willingness to accommodate local project costs has generally been limited, with the major exception of the International Development Association. By their own standards, however, most donors accorded Malawi generous treatment. Even so, it is clear that Malawi's development choices would have been severely restricted if it had had to rely solely on such donors. With IDA and West German aid, Malawi would have been able to pursue the development of agriculture but not on a widespread geographical basis, as with British aid. It would most probably have only been able to use the other aid receipts, if at all, for investment in physical overhead capital — and in the absence of the various development services financed by British aid, these investments would have had low returns. This assumes that in the absence of British aid, Malawi would have been unable to attract other donors' aid which, with the exception of South African 'aid', is doubtful. British aid was largely responsible for the administrative and economic framework which enabled Malawi to formulate and execute projects acceptable to donors and so to attract aid.

All Malawi's major donors with the exception of the African Development Bank and South Africa have provided financial aid on soft terms. Some of this aid has been on-lent on near commercial terms to public sector corporations by the Malawi government. But neither that nor the remainder spent directly by the Malawi government has on the whole been used wastefully or inefficiently, as Bauer would predict. And of Malawi's large infrastructural projects, the two most likely to attract criticisms of resource wastage — the new capital and the Nacala rail link – were both financed by South Africa on relatively hard terms. If anything, it is a donors' lack of interest or ignorance of the developmental returns to the various projects and policies pursued by the recipient rather than the concessionality of finance which permit its misuse. Certainly, Malawi's awareness that most of its donors based their decisions on future aid allocations on its development performance has been an important incentive to effective aid use. And the concessionality of the finance received has enabled Malawi to proceed at a faster rate than would have been possible had its balance of payments been burdened by substantial debt servicing.

The terms and conditions of British aid reflect the concern for Malawi's development which underlies Britian's aid programme to the country. This concern had its basis in Britain's sense of moral obligation towards Malawi as an ex-colony, whose weak position at independence owed much to past neglect and Britain's misguided policy on federation. At that time Britain made a commitment to provide Malawi with financial and technical assistance for both the support and the development of its economy. This adoption of a quasi-colonial role was seen by Britain as necessary but unwelcome. It involved an open-ended commitment to support Malawi over which the British government could have only limited control if it were to avoid undue interference with the affairs of a sovereign state. The desirability of ending such a commitment, specifically on budgetary aid, without damaging Malawi's economy, added to Britain's generally stated interest in development. In Malawi this was seen as a means to ending budgetary support, and also of attracting other donors to share the responsibility of assisting further development. Accordingly, the aid programme to Malawi, both in size and quality, was geared to the promotion of development. It was largely unaffected by the various non-developmental commercial and political interests which have tended to influence the volume, direction and quality of British bilateral aid elsewhere and have reduced its potential stimulus to development. If aid to Malawi was to bring commercial and political gains to the UK, they would be indirect, through the country's economic development.

The British government has not simply been a passive aid giver. Because of public accountability for spending, the British aid programme has always had built-in checks to ensure that aid was needed and used for the purpose requested. These checks were less rigorous in the case of independent developing countries than for Britain's colonies – and so far as ex-colonies were concerned, the reason lay in Britain's unwillingness to appear to be interfering with the sovereign rights of such countries, who could be expected to be more than usually sensitive on such an issue. In the sixties, however, the British government moved away from this position. It stressed its right to ensure that aid should be well used, and the benefits to both parties in the aid relationship of a joint approach in identifying development needs that could be met by aid. In Malawi's case, Britain's interest in such an approach was reinforced by the scale of its support and its desire to eliminate budgetary aid.

Assessment of the need for aid was based on a scrutiny of the Malawi government's expenditure plans, and appraisal of individual projects submitted for British finance and of the government's past performance in using aid and mobilising its own resources. The assessment was carried out by ODM independently and in consultation with the Malawi government, in both Britain and Malawi. And efforts were made to help the Malawi government in its own assessment of its needs, through technical assistance. ODM's contacts with Malawi also provided a means of checking on the use of aid and so was a further incentive to effective implementation. The policy of providing project aid on a reimbursement basis, combined with a requirement that changes in agreed projects were subject to British approval, allowed further checks, while the policy of over-commitment of project aid assisted implementation.

As Malawi's most important aid donor, Britain's active involvement in assessing the need for and use of aid has had some influence on the kind of development strategy pursued by Malawi. The extent of this influence is hard to identify. Clearly Malawi would have behaved very differently without British aid. But to say that aid changed Malawi's development prospects is very different from saying that Britain actively influenced Malawi's choices with aid. Nevertheless there is some evidence to suggest that despite the apparent broad agreement between the two parties on development priorities and policies, Britain sought, with some success, to influence sich policies at both general and project levels.

At a general level, the evidence is partly circumstantial. The broad policy agreement that existed could have stemmed from independent assessments of Malawi's position: certainly its resource base was such as virtually to dictate the areas for major development efforts. On the other hand, Malawi depended on British aid to pursue its strategy and had it adopted policies which significantly conflicted with British views, then that aid would probably not have been available.

More specifically, there can be little doubt that the compulsive elements in Britain's policy of eliminating budgetary aid helped to ensure that the Malawi government kept up its tax effort and its restraint on recurrent spending. But this policy of eliminating budgetary aid was not wholly beneficial in its effect. Certain imbalances emerged in the pattern of government expenditure – a relative neglect of health and primary education and of some maintenance spending on capital stock

172

especially roads, which has partly been remedied through the somewhat expensive means of capital expenditure. Such imbalances are not wholly attributable to the British policy: manpower shortages, the preferences of other donors for capital projects, and the Malawi government's priorities in respect of its non-revenue account, local resources and its development programme generally, are all important factors. And even if Britain had been more generous in providing general budgetary support, the resultant increase in recurrent spending would have occurred not only in the areas where, in development terms, the deficiencies were most marked. Nevertheless Britain could have reduced these imbalances by a different policy on budgetary support.

Apart from this broad impact on the pattern of government spending, Britain has clearly wielded some influence on development spending by virtue of its dominant position: its refusal formally (or more often informally) to provide support to particular projects has affected the composition of Malawi's development programme. However, partly on principle and partly because it could not do otherwise, Britain has not generally attempted to exert leverage on projects it was not prepared to finance. In the few cases where overt leverage of this kind has been attempted, Britain has not been conspicuously successful. In the two major cases – the Nacala rail link and the new capital at Lilongwe – when Britain went beyond a straight refusal of projects, these were only deferred until alternative finance became available from South Africa. Even so, by effectively delaying the projects until output and incomes were higher Britain may well have prevented some resource wastage. And, while not preventing certain dubious developmental projects financed from local resources, Britain has restricted resource availability for their implementation by introducing the requirement, in 1969, that Malawi finance 10 per cent of the costs of British-aided projects.

Britain has succeeded through formal and informal contacts in modifying some projects and policies directly supported by British aid both before and after their implementation, with largely beneficial effects. And Britain's interest in project preparation and implementation, which has been backed by British-financed technical assistance, helped to increase the effectiveness of aid and generally reinforced Malawi's own efforts to increase its efficiency and capacity for planning and implementation. British interest has, however, led to some delays not simply because disagreements have had to be resolved – for instance, between the Malawi Housing Corporation and ODM – but also because of the procedures involved in British checks on its aided projects. The policy of reimbursement and the fact that most aid administration has been carried out from London, albeit backed by field level contacts, has delayed implementation on occasions. But the costs of such delays are outweighed by the benefits derived from donor interest in the use of aid. However, they could have been avoided to some extent by administrative decentralisation. The recent establishment of the Development Division in Blantyre could provide such a remedy.

Some traces of Britain's non-developmental interests are to be seen in its project selection — for instance, there is tacit agreement with Malawi that projects submitted to Britain should include some with a high import content, and the average import content of British-financed projects has in fact been increasing. Malawi officials maintain, however, that this agreement has not led to any distortion in their development programme: the terms of different donors' aid allow them sufficient flexibility to parcel out projects without changing its composition. And from the composition of its aided projects — many of which support agricultural development — Britain's developmental interest appears to be paramount. The pursuit of this interest has been both dependent on and constrained by the maintenance of good diplomatic relations. At least one project has been accepted without the full appraisal thought necessary by ODM, for diplomatic reasons. And diplomatic caution has limited British attempts to influence Malawi in areas not supported by British aid.

There has been some resentment in Malawi at Britain's generally close interest in the projects it supports, or proposes to support, and at its scrutiny of government expenditure plans prior to agreeing budgetary support. Yet Britain has rarely gone beyond its prerogative as a donor to ensure that its aid is well used. Indeed, given that its aid was of the nature of general support to the Malawi government, it has stayed well within the bounds of what it might justifiably have done. Britain's interest in the country's development has on balance had beneficial effects and must be regarded as responsible for the quality of its aid which performed a fundamental role in permitting and encouraging Malawi's economic development.

Implications for Future Aid Policy in General

A consideration of the implications for general British policy follows naturally from the finding that in Malawi at least aid was successful in promoting development. Uppermost in the mind of any sceptic, who has accepted this conclusion, must be the question 'was Malawi a special case?'

Obviously, all countries are special cases. But so far as the role of aid in development is concerned, one of the major factors making Malawi a 'special case' was the exceptional, if not unique, treatment it received from Britain. From this, certain lessons for aid policy may be drawn.

Britain's chief interest in providing aid to Malawi was to promote development. Its aid programme was largely untrammelled by conflicting non-developmental objectives. The predominance of the development objective was fundamental to the success of the programme. A necessary, but not sufficient condition for such a success to be repeated is that the various short-term political and commercial objectives pursued elsewhere in the British bilateral aid programme are downgraded in relation to the objective of assisting development.

In Malawi's case, Britain's aid in support of local and recurrent expenditure was crucial to its development. Britain's aid here was in marked contrast to its usual provisions, which tend to have strict procurement conditions and to be supplied for capital rather than recurrent expenditure. It is true that Malawi was particularly in need of such aid and that for other ldcs, less poor and not on the verge of collapse for want of domestic resources, it would be less appropriate. But the kind of aid most frequently on offer – tied to procurement and to usually large capital projects creates an incentive to capital-intensive expenditure. Such expenditure is unlikely to be appropriate to the rural areas where it is increasingly recognised that efforts should be focused if mass unemployment and inegalitarian development are to be avoided. If Britain is to encourage such efforts, then its aid recipients should be allowed greater flexibility in the use to which aid may be put. Britain should be prepared to finance small diffuse items of expenditure as well as large projects, local costs as well as offshore costs and recurrent as well as capital expenditure.

This would involve changes in certain aid practices. Procurement tying obviously would have to be relaxed at least to the extent it was relaxed in Malawi's case (and also for some other British aid recipients). Techniques of aid giving would have to be adapted, and accountability requirements reviewed. Moreover Britain's long standing policy of reducing 'open-ended' commitments would apparently be broken. Would these changes be very difficult?

A relaxation in procurement tying would clearly reduce the extent to which Britain can protect its balance of payments position and, while providing aid, subsidise its exporters. But it is the intrusion of just this sort of non-developmental concern which should be avoided in determining the terms and conditions on which aid is provided. In any case, the limited form of untying proposed here would not have major effects on the balance of payments position and could be countered by the increased export orders which would be generated if aid were used more effectively.

Administrative tidiness would clearly be lost if the trend towards larger projects was reversed (in allowing greater flexibility on the use of aid). However the increase in the administrative burden could be minimised by delegating more responsibility to field level representatives who could substitute at least some of the paper-work by maintaining less formal checks on aid proposals and on implementation. Such decentralisation would have additional benefits – decisions would be more informal and timely and the possibilities of monitoring general development performance in the recipient would be increased.

This latter point has a bearing on the accountability issue. Large identifiable projects provide, apparently, clear evidence of the use to which aid is put. Thus, leaving aside the political *kudos* which is believed to accrue from such projects, it is easy for the donor government to account for its use of public funds. With small, diffuse projects often part of some larger programme of expenditure, this is apparently less easy. But the notion that aid may be identified or evaluated by reference to the purpose for which it was approved is frequently erroneous. Shunting – the freeing of resources for other uses by the addition of aid – is a common occurence in all forms of aid. Although in Malawi it was not significant in relation to project aid, this was mainly because of the unique and dominant role played by such aid. Project aid, as with other types of aid to Malawi, clearly had a major impact on total resource availability. It is reasonable to suppose that in any aid programme, whether consisting solely of project aid or not, such an effect will occur. It will therefore usually be necessary to consider the broader effects of aid as well as the precise purpose for which aid is given, if real accountability is to be achieved.

Since this approach clearly extends the donors' range of legitimate interest, it could weaken the recipient's sovereignty. But this would be more apparent than real. The recipient's broad choice of development policies, as well as of particular projects, is open to influence so long as its aid receipts depend on more than its ability to prepare and implement a given aid-financed project. Unless donors are prepared to ignore the context in which aid is given – in which case they may as well forget the accounting fiction of projectising aid except in the limiting case when the project would have been foregone without aid – they are bound to exercise a more general influence. Nevertheless the diplomatic value of linking aid to apparently specific uses remains especially if aid is small in relation to total government expenditure. The donor is more likely to make a positive contribution to development policies if he confines his interest to the specific areas where his aid is ostensibly employed. It does not follow therefore that donors should relinquish the practice of attaching aid to specific uses. It does follow, however, that accountability is a weak argument for such a practice. This being so, it makes little *real* difference – except administratively – to go for large identifiable projects or small, diffuse projects.

The question of the open-endedness of any support involving

recurrent expenditure remains. The British government's dislike of open-ended commitments to sovereign states — or even its own citizens — is understandable, for such commitments may limit its options at a later date. While it was true that general budgetary support usually entailed such a commitment, it did so because Britain felt morally obliged to prevent the adverse economic consequences of the withdrawal of such support. Even so, in Malawi's case, as the scale of the support was reduced, Britain was able to limit the period of future aid, and it became no more open-ended than other aid commitments. There is little reason why recurrent projectised support should not be given subject to an agreement between donor and recipient that it be phased out over a given period. The argument against — that the recipient might break its side of the agreement, leaving the donor with the choice of cutting off aid as agreed and so ending the on-going service that has been built up or continuing aid on an open-ended basis — is weak. The donor is under no more obligation to continue aid in this case than he is to provide recurrent aid finance for an aided capital project which the recipient will not or cannot maintain on completion. The second argument against, that problems would arise because the phasing out period of a recurrent project would probably be longer than the present length of aid commitments to ldcs, is also weak. Only if there were a dramatic cutback in aid would there be any difficulty in maintaining such commitments. And their existence would only impinge on Britain's flexibility in the unlikely event that it wished to make a large reduction in the aid to a country or countries receiving recurrent project aid, while honouring existing commitments.

One last and more general point that emerges from Malawi's experience is the beneficial effect of Britain's active interest in the use of its aid. It is true that Malawi resented this interest to some degree, particularly in the case of the budget scrutiny that accompanied budgetary aid. But the latter resentment arose from the extent of involvement the practice entailed in Malawi's affairs; a point which reinforces the case for maintaining projectised aid. On the whole, however, this interest not only enabled Malawi to receive suitable aid but also encouraged domestic development efforts. It is notable that in the sphere of technical assistance where British interest was, until recently, somewhat perfunctory Malawi's performance was least energetic. Obviously when non-developmental considerations govern the donors' concern with recipient behaviour or when the donor is insensitive to, or ignorant of, the recipient's development needs, an active interest in the use of and need for aid can be detrimental. Further, the extent of beneficial donor involvement will vary according to the capacity of the recipient to formulate and execute development policies. But given sensitivity to a recipient's needs and respect for its sovereignty, such an approach is clearly beneficial.

Implications for Aid to Malawi

What points emerge for future British aid policy in Malawi? Certain steps have already been taken to remedy points of criticism in the aid programme.

The need to decentralise aid administration, more to end delays than to improve the quality of decision making, has been reduced by the establishment of the Southern African Development Division in Blantyre. With its establishment, the High Commission was given delegated authority, on advice from the Development Division, to approve any individual projects costing less than £100,000 — recently raised to £150,000. And the presence of the Development Division has increased the extent to which projects may be informally discussed prior to submission to ODM, and implementation progress may be monitored. It is, however, too early to tell how far the presence of the Division has affected or will affect the quality of administration or of decisions.

The somewhat lax approach to assessing Malawi's technical assistance requirements — in part, it is true, stemming from factors beyond Britain's control — has been altered with the introduction of the manpower reviews. The first review team concentrated on assessing Malawi's needs for supplemented personnel but it is hoped (and it is certainly desirable) that the assessment can be extended to Malawi's overseas and internal educational and training needs.

Finally the British government has taken over the main burden of pension, commutation and compensation payments arising from its obligation to those previously in colonial service. Although these payments are made out of the aid budget — where arguably they do not belong — they are regarded as additional to the aid programme.

There are, however, signs that with the elimination of budgetary aid, the special treatment of Malawi is weakening. Because it is poor and a good performer, has a stable government committed to development and an efficient administration and offers opportunities to British investors and exporters, Malawi is currently assured of a continued and relatively large inflow of British aid. But certain disturbing shifts — more in intention than execution as yet — are apparent in British policy. The projectised recurrent support to Malawi's development account (representing over a quarter of British project aid commitments in 1974-5) that was a key element in preventing serious distortion in Malawi's development spending, is to be gradually taken over by the Malawi government and efforts are to be made to identify larger 'integrated' projects for British support. While Britain intends to retain the sectoral emphasis of its programme on natural resources, it is evincing greater interest in finding projects which will benefit British exporters and investors, subject to developmental considerations. It has to be emphasised that these shifts are barely perceptible in Britain's programme and that taken in isolation they are not overly important. But in the context of Malawi's likely position over the next ten years or so, British policy could be tending in the wrong direction.

Although Malawi's economy has expanded considerably and has achieved a significant growth momentum, its development prospects are still subject to the same kind of constraints that faced it in 1964. In relative terms. Malawi now relies less on external support than in 1964, but it is still dependent on such support, both of finance and manpower. The agricultural sector is less dominant but it still accounts for some 95 per cent of merchandise export earnings. And, since employment opportunities in other sectors are unable to keep up with the increase in new entrants to the labour market, the agricultural sector must continue to provide a livelihood for increasing numbers of Malawians. Although new growth points have emerged, and may yet emerge in the development of processing industries, for instance, of a pulpwood industry, the exploitation of Mulanje bauxite and tourism, the key to Malawi's future development lies in agriculture. These points are stressed in Malawi's ten-year perspective plan, Devpol. Yet certain factors cast doubt on Malawi's ability to maintain its growth momentum.

The country's scope for mobilising domestic resources for development is closely related to its balance of payments position. In 1973, this looked extremely healthy. However, there were already signs of a deterioration in the terms to trade and the adverse effects of the oil crisis had yet to be fully felt. With these, Malawi's import prices are likely to rise still further. Oil and petroleum products constitute only a small portion of Malawi's imports of goods and services, and additional direct costs are likely to be only 5 to 10 per cent of the country's total import bill. But freight charges, relatively high because of Malawi's landlocked position and the nature of its exports, will also increase as a direct result of the oil price. And the latter will generally push up the cost of imports, already rising because of global inflation. To some extent, these rises have been and will be offset by increases in Malawi's export prices. But with 'stagflation' in Malawi's main developed country markets, it is unlikely that the terms of trade will move in its favour, and the volume growth of its exports may also suffer. Malawi's relative unimportance in the world trade of some of its major exports will be an offsetting factor, as will its improved access to the EEC, assuming that the association negotiations are successful. But since Malawi's main exports – cotton, tea and groundnuts but not tobacco –

already enjoy duty free access to the EEC, association is unlikely to change its export opportunities substantially. Overall it seems probable that Malawi will have difficulty in maintaining its present trade position.

Malawi has in the past benefited from favourable movements in its terms of trade. Adverse movements increase the importance of raising the volume of its agricultural exports. The agricultural development strategy outlined in Devpol concentrates on raising yields (further extension of the cultivated acreage would be expensive and, if uncontrolled, could result in major conservation problems). Besides the encouragement of estate farming by both expatriates and Malawians, efforts to raise cash crop production in Malawi have been increasingly focused on both large- and small-scale development projects, with smallholders outside the schemes being provided with less intensive farmer education and marketing services and improvements in the transportation network. Devpol proposes the continuation of such policies. Yet a conflict is likely between maintaining widespread agricultural development and increasing the volume of cash crop production — both for export and to meet domestic food needs — at a pace sufficient to sustain the present rate of economic growth. Since the volume of smallholder cash production has grown only slightly since independence — and this has mostly occurred in development project areas — raising the volume of cash crop exports is likely to entail greater emphasis on development projects and the encouragement of estate farming. The latter is, anyway, clearly favoured politically. But the longer-term consequences could be serious. If smallholders outside schemes are relatively neglected their marketed output is likely to fall. Subsistence demands would increase with the unchecked growth of population, and in some areas that population pressure would probably reduce land productivity. Urban migration — and probably unemployment — would increase, creating political tensions there while land hunger and inegalitarian agricultural development would provide a focus for rural discontent.

Migration abroad, a major safety valve since independence, is an unlikely solution to such problems. Political difficulties in southern Africa and Dr Banda's recent banning of recruitment of Malawians for South African mines suggest that migration will decline rather than increase. Whatever actually happens to Malawi's agricultural development, this factor by itself will exacerbate urban and rural unemployment or underemployment. And by reducing the inflow of workers' remittances — over K12m or roughly 10 per cent of current account receipts in 1972 — it will aggravate the balance of payments problem.

Malawi's ability to continue its public-sector-led development depends on local resource mobilisation and internal and external support for the government. Local resource mobilisation will continue to be constrained by the country's poverty and the limited scope for deficit financing. With average income still at under £45 a head, and tax revenue amounting to 11 per cent of GNP in 1973, the government has reasonably decided that, rather than impose new taxes, it will rely on the fact that the tax take will increase as incomes rise. Given a buoyant economy with GDP and domestic exports growing respectively at 8.2 per cent and 10.5 per cent in real terms, Devpol estimates that local resources should be able to finance around 75 per cent of the total planned public spending of K1,078m over the decade 1971-80. About 65 per cent of this spending is of a recurrent nature, including some K40m on the government's development account, and the major part of local resources is to be used for this purpose. External borrowing and grants are expected to cover over 70 per cent of public sector investment spending. Although Malawi's planned spending for 1974-5 exceeds Devpol estimates for 1975, adverse movements in the balance of payments could threaten its implementation.

A reduction in public sector spending would not necessarily be harmful. Certain large items now in Malawi's expenditure plans – for instance, the new international airport at Lilongwe and some road and rail investment – are unlikely to bring significant benefits over the next decade and may even yield negative returns to the economy. However, the priority apparently attached to these items and, other things being equal, the type of finance available to Malawi, suggest that they would not be the first to be axed. Any shortfall in local resource availability is most likely to hit the planned expansion of general development services to the rural areas – primary education, agricultural extension, health. Meanwhile if, as suggested, urban problems increase, there would be a political incentive to divert scarce resources to improve urban conditions.

Recent changes in the political conditions in Malawi have in some ways made the country less attractive to its outside supporters, for instance, the repression of minority groups, and the apparent increase in popular hostility towards expatriate Europeans and Asians and in government pressures on foreign enterprises. And the growing economic power of politicians, while in keeping with longstanding government policy to encourage private enterprise, suggests a move away from the broadly based development efforts that have characterised the country's progress since independence. Although implicated in these changes, Dr Banda has probably been more a moderator than an initiator; the question of his succession inevitably casts a shadow on the political future of the country and the extent to which outside support will be forthcoming on his demise. In particular foreign private investors may be deterred – even to the extent of withdrawing from existing interests in Malawi. Yet even if the rather gloomy predictions about Malawi's *economic* state are not borne out by events, Malawi will remain dependent on external support.

Malawi has in the past been fortunate in the type of aid it has received. The terms have generally been soft, with the result that the public debt service burden – though somewhat high at 9 per cent of exports of goods and services in 1972 – is manageable assuming a continued good balance of payments performance. And Malawi's inclusion in the recent UN list of least developed countries enhances its chances of receiving further soft aid.[4] Meanwhile most of its donors have been prepared to take on a share of local expenditure. But, aside from Britain, most have exhibited a preference for large projects and only West Germany and IDA have, besides Britain, made significant contributions to rural development services. This pattern of aid giving by other donors is unlikely to change, notwithstanding Malawi's prospective eligibility for aid from the EEC fund. Consequently any expansion of rural development services outside major project areas will have to be financed from local resources or by Britain. And, as pointed out earlier, any diminution in local resource availability is likely to threaten precisely these services despite their importance to Malawi's development. Britain's aid therefore will continue to be of major significance to Malawi.

The problem is, however, that Britain's aid may not be available to finance expenditure in the areas where it is most needed. The support of countrywide rural development services, for instance, health, rural road maintenance and agricultural extension, is needed to counter the bias towards inegalitarian rural development and to redress the balance of spending away from some of the large-scale and possibly unproductive infrastructural projects currently proposed. Such support accords with Britain's sectoral priorities, particularly Britain's recent albeit somewhat belated, interest in aiding the development of rural health services (which could form the institutional framework for a much needed population policy when political objections within Malawi cease). But Britain's stated intention of reducing recurrent projectised aid, of seeking out 'integrated' projects in the natural resource sector and of raising the import content of British-financed projects would seem to limit the possibility of British aid being used for broadly based rural development: support for rural development services entails a readiness to provide aid for somewhat diffuse projects, involving a significant local, and often recurrent, cost element. It may be argued that by financing such expenditure Britain is simply releasing local resources for the kind of development expenditure which it seeks to avoid. The possibility of this is reduced, however, by the fact that Britain would probably be supporting expenditure which would not otherwise have occurred on the same scale. Secondly, by requiring an immediate local cost contribution — perhaps greater than the 10 per cent currently required for British-aided projects — and by gradually increasing the level of this contribution, Britain can pre-empt local resources that might otherwise have been used with less developmental effect and prevent its support from becoming open-ended. Larger, better defined, projects may be more attractive for political and administrative reasons but it would be unfortunate if such factors came to over-ride Britain's previous and effective interest in Malawi's development.

NOTES

1.   This included some recurrent as well as capital expenditure.
2.   See P.T. Bauer, *Dissent on Development*. Weidenfeld and Nicolson, London, 1971, p. 95ff.
3.   See, for instance, K. Griffin and J.L. Enos, 'Foreign Assistance, Objectives and Consequences,' *Economic Development and Cultural Change*, Vol. 18, No. 3, April 1970.
4.   Britain has already improved its aid terms to Malawi to meet international requirements.

INDEX

Treasury Fund, 81

United Kingdom,
    aid, *see* Aid, British
    colonisation of Malawi, 3-7
    and Federation, 7-11
    political and commercial interests
      in Malawi, 59
    as trading partner, 41-2, 59
United Nations, 182
United States,
    as aid donor, 16-17, 32, 62, 70,
      122-3, 127
    as trading partner, 41-2
Universities' Mission to Central
    Africa (UMCA), 3
University of Malawi, 19, 67, 110,
    117, 128-9, 138
U.S. Sugar Agreement, 41

Vipya Tung Estates, 76-7, 126

White Papers,
    *Overseas Development: The Work
    of the New Ministry* (1965), 71,
    92
    Public Service Overseas (1969),
    140
World Bank, 16, 115

Zambia, 3, 39, 41, 116
Zomba,
    centre of insurrection, 24
    proposed University site, 129
    road link with Lilongwe, 43, 101

For Product Safety Concerns and Information please contact our EU
representative GPSR@taylorandfrancis.com Taylor & Francis Verlag GmbH,
Kaufingerstraße 24, 80331 München, Germany

Printed and bound by CPI Group (UK) Ltd, Croydon, CR0 4YY
02/05/2025
01859615-0001